IHS

That through the Church the manifold wisdom of God might now be made known.

GLORY TO GOD PEACE TO MEN

AL
BA

The Daughters of St. Paul
50 Years of Service in the U.S.A.
1932—1982

The Daughters of St. Paul

50 Years of Service in the U.S.A.

1932-1982

by the Daughters of St. Paul

ST. PAUL EDITIONS

ISBN 0-8198-1805-4

Printed in the U.S.A. by the Daughters of St. Paul
50 St. Paul's Avenue, Boston, MA 02130

The Daughters of St. Paul are an international congregation of religious women serving the Church with the communications media.

The Daughters of St. Paul
of the United States Province
dedicate this album

To their
Founder, the Servant of God
JAMES ALBERIONE, S.S.P., S.T.D.
(1884-1971)
whose Process for the cause of Beatification and Canonization
had its solemn opening
on June 19, 1982, in the Church of St. Paul in Alba.
His daughters rejoice with all the Pauline Family for this great news
which happily coincides with the 50th Anniversary
of their Foundation in the United States.
In this moment, particularly meaningful
for the history and life of the Pauline Family,
they renew their commitment to walk toward sanctity,
mindful of his oft-repeated words:
"I ask of you Pauline saints from the U.S.A."
With renewed fervor and faith they repeat the prayer:
"Lord, glorify him in Your Church."

To their
Co-Foundress, the Servant of God
MOTHER THECLA MERLO
(1894-1964)
whose cause for Beatification is proceeding rapidly
and whose life was a continuous "yes" to God,
through the directives of the Founder.
They pledge their unswerving fidelity,
ever mindful of the inspiring words of St. Paul:
"Remain faithful to what you have learned,
for you know who your teachers were."

To their beloved
MOTHER PAULA CORDERO
who in 1932 was chosen by the Founder and Co-Foundress
to begin the mission of evangelization with the media of social communication
in the United States of America,
and who has worked tirelessly since then
for the development of the Pauline spirit and apostolate.

And to their
FIRST SISTERS
who made the initial sacrifices with great faith and generosity
and who still work with zeal
to accomplish God's plan of love for America's millions.

CONTENTS

Upon the Daughters of Saint Paul of the United States Province, with gratitude for their zealous collaboration in the Church's mission of proclaiming the Gospel, I invoke the joy and peace of our Lord Jesus Christ and cordially impart my Apostolic Blessing.

At Castelgandolfo, September 23, 1981.

Joannes Paulus PP. II

SECRETARIAT OF STATE

FROM THE VATICAN, December 5,1981

Dear Sister Mary Domenica,

The Holy Father was pleased to be informed that the Daughters of Saint Paul of the United States Province are celebrating in 1982 the Fiftieth Anniversary of their Foundation in America.

On this joyful occasion His Holiness extends his best wishes to you, to Sister Paula Cordero and to all the Sisters. He prays that all of you will ever maintain fervent zeal for proclaiming the Gospel by the faithful witness of your consecrated lives and through your special apostolate in the mass media. He urges you to have a deep trust in God's power at work in your hearts which "can do infinitely more that we can ask or imagine" (Eph 3:20).

With affection in our Lord Jesus Christ, the Holy Father entrusts the Daughters of Saint Paul of the United States Province to the loving protection of the Blessed Virgin Mary and cordially imparts his Apostolic Blessing.

Sincerely yours in Christ,

+E. Martínez
Substitute

Sister Mary Domenica Vitello, D.S.P.
Provincial
Daughters of Saint Paul
50 St. Paul's Avenue
Jamaica Plain, MA 02130

APOSTOLIC DELEGATION

UNITED STATES OF AMERICA

3339 MASSACHUSETTS AVENUE, N.W.
WASHINGTON, D.C. 20008

October 28, 1981

Dear Mother Paula:

I am pleased to inform you that our Holy Father, Pope John Paul II, graciously bestows his Apostolic Blessing upon the Daughters of St. Paul in the United States province who are celebrating their Golden Jubilee of Foundation on June 27, 1982 in Boston, Massachusetts.

The Holy Father thanks the Daughters of St. Paul for their unceasing contributions to the spread of the Gospel by their use of the social communication's media.

Speaking on this topic, our Holy Father remarked:

"It is undoubtedly true that the social communications media can be a most valuable source of cultural enrichment for the family and for its members. Well-ordered reading, listening and viewing can contribute greatly to the stimulation of dialogue and interchange within the little community, and can create a broadening of interests which will involve the family in the activities of the larger family outside...

"The question arises: where are the mutual connections between the Church and art, the Church and journalism? The answer to this is: the subject of the Church and the subject of both artists and journalists is man, the image of man, the truth of man, the 'ecce homo', including his history, his world and environment, as well as the social, economic and political contents...

"As the conveyor of the message of Christian faith, the Church will always speak out in reminder of the fact that the reality of man cannot be fully described without the theological dimension.."

This theological dimension of which the Holy Father speaks is the concern of the Daughters of St. Paul as they serve God and the Church.

To the Blessing of the Holy Father, permit me to add heartfelt congratulations. It is my prayer that in your service of the truth, you will unceasingly find Truth itself.

Sincerely yours in Christ,

Pio Laghi

Apostolic Delegate

Mother Paula, D.S.P.
Founder of the Daughters of St. Paul
in the United States

SACRA CONGREGAZIONE
PER I RELIGIOSI
E GLI ISTITUTI SECOLARI

Rome, December 25, 1981

Dear Sister Mary Domenica,

The Golden Jubilee of your coming to the United States of America is an occasion for reflection on the past, gratitude to God for what has been achieved and renewed commitment to your apostolate of evangelization with the media of social communication.

Looking to the past means drawing inspiration from your Founders, Don James Alberione and the Servant of God, Mother Thecla Merlo, as well as from Mother Paula and those who pioneered your presence in the United States; being imbued with their spirit and pledging fidelity to their charism in the service of the Church.

These fifty years of presence in the United States of America have been blessed with fruitfulness, and for this your prayer of praise and thanksgiving goes to God, the giver of all good. The seed was sown by Mother Thecla and her first companions, supported by the prayer and faith of your Founders, but it was the Lord who gave the increase.

Your aim is the glory of God and the salvation of souls through evangelization with the media of social communication. Your apostolate is a continuation of the apostolate of the Divine Master, who commanded his disciples to preach the Gospel to all creatures. "The diffusion of the Sacred Scriptures must be the primary and most important aspect of all our apostolic activity", is the injunction of your Founder, Don James Alberione, and he goes on to say: "We were born of the Word, for the Word and in the Word. We must ensure, then, that all our books, films, transmissions and recordings be always merely an extension, an echo, a continuation, an irradiation of the divine book, but especially of the Gospel".

Don Alberione looked on your apostolate as "a priceless treasure, one that the angels envy". But because it is of such importance, he stressed the need for holiness in those engaged in it. No one who has not lived the Word can really transmit the Word. "An apostle", he says, "is one who carries God in his soul and irradiates him to others". Indeed, his greatest wish was that among the members of his Institutes there should be saints.

In congratulating you on these fifty years of dedicated work in the field of social communication and in thanking you for your loyal service to the Magisterium, our prayer and our wish is that God will continue to bless your efforts, and that the will make you "a society of souls who love God with your whole strength, with all your mind and heart, and who work for the Church, looking for no other reward than that of the divine reward" (Don Alberione).

Yours sincerely in Christ and his Blessed Mother,

E. Card. Pironio, Pref.

+ Augustine Mayer O.S.B.
Secr.

Sister Mary Domenica, D.S.P.
Provincial Superior
50, St. Paul's Ave.
JAMAICA PLAIN, Boston, Ma. 02130

U.S.A.

SACRA CONGREGAZIONE
PER IL CLERO

December 3, 1981

Daughters of St. Paul
United States of America

In the celebration of the Fiftieth Anniversary of the Foundation of the Congregation of the Daughters of St. Paul in the United States of America, I do not intend to exalt its works and accomplishments, but rather to emphasize the spirit which aroused them and the love which accompanied them.

It is not a human adventure, but rather a supernatural mission which the venerated Founder, Father James Alberione, and the unforgettable Co-Foundress, Mother Thecla Merlo, entrusted to the young Sister Paula and her fellow Sisters, in sending them out into the vast and difficult field of labor of the United States.

A mission of faith and love. Of faith, because the foundation of this work was and is faith; of love, because the spring of action was and is love. In fact, this work and action strive directly for the building up of the Church and the edification of souls; it is not human vision and natural actions which count and operate, but rather the light of faith and the power of grace. All the mass-media which can be imagined are and will be always simple and poor instruments in comparison to the divine work of the edification of souls.

And it is the spirit which is of value when souls are to be reached; in this lies the secret of success and the key of perseverance.

Justly the Daughters of St. Paul can say with the Apostle Paul: "The love of Christ impels us" - Charitas Christi urget nos (2 Cor. 5:14), because it is in view of and in the supernatural power of the love of God that their action was illuminated and strengthened.

This action is eminently directed to bringing the knowledge and love of God, because one who loves God desires that together with himself all love Him, and one who loves his neighbor uprightly intends to work so that the neighbor, too, will love God. St. Augustine affirms: "Whoever loves his neighbor rightly, must work with him, so that he too may love God with his whole heart, with his whole soul, with his whole mind" (*De Doctrina Christiana*, lib. I, c. 22). This in fact is the supreme ideal, and the first duty of the love of God and of neighbor: to diffuse and to enkindle in everyone the fire of divine love - unless, I wish to remind again with St. Augustine: "we are so foolish as to think of having to run more swiftly with the bread, with which to fill the stomach of the hungry man, than with the word of God, with which to instruct him who eats it - Nisi forte tam stulti sumus, ut alacrius arbitremur cum pane currendum, quo ventrem esurientis impleamus, quam cum verbo Dei quo mentem istud edentis instruamur" (*De Catechizandis rudibus*, XIV, 22).

In this spiritual vision and supernatural action of the Congregation of the Daughters of St. Paul, the action must be rightly united to the spirit of love, because it is precisely in the love of God that there lies and will always lie the secret of fruitfulness and of perseverance.

In the meantime, I invoke the Lord's blessing upon your ceaseless action and multiform activity, but above all I implore for you perseverance in this spirit of love of God, which has aroused, made fruitful and sustained many of your works and admirable undertakings.

With the blessing of the Lord and my most fervent wishes for the celebration of a happy and fruitful *Golden Jubilee* of the American foundation of the Congregation and of the so worthy Sister Paula!

In Christ Jesus,

Silvio card. Oddi

(Silvio Cardinal Oddi)

ADVENIAT REGNUM TUUM

CARDINAL'S RESIDENCE
2101 COMMONWEALTH AVENUE
BRIGHTON, MASSACHUSETTS 02135

December 7, 1981

Sister Mary Domenica
Daughters of St. Paul
50 St. Paul Avenue
Jamaica Plain, MA 02130

Dear Sister Mary Domenica:

As the Daughters of St. Paul celebrate the Golden Jubilee of the Foundation of their Congregation in the United States of America, I am delighted to offer my most sincere congratulations and my heartfelt best wishes.

The history of the Daughters of St. Paul is an inspiration to me, and I know it is the same for the Bishops, priests, religious and faithful of the Archdiocese of Boston. The work the Daughters of St. Paul have done for the spread of the Catholic faith with such zeal and devotion will certainly constitute a most impressive page in the history of the Catholic Church in the United States. Your loyalty and devotion to the Holy Father and the Bishops of the United States have been and continue to be a shining example and a source of great encouragement for all of us.

I wish to take special note of the unique and overwhelming contribution made by Mother Paula Cordero, whose deep, simple faith and undying trust in God have enabled her to overcome countless obstacles which have been placed in her way. Motivated by the love of her Lord, Jesus, she has given all of us a conspicuous example of tireless service and fidelity for which the Church in the United States is deeply indebted to her. The beautiful witness of her life is a constant source of strength and joy to all of us.

We are privileged to have the Provincial House and the Novitiate of the Daughters of St. Paul in our Archdiocese, and it is a joy for me, as the Archbishop of Boston, to assure you of my abiding gratitude for what your Community does for the glory of God and the salvation of souls through enlightened and faithful evangelization with the media of social communication.

With my blessing and kindest personal regards, I remain

Devotedly yours in Our Lord,

+ Humberto Cardinal Medeiros
Archbishop of Boston

PIA SOCIETÀ SAN PAOLO

SUPERIORE GENERALE

VIA DELLA FANELLA, 39 - 00148 ROMA TEL. 51.46.053

TO THE SISTERS DAUGHTERS OF ST. PAUL
OF THE UNITED STATES PROVINCE

My dear Sisters,

I accept with sincere thanks your invitation to participate in the jubilarian celebrations of your Foundation. I desire and hope to be present personally.

From this very moment I comply, by means of this brief written message, with your expectation and preparation for that event which marks an important date in your life.

I find stupendous and truly inspired your proposal, contained in these your words: "In this 50th we want to renew ourselves in spirit and in apostolate." I believe that there cannot be a more appropriate attitude for a jubilee celebration than yours: to renew the zeal of the mission and of your own consecration; to start out again and witness with more luminous evidence the mission of the apostle Paul.

In this year, in which the Paulines are invited to deepen the values and the awareness of their own mission, I hold as fundamental the contribution which you are destined to give, thanks to the total dedication which you show towards the Word of God, and to the courageous missionary zeal which animates you.

I fervently pray the Lord to bless your resolutions and apostolic projects. I pray above all that in the Pauline mission, the reason for all our consecrated life, the women and men Paulines can walk together, to reach together that goal of service to the Church to which the Divine Master has called us to collaborate.

The rest I will have the joy of saying by word of mouth. In the meantime I entrust you to the protection of the Apostle Paul and to the blessing of the Virgin Mary, Queen of Apostles.

Sac. Renato Perino

Superior General

ISTITUTO PIA SOCIETÀ FIGLIE DI S. PAOLO
Via San Giovanni Eudes, 25 - 00163 ROMA
Tel. 6254957 - 6255098

Casa Generalizia

JUBILARIAN FEAST OF THE UNITED STATES PROVINCE

Dearest Sisters,

I present you the greeting and the gratitude of the sisters of the whole world who, in this moment, are close to you and with you praise the Lord for the many graces which He has granted to you.

The spirit of all is full of gratitude toward God for so much good and therefore together we sing our magnificat because the Lord "has done great things."

After the Lord, our gratitude goes to the first sisters who arrived in the United States to sow the seed of the Pauline charism. They "believed" when there was still nothing and they abandoned themselves to the powerful action of the Lord.

Thanks also to the first United States sisters who with sacrifice "left all" to enter to form a part of a family which, at the time, was still foreign.

Thanks to all the people of the United States which has been the "good earth" upon which the seed sown took root and bore fruit.

Thanks to the ecclesiastical authorities and to the civil authorities which have always appreciated and encouraged our Congregation and our apostolate.

Thanks to the friends, cooperators and benefactors who have sustained us in difficult moments and have helped us to overcome the inevitable difficulties.

Thanks also to all the sisters who have come in the "second and in the third hour" and to those who will come in the future: the work of God is not yet fulfilled, the confines of the world have not yet been reached, the seed sown has not terminated in giving its fruit. If the first have tilled the soil, to the others is the duty to continue the work by realizing it with dynamism and renewed courage. The Lord, who is faithful, will not let His grace be lacking.

Affectionately,

Suor Maria Cevolani
Superior General

How can we thank God for all His graces and blessings of these past fifty years of our existence in the great United States of America!

The best way to show our gratitude is to promise our Divine Master to continue to strain forward in performing our apostolate of evangelization, given to us by our Founder—go to all, no matter the race, color or creed.

We humbly express our sincere gratitude to their Eminences, the Cardinals, and to their Excellencies, the Archbishops and Bishops of our country, as well as to the Priests and Religious, for the opportunity they have given us to cooperate in the spreading of the Word of God with our apostolate among their faithful.

We also ask our Lord to abundantly bless our good benefactors for their generosity and cooperation.

"Glory to God and peace to men" is our motto. May our patron, St. Paul, give to each of us his love of God and zeal for souls, so that we may be his worthy daughters.

May we always be docile instruments in the hands of God and of our Superiors, so that we may be able to help promote the greater glory of God, the exaltation of His Church and the salvation of souls.

Sister Paula

Riflessione su la chiamata da Dio, come sono stato illuminato
dalla voce di Dio e dalla parola del Direttore spirituale:
I vari passi: la stampa ed organizzazione,
il cinema gradualmente,
la radio-Televisione,
il disco iniziato.
Meditare a lungo, in continuo progresso, secondo
l'ora "la Costituzione della comunicazione sociale"

meditare ogni mese su questa vocazione.
— La preghiera quotidiana per corrispondere all'apostolato =

"Reflections on the call of God,
as I was illumined by the voice of God
and by the words
of my spiritual director:
The various steps:
the press and organization,
gradually the cinema,
radio, television,
launching of records.
Meditate long and progressively,
depending on time,
on the 'Constitution (decree)
of Social Communications.'
Meditate every month on this vocation.
Daily prayer in order to correspond
to the apostolate."

—Father James Alberione, SSP, STD
Founder

Alba, Italy — 1915

A Look at the History of the Congregation

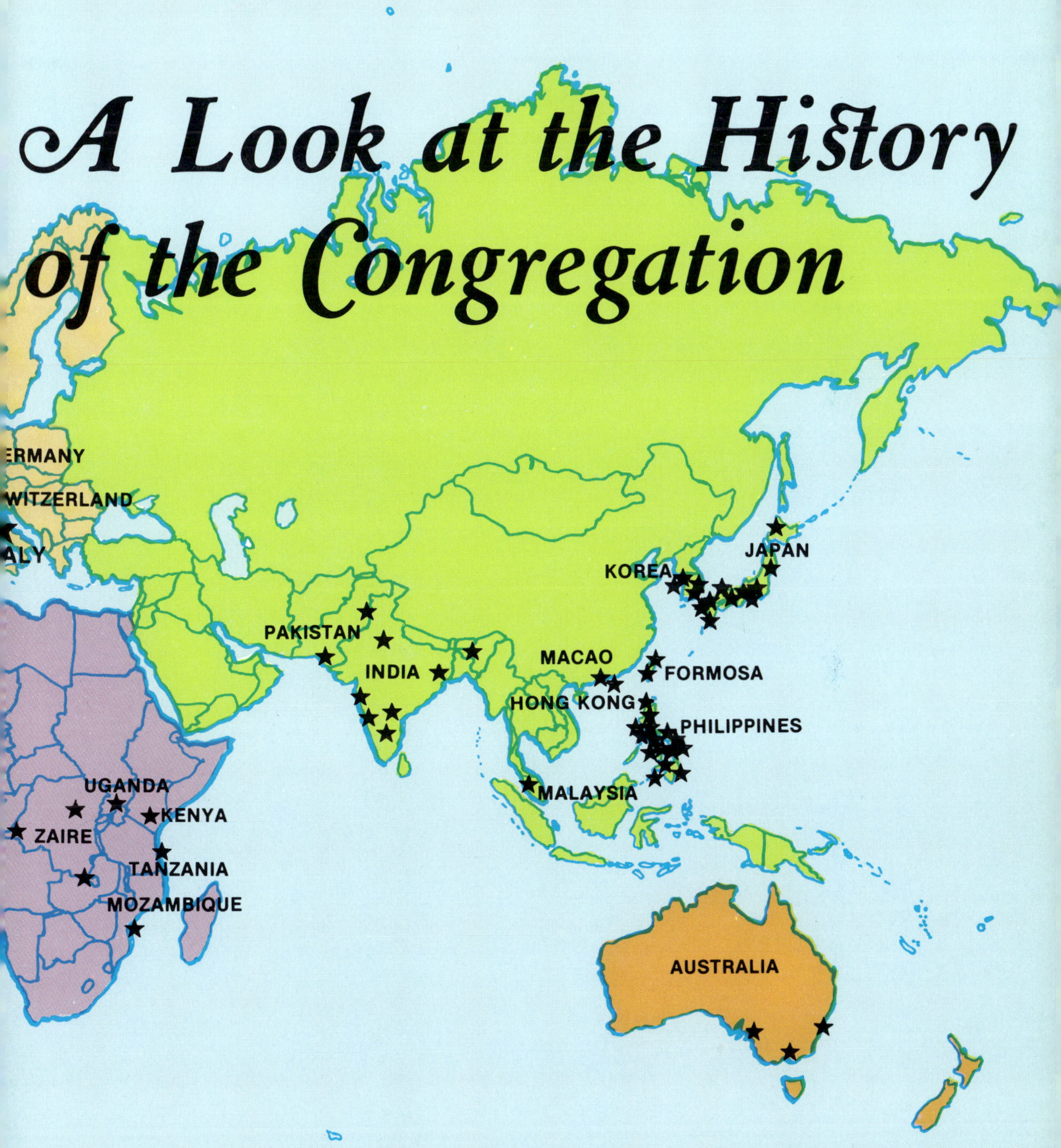

The Daughters of St. Paul in the World Today

It was in 1932 that I entered the religious congregation of the Daughters of St. Paul in Rome. It was during the same month—June—that I saw Mother Paula, who was then a young sister, twenty-four years old, with another sister younger than she, leaving for the United States of America, for the great city of New York. They were sent to begin our mission in this new world.

The year before—1931—two other young sisters had left for Brazil to launch our congregation in São Paolo, followed by others who went to Argentina. Up to this point these were the only three nations to which our sisters had been sent. In Italy, however, our congregation had already begun to spread to different cities.

Our Founder, Rev. James Alberione, had started our religious congregation in Alba, Piedmont, in 1915, only seventeen years before my entrance. He had chosen Teresa Merlo as the leader of the first group of young women. Her name in religion was Thecla.

In 1914, before beginning the Daughters of St. Paul, Father Alberione had founded the Society of St. Paul, the priests and brothers of the newborn Pauline Family. Both religious congregations have the same mission: to evangelize, that is, to diffuse the Gospel, with the media of social communication. At that time only the press was available, while the radio and films were being developed. TV and the mini-media did not exist. But the Founder already knew that his congregations had the mission from God to use all the modern media of communication that technical progress would provide in the future to spread the Gospel. "Go and teach all nations what I taught you" (Mt. 28:19) were Jesus' own words.

Father Alberione was inspired to do just that when, as a sixteen-year-old seminarian, he spent four hours in adoration before the Blessed Sacrament on the night between the 19th and 20th centuries. During this time of adoration he was inspired by the Divine Master to do something for the men of today.

In his written remembrances of that decisive night, he tells us what he decided to do:

"I had read Pope Leo XIII's invitation to pray for the century that was about to begin." The Pope "had stressed the needs of the Church, the new means of evil, the duty to oppose the press with the press, organization with organization, the need to bring the Gospel to the masses, the social questions....

"I prayed that the new century might be born in the Eucharistic Christ, that new apostles would reform laws, schools, literature, the press, customs; that the Church would launch a new mission campaign, that the new means of apostolate would be used well....

"These things were so deeply impressed on my mind and heart that from then on they would always dominate my thoughts, prayers, interior work and aspirations. I felt obliged to serve the Church, the men of the new century and to work with others.

"At first I thought of a Catholic organization of writers, technicians, book dealers and salesmen—all Catholics to whom I would give direction, work and the spirit of the apostolate.... But soon, in a greater light, toward 1910, I took a definite step: writers, technicians and propagators, but *men and women religious.*"

Very seldom did we see our Founder or our Co-Foundress, Mother Thecla Merlo, in Rome, because until 1935, they remained in Alba to consolidate the beginnings of the congregation. There were many of us in Rome—in fact, we were sixty postulants and a number of pre-novices. Already we were working with much enthusiasm to print the Word of God. We did everything: from setting the type to printing, sewing the books and binding them. We also prepared many monthly parish bulletins. For a good number of years, we also produced weekly Catholic newspapers for five dioceses. In addition, we published many books on the writings of the Fathers of the Church, on religious instruction, and on the lives of the saints. Everything was for evangelization. We were taught from the time we entered the convent what our mission was: evangelization with the media of social communication. Father Alberione told us: "The apostolate consists in giving salvation to humanity: Jesus Christ, Way, Truth and Life. Preach with modern means."

Young as we were (the oldest among us was perhaps eighteen years old), we worked with great fervor. We knew what we were doing in the Church for the People of God, in fact, for everybody. Two by two we visited families, schools, parishes, everyone—and this was our main purpose—to *bring* the Word of God. We felt that we had the mission of Jesus. He had gone about preaching the kingdom of heaven, and that was what we were doing. That was what the Apostles did: they went to preach the same doctrine, the same Word of God that Jesus had preached for the salvation of all. This was our call: to continue this mission, to bring the Word of God, the Word of salvation, to all.

Did the people understand what we were doing? Not always. Did we find difficulties? Yes, we did, because it was a new mission in the Church. Neither the laity, nor the priests, nor even all the bishops understood our mission in those beginning years.

But we went in the name of the Lord, and soon enough, as the Founder had predicted, the bishops and pastors were calling us to bring the Word of God to their people, for their religious instruction and salvation. As St. Paul says, to be saved we are to believe. But then he asks: how can they believe if there is no one to preach? Yes, there is preaching in the Church, but at that time, even in Italy, a

Catholic nation, how many people did not go to church! And the Founder said that we were to go to all, to bring everyone to God.

Soon enough grateful pastors were writing beautiful letters saying that after the Daughters of St. Paul had visited, diffusing their religious magazines, their books and, naturally, leaving a word of encouragement, many more people were going to Mass and the sacraments. The Founder would always repeat, "Bring people to church; bring them to the sacraments. We must always lead souls to paradise, not those who lived ten centuries ago, but those who are living today. We must take the world and men as they are today, to do good today." And we saw many, many entering or returning to the Church, the font of grace.

The congregation progressed steadily, first of all in Italy. There, each of the major cities was soon blessed with a "St. Paul Catholic Book and Film Center," and a number of sisters eventually visited all the dioceses in the nation. On December 13, 1943, the congregation received approval of its Constitutions by way of experiment. Final papal approval came on March 15, 1953.

In the meantime, Father Alberione and Mother Thecla sent sisters to begin our mission in different nations. As I mentioned:

1931—Brazil and then Argentina
1932—United States of America
1935—France
1938—Philippines
1948—Chile, Colombia, Japan and Mexico
1950—India
1952—Canada and Switzerland
1955—Australia and England
1956—Spain and Venezuela
1957—Portugal
1958—the Congo (Zaire)
1959—Formosa (Taiwan)
1960—Korea and Peru
1961—Malaysia

By this time Father Alberione and Mother Thecla, still in good health, had visited this worldwide congregation five times. Mother Paula herself had also been sent from the U.S.A. to begin three of these foundations: Mexico, India, and Canada. In 1963, a foundation was begun in Bolivia, and then after the death of Mother Thecla in 1964, the Daughters of St. Paul spread to other parts of the globe:

1964—Germany, Uganda, and Uruguay
1965—Pakistan
1967—Mozambique and Puerto Rico
1969—Macao
1970—Tanzania
1976—Kenya
1978—Hong Kong

For these various foundations, the first sisters were sent from Italy, and the native vocations who joined them worked with the same zeal as their pioneer sisters.

Continued on p. 56.

Alba—birthplace of the Pauline Family...

"The work of evangelization of the Pauline Family had its "Alba" (dawn) here, or its beginning: it is progressing; and with the press, film, radio and television, it serves the Church in the mission entrusted to it by the Divine Master."

—Fr. Alberione,
on the 40th Anniversary
of the Foundation
of the Pauline Family (1954)

When the Daughters of St. Paul asked Fr. Alberione for a picture of himself, he gave them this one, to indicate the primary place of the Eucharist in their lives and Its relation to the Gospel—the inspiration of the apostolate.

On August 20, 1914, with an hour of adoration to the most Blessed Sacrament and the blessing of the small typography, the Pauline Family was begun under the title of *Typographical School of the Little Worker.* Few rooms, few youths, a tiny chapel. The preparation had been long in the expectation that in the light of God everything would be clarified and become concrete, and divine Providence would give the means.

"When the first youths were accepted...a curious fact occurred, which was almost an alarm: 'They are depriving work and bread from the printers.' They even had recourse to the authorities. Therefore, it was necessary to be born even smaller, and not even let a wail be heard.... Then a simple title was given to these newly born apostles, ***Typographical School of the Little Worker.*** A crib. We must always and only...consider ourselves ***little workers of God*** in respect to the entire world."

—*The Founder*

Poor means of transportation were used by the new apostles of the press.

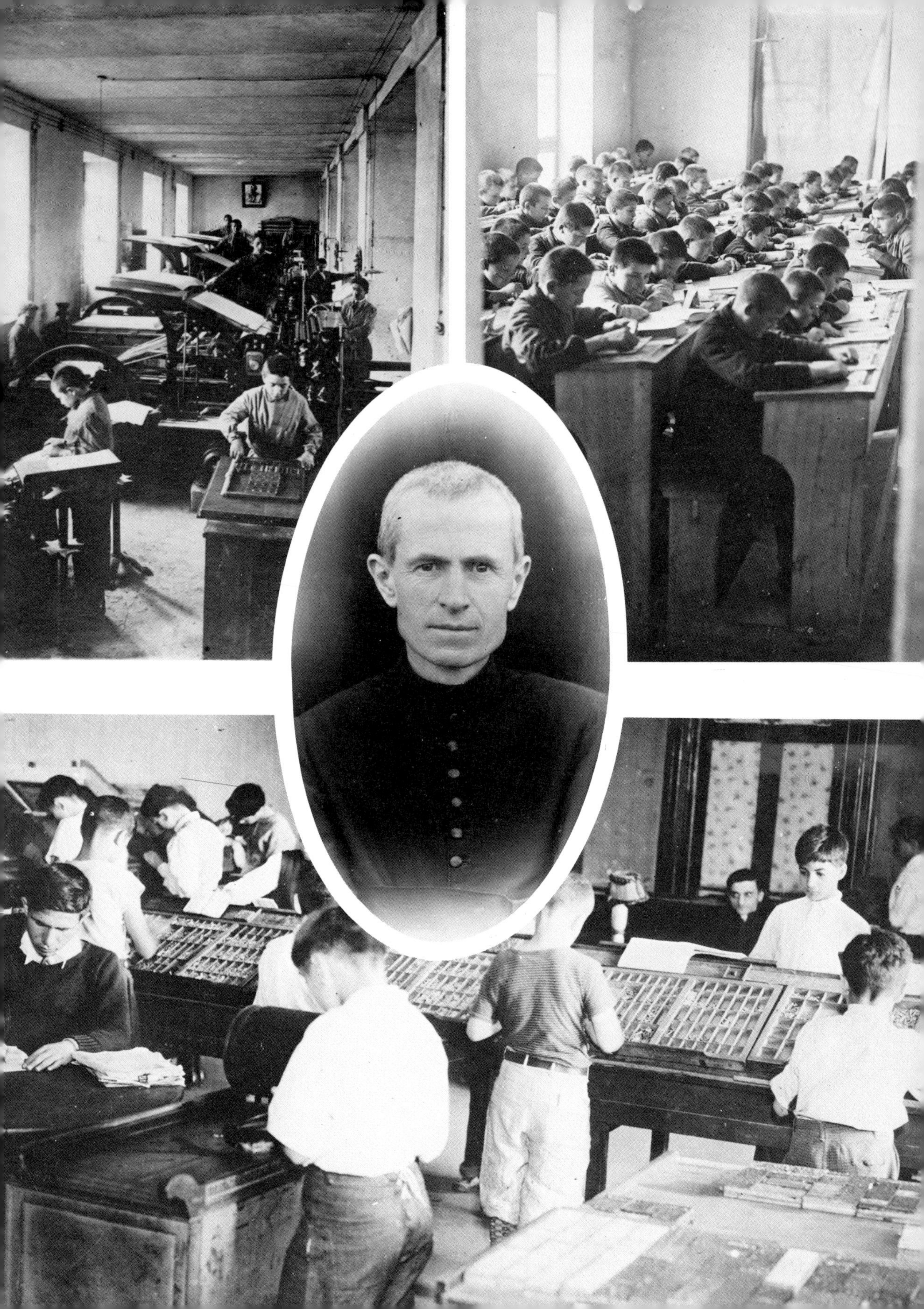

The first years and the constant growth of the Society of St. Paul. The Founder composed a chaplet to St. Paul to be recited to obtain vocations. And did the vocations come!

The first house of the Daughters of St. Paul in Alba.

Involved from the very beginning in preparing and diffusing the Word of God in book form

Mother Thecla Merlo, Co-Foundress

"She has been a constant help to me: in giving the Daughters of St. Paul a good spiritual, intellectual and apostolic formation; in developing their specific apostolate; in overcoming the many difficulties."

—The Founder

The first Daughters of St. Paul: Mother Thecla is seated, the first from the left.

In 1928, the Daughters of St. Paul first donned the religious habit.

The Sisters, true Daughters of St. Paul, were very devoted to their father and patron, and he in turn blessed their devotion with growth in numbers and apostolate.

Holding the picture of St. Paul at left is Sr. Paula Cordero who, in 1932, was chosen to begin the mission of the congregation in the United States.

The Daughters of St. Paul were started by the Founder in their mission of evangelization in 1929. Two by two, they visited the families of the Piedmont, bringing the life of St. John Bosco, on the occasion of his beatification.

This form of distribution was to be extended to all nations, together with many other forms.

SONO LA VERITÀ
LA VIA E LA VITA

"We were sixty postulants and a number of pre-novices. Already we were working with much enthusiasm to print the Word of God.

"Young as we were (the oldest among us was perhaps eighteen years old), we worked with great fervor." *(See p. 24.)*

Sisters and postulants work side-by-side in the apostolate rooms, under the fatherly gaze of St. Paul.

During World War II when Rome was bombarded, the statue of St. Paul (upper right-hand corner) was gouged by shrapnel, but this good father kept his daughters and their machines completely untouched. At the request of Mother Paula, the statue was donated to the Daughters of St. Paul of the United States where it can still be seen in a niche of their chapel in Boston.

The mission of evangelization has its climax in the distribution stage. "If the apostle would not directly bring the good book, the good magazine, very many would not have it."

—The Founder

The Daughters of St. Paul visit inmates at a women's penitentiary to give them "the truth that sets them free."

Among God's little ones, Il Giornalino *(The Little News paper) was a favorite. Its American counterpart is* My Friend

Workers flock to a book exhibit which the sisters had set up in the yard of the factory.

Chosen by God for a New Mission—Evangelization with the Media of Social Communication

An Encounter with the Founder and Co-Foundress

Like the boys of the "first hour," so the boys who came later were also conquered by the dynamism of Father Alberione who, when he was only 16, decided irrevocably "to do something for the people of the 20th century."

His office. On his desk stood:

—a statue of the DIVINE MASTER: "Jesus Master, sanctify my mind and increase my faith. Jesus, Way of holiness, make me Your faithful imitator";

—and a GLOBE: "We were born to give Jesus Christ, the Way, Truth and Life. We are here to accomplish an apostolate with the spirit and strength of St. Paul."

Explaining the Constitutions to the Daughters of St. Paul in 1961, at a 20-day retreat in Ariccia, Rome

Five times he traveled around the world to visit his sons and daughters, making himself, like St. Paul, "all things to everyone."

Following the Divine Master's example and stimulated by St. Paul, Father Alberione searched for the adequate method and means of communicating the Good News to people of the electronic era.

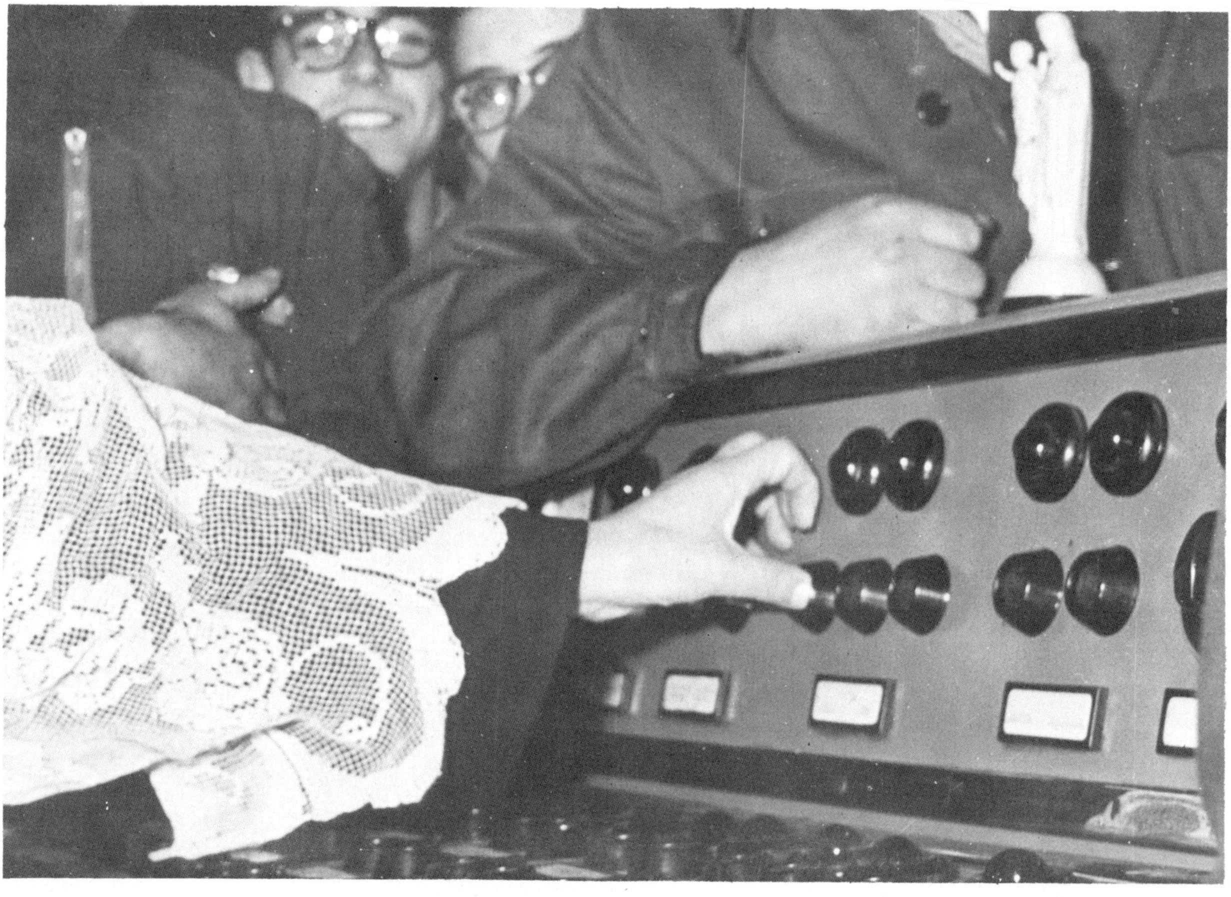

He did it by pioneering the use of the mass media. It wasn't easy, but history and Vatican II have validated his vision.

With His Holiness, Pope Pius XII

With His Holiness, Pope John XXIII

Due to the esteem that Pope John XXIII nourished for Father James Alberione, His Holiness invited him to be among the superiors general participating in the assembly of the Council Fathers of Vatican II. Very grateful for this honor, Father Alberione would arrive on time for each session; in humility he offered his contribution of prayer and witness.

Father Alberione shunned personal recognition. But because of his great love and service for society and the Church, high authorities in turn honored him...

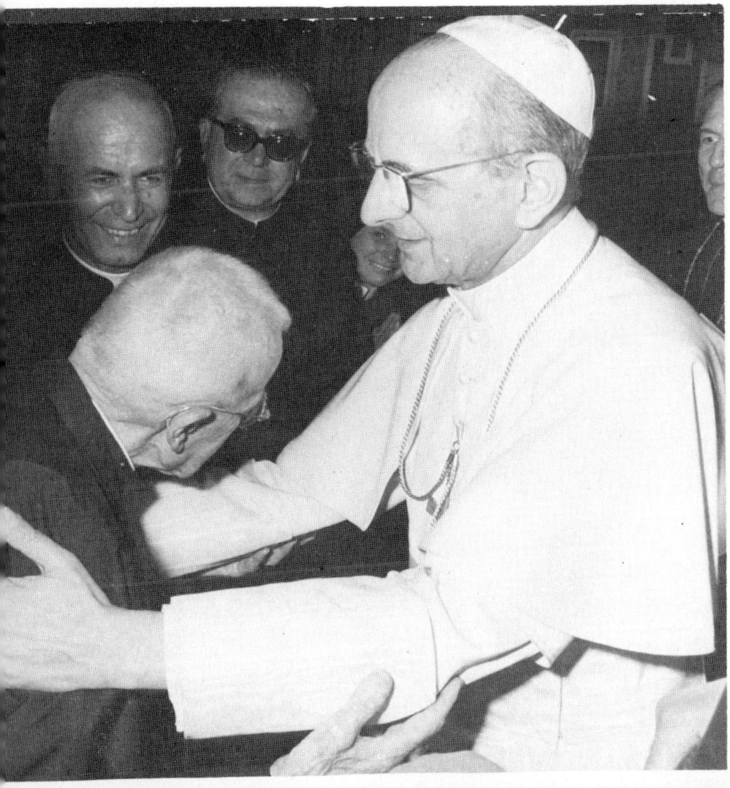

June 28, 1969:

"As a sign of our benevolence and recognition, and for the comfort of all the Pauline Family, as a stimulus to those who dedicate themselves to the Catholic apostolate through the generous promotion and the right use of the instruments of social communication, We want to confer today on the venerated and venerable Father James Alberione Our medallion: *Pro Ecclesia et Pontifice!*"

—Paul VI

August 15, 1967:

Father Alberione poses with the late Augustin Cardinal Bea, President of the Secretariat for Christian Unity, and with officials of the World Council of Churches at the retreat house of the Society of St. Paul, Ariccia (Rome).

January 26, 1958:

On the occasion of the 50th anniversary of the Founder's ordination, the president of the Italian Republic, Giovanni Gronchi, conferred an award on Father Alberione in merit of his contribution to education, culture and art.

He receives the medal from Professor Nazareno Padellaro.

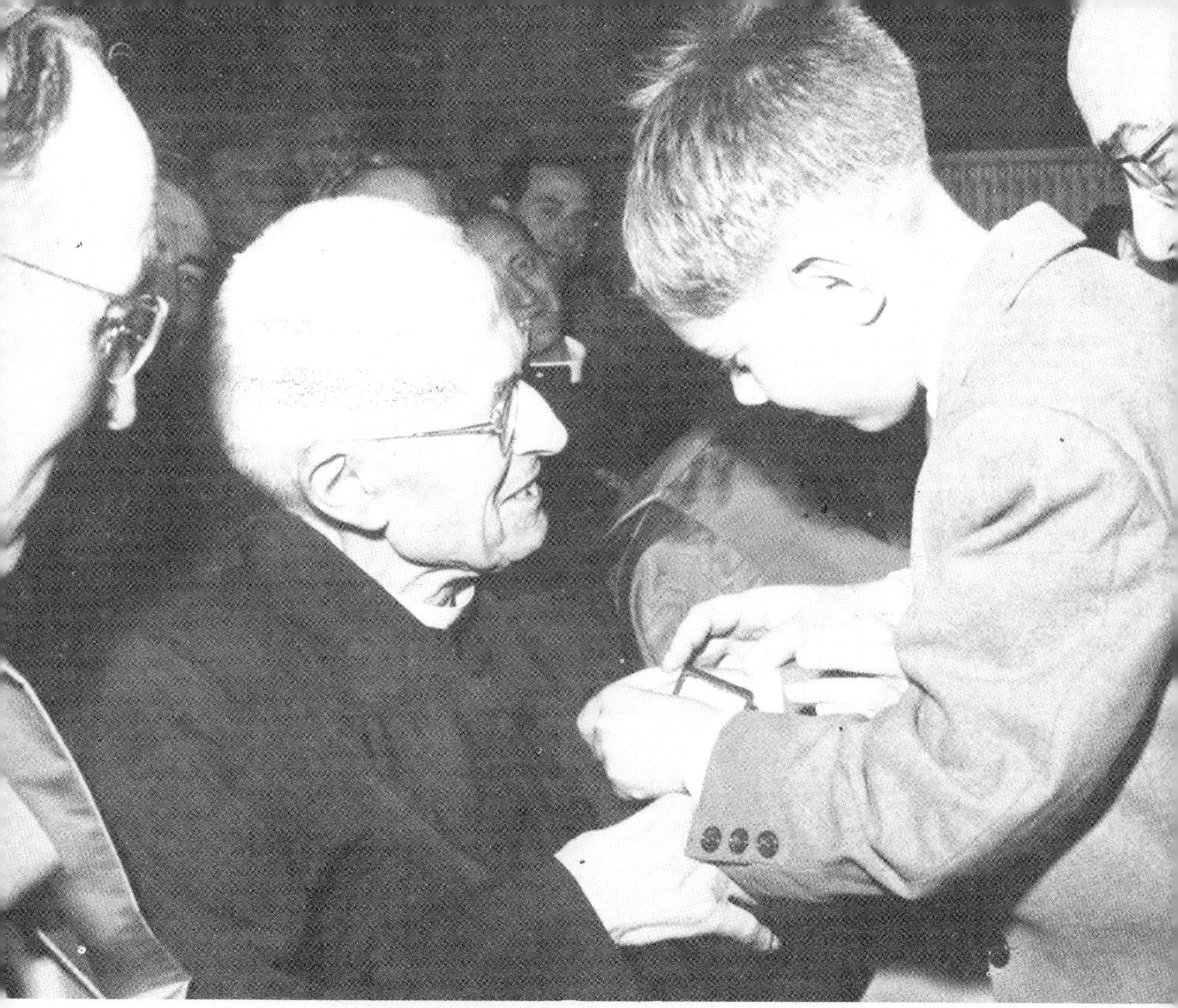

Rome, May 16, 1964: Receiving the "Gold Star."

September 27, 1964:
The mayor of Alba confers honorary citizenship on Father Alberione.

Father Alberione looking at the shrine dedicated to Mary, Queen of Apostles. This magnificent church is the fulfillment of the vow he made to our Lady during the Second World War: if she would spare all the sons and daughters of the Pauline Family throughout the world, he would build a temple in her honor in the Holy City.

At the main altar of this church appear the words spoken to him by Christ in a vision: "Do not be afraid; I am with you. From here (i.e., from the tabernacle) I want to enlighten. Be sorry for your sins."

These words of reassurance also appear in all the Pauline churches and chapels throughout the world.

Albano Laziale (Rome),

In August, 1963, two months after his election, Paul VI visited the clinic of the Queen of Apostles, which Father Alberione had designed for the physical and spiritual health of the members of his Pauline Family.

Father Alberione and his successor, Father Luigi Zanoni, welcome His Holiness to the hospital.

The Pope visits the sisters. Among them was Sr. Domenica Dolcini, a Daughter of St. Paul from the United States, who died of cancer less than a month later, at the age of thirty-seven.

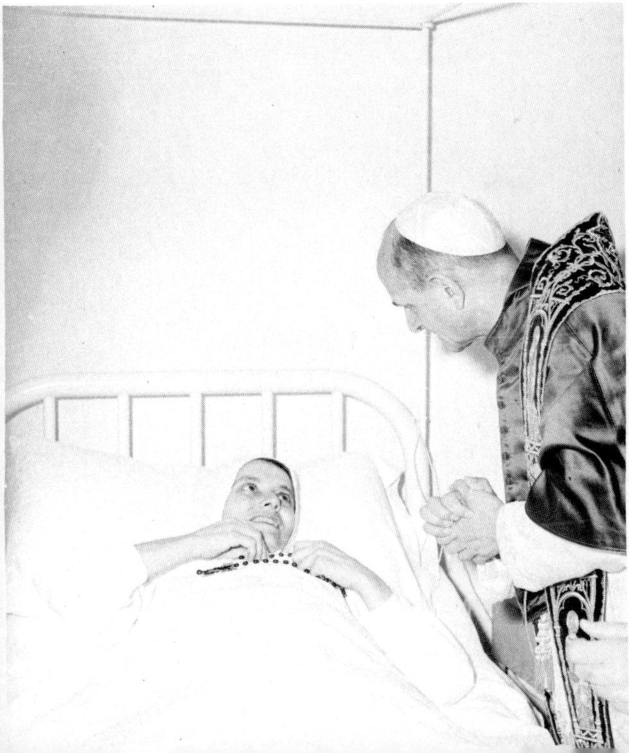

The Holy Father with Mother Thecla and her vicar, Mother Ignatius Balla

Like Father Alberione, Mother Thecla blended contemplation and action. This was the source of her strength in the heavy responsibility she had of governing a world-wide congregation from 1915 to 1964.

Mother Thecla had at heart the clinic staffed by her daughters. She often visited the sick sisters there and brought much joy with her maternal presence.

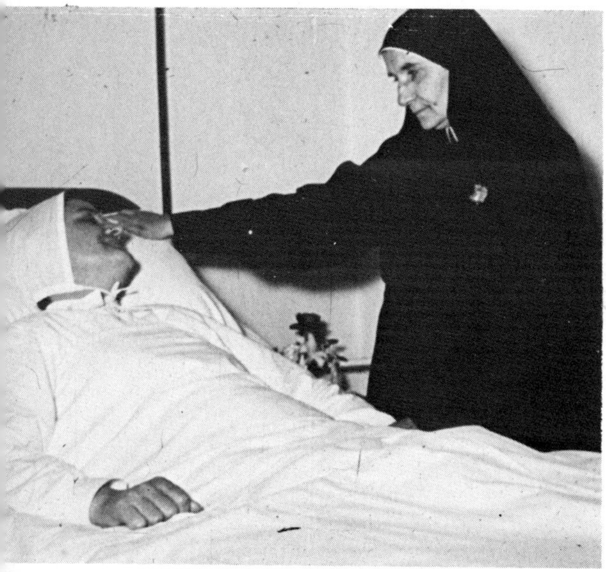

She corresponded weekly with her daughters around the globe.

"Be serene, joyful; show yourselves to be strong women, superior to the little adversities which are never lacking in life. Overlook them. This house must be a house of observance."

—Mother Thecla

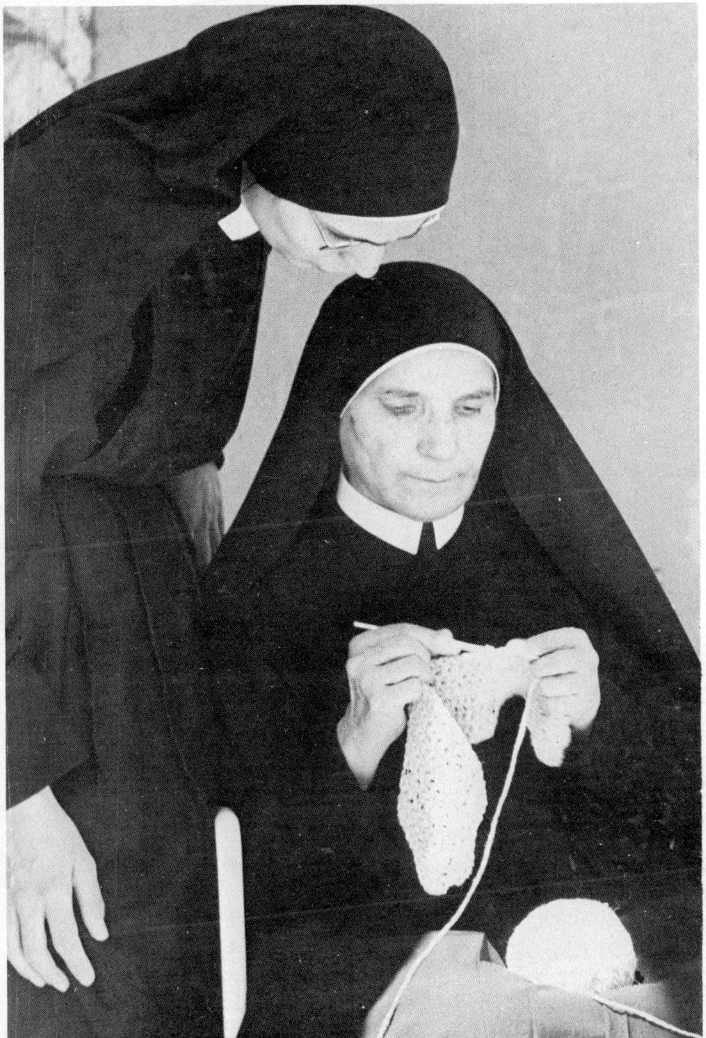

Despite her busy schedule, Mother Thecla always found time to be in the midst of her sisters, a real inspiration to young and old alike.

Like the Founder, she traveled around the world five times to visit her daughters.

Strong, yet very maternal, Mother Thecla found herself at home with her daughters in every part of the world. Here she welcomes her vicar, Mother Ignatius, after her visit to the U.S. Province.

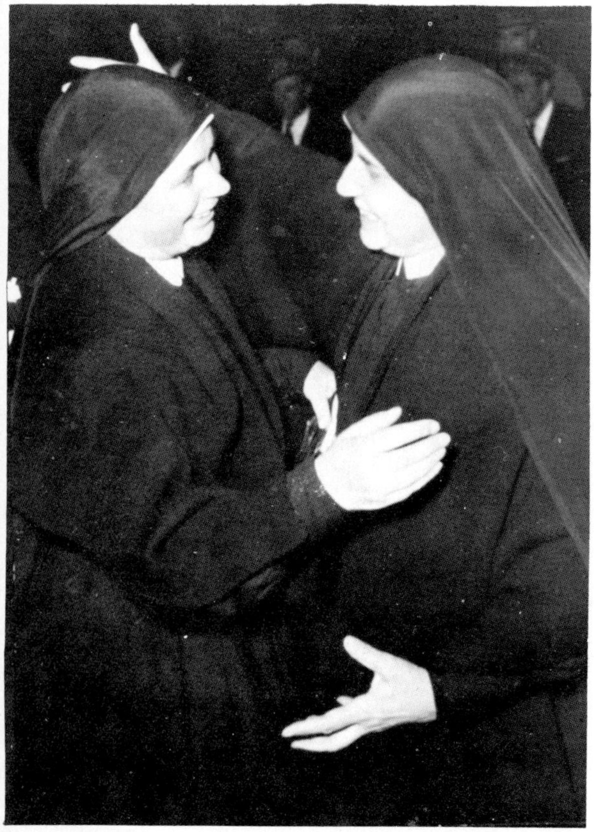

On her last trip to the African missions, she was accompanied by Mother Paula.

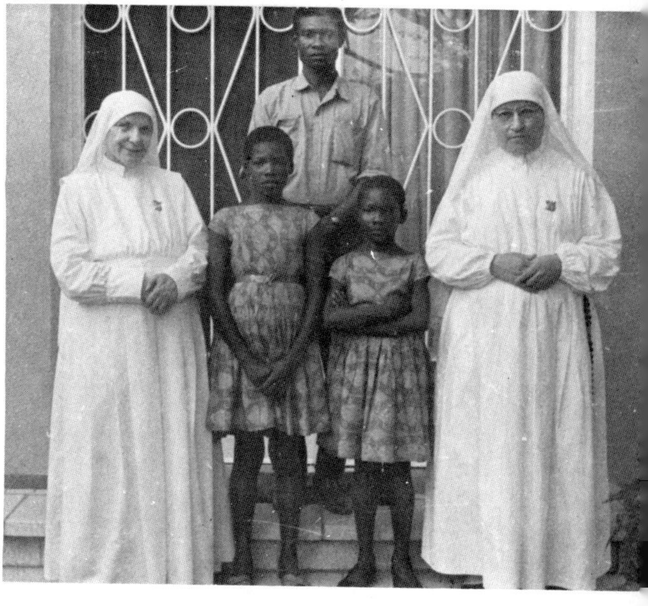

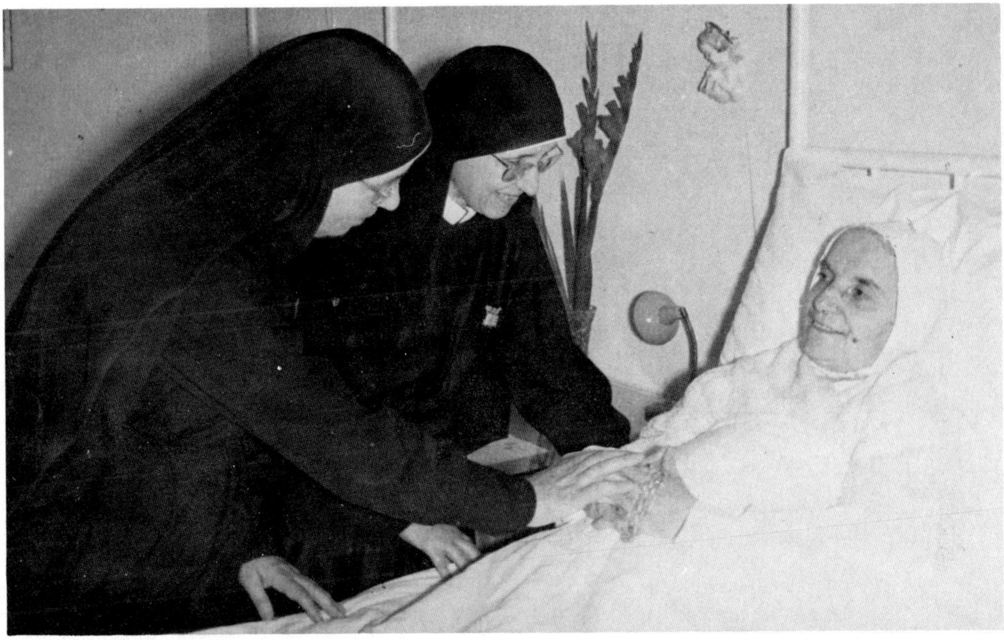

Above: Mother Paula and Sr. Nazarena visit Mother Thecla during her last illness. She died on February 5, 1964.
Below: During one of his trips to Rome, Cardinal Cushing stops to see Mother Thecla and thoughtfully leaves her his autographed zucchetto.

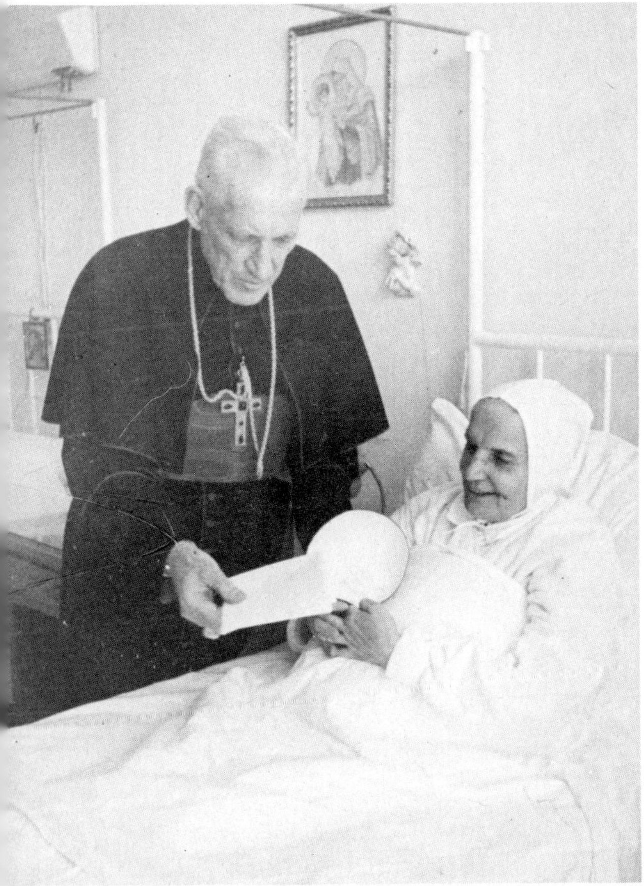

"I want to offer my life that the Daughters of St. Paul may all become saints." —*Mother Thecla*

"Jesus, I hope in You, I believe in You, I love You with all my heart."

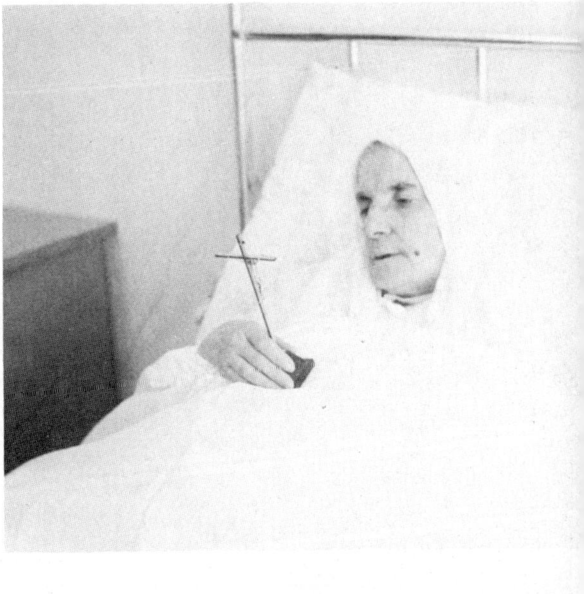

The Founder's brief moments of rest on the terrace of the General House, Rome. His poor chair was donated to the Daughters of St. Paul in the United States and is kept as a precious remembrance in the house of formation in Boston.

Until the end of his life, almost eight years after the death of Mother Thecla, Father Alberione kept informed about the needs of his sons and daughters throughout the world and supported them with his sufferings and his prayer.

The concluding chapter of Father Alberione's life, marked by intense pain, was sanctified by an ever-increasing union with Jesus Master and with the Pauline Family:

"I remember everyone in every Mass, and as the last act of the evening, I send my blessing to all. I ask prayers as the conclusion of my poor life draws near."

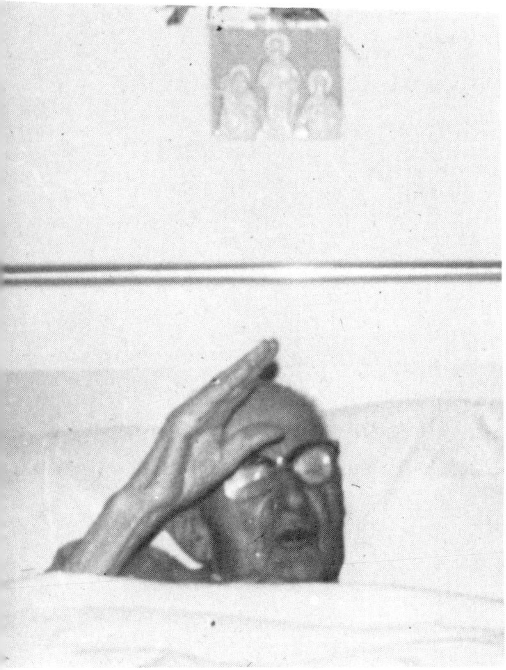

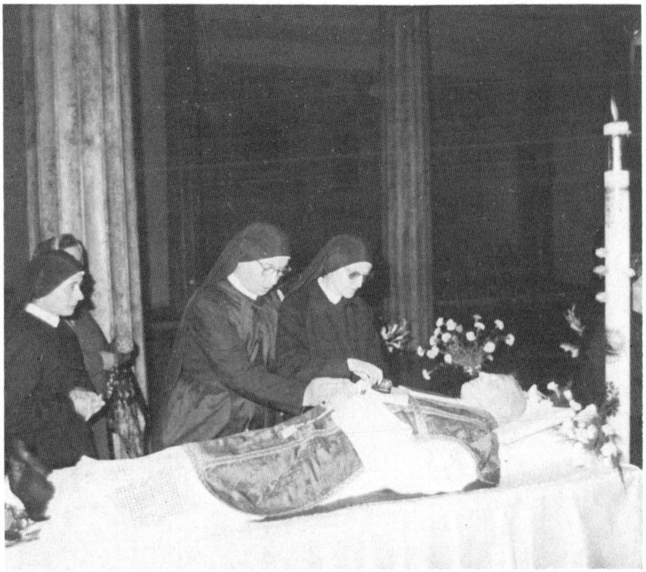

Divine Providence had arranged that, at the time of the Founder's death, the Daughters of St. Paul from around the world would be assembled in Rome for their general chapter. Mother Paula was among the delegates.

A Bible rests under the Founder's head—a symbol of his devotion to the Word of God.

Father Luigi Zanoni, Father Alberione's successor, pays his respects to the Founder of the Pauline Family, now entrusted to him. At his right is Father Renato Perino, the present superior general; at his far left, Father Stanislaus Crovella, who had come to the United States in 1932, and had become the provincial superior of the Society of St. Paul in America.

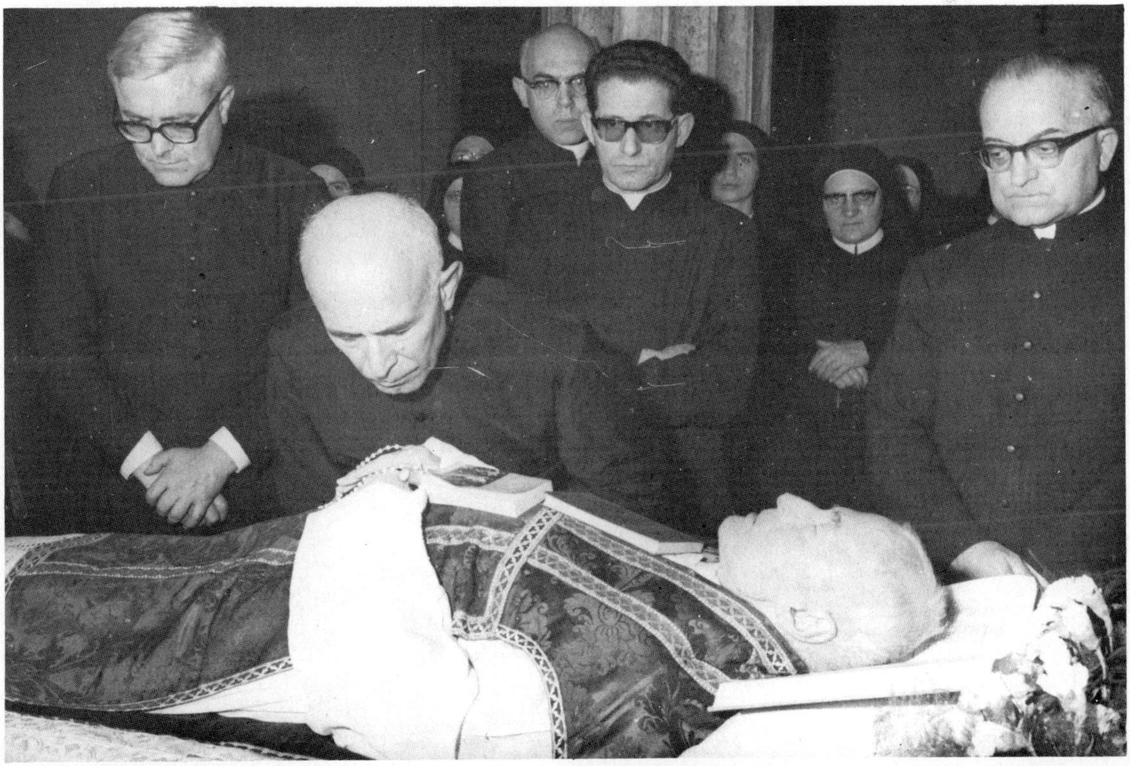

VOSOTROS
TENED EL DOLOR

局書日

LIBRERIA SAN PABLO
apostolado de las ediciones

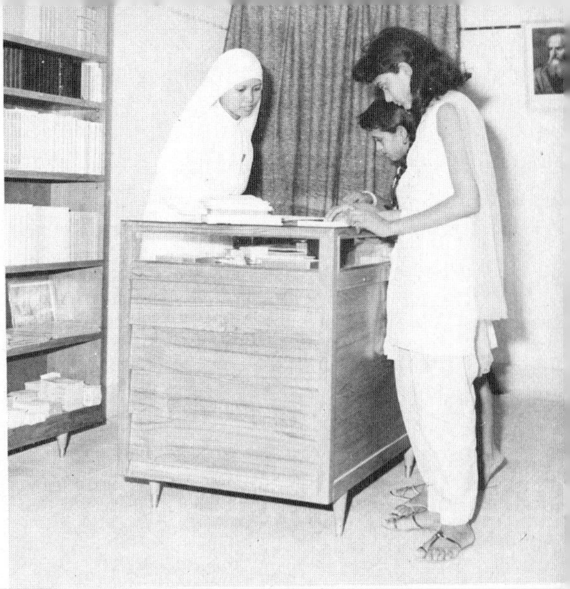

Even though Mother Thecla had poor health throughout her life, she never granted herself any rest. She often visited her daughters in every nation, bringing to them her maternal love and encouragement.

Continued from p. 25.

The secret of this great fervor is the solid spirituality given us by our Founder, a spirituality centered in the devotion to the Divine Master, the Way, the Truth and the Life. In the words of the Founder, this spirituality is the living of every verse of the Gospel, emphasizing all of it—every word and every example given by our Divine Master. There we find the truths to believe, the morality to live by, and the means of grace to strengthen and sanctify us.

Father Alberione says, "You were born of the Eucharist." He always recommended, too, the daily hour of adoration before the Blessed Sacrament. In this hour he included spiritual reading, especially from Sacred Scripture. The New Testament was to be preferred and in particular the Gospels and the Letters of St. Paul, since St. Paul is the best interpreter of and commentator on the Gospel.

Father Alberione also gave us a great devotion to Mary under the title "Queen of Apostles," because Mary formed the first Apostle of the Father, her Son Jesus, and then the Twelve, especially after Jesus' ascension, and continues to form all apostles throughout the ages. The Founder chose this devotion, however, especially because of our mission, which is the same as Mary's: to give Jesus to the world.

St. Paul, the great Apostle, was given to us as our protector, our father, and as Father Alberione says, even as our Founder. What is most important in this devotion to St. Paul is to do what he would do if he were living in our own times: to use the most effective means to bring the Word of God to this world for the salvation of all peoples. After the Founder's death, the praise most often repeated was that he had been instrumental in having twenty million copies of the Bible diffused.

This rich spirituality was passed on to the whole Pauline Family (the ten institutes founded by Father Alberione: five religious congregations, four secular institutes, and the Pauline Cooperators).

When in 1949, I was sent to this country, I was primarily impressed by the first sisters' bringing here our spirituality: the Divine Master honored with the hour of adoration especially, and the love and imitation of Mary, Queen of Apostles, and of St. Paul the Apostle. Oh, it was so genuine, so felt and so lived by the sisters!

The first time I met our Cooperators in New York was on the feast of St. Paul, June 30th. Besides planning a spiritual day, the sisters also had a bazaar for the entertainment of these good people. But both men and women were just as interested in going to pray in chapel. How much devotion they showed to our patron and father, St. Paul!

Daughters of St. Paul—this name was given to our sisters in the very beginning by the people themselves. Up to that time our congregation had no title yet. But because there was a large framed picture of St. Paul hanging in their little book center in Susa, near Turin, people connected the sisters with that saint and started to call them "Daughters of St. Paul." This name means that we are to live as St. Paul lived—for the glory of God and the salvation of souls. We are to have the same zeal he had in traveling the whole then-known world, to bring Christ—Christ crucified—to all people.

From the very beginning the sisters were taught that as Daughters of St. Paul they were to bring the Word of God to all, regardless of creed or race, for Jesus had come on earth to suffer and die to save all. So our sisters here in the United States approach not only Catholics, but people of all faiths and those of no faith at all.

Even though I had been in the general motherhouse in Rome for seventeen years, close to our Founder and Co-Foundress, I felt immediately at home here in the States because I found the same Pauline spirit.

At the time I arrived—1949—even though the sisters had been here for seventeen years already, there were only two convents: Staten Island, New York, and Youngstown, Ohio. Vocations were few. Although there was no novitiate yet, the sisters were very fervent. When I asked why the expansion of the congregation here in the States was taking place so slowly, I came to realize that even the works of God are sometimes hindered by higher authorities; He permits this in His providence.

In 1932, when the sisters had arrived in the United States, penniless and without knowing the language, they had encountered the same difficulties that the congregation had experienced in Italy: a new vocation, a mission in the Church unheard of before, about which even ecclesiastical authorities were dubious. So the sisters had been told there was no need for the Daughters of St. Paul here; they could, therefore, go back to Italy from where they had come, or they could try another place.

Living in humility and sustained by the faith that God's representatives had sent them here, the sisters had kept praying. The Superior of the little community herself, Sr. Edvige Soldano, after four years was destined first to China and then to the Philippine Islands. Sister Paula Cordero was chosen to replace her, and after two more years of prayers and sacrifices, finally the long-awaited permission to remain in the great Archdiocese of New York was granted.

After having moved from one place to another—always in cramped rented quarters—with great sacrifice they had bought the property in Staten Island which we still have today. (In fact, now we have a new convent there.) After this the sisters were able to perform our mission without hindrance.

Already in 1949, our sisters were visiting not only families, but also factories. For a few days I myself had the experience, and it was a beautiful experience, of going to visit so many people crowded in those large factories—hundreds and hundreds, and thousands and thousands. It was a beautiful experience, I repeat, because I felt once again the greatness of our divine mission—to bring the Faith to those people, who at times were searching for it without even realizing it.

It was not only the various parishes in New York City that our sisters visited, but also those in upstate New York, as well as those in New Jersey, Connecticut, Rhode Island and Massachusetts; they even took on the parish census when pastors requested it. These first sisters, who were still learning English, brought so many people back to the sacraments! Many couples had their marriages blessed. A number of children were baptized. Countless elderly people—who had not gone to church for perhaps twenty, thirty, forty or fifty years—returned to the sacraments.

Again, however, the Daughters of St. Paul experienced difficulties in opening convents in the different dioceses.

The Founder, Father Alberione, and the Co-Foundress, Mother Thecla, came quite often to visit us. When the Founder was asked, "What can we do to open convents? Our requests are not answered positively"—he who desired a convent in each one of the states replied: "Well, the bishops have to see what you do in the Church. So start to send them a few publications from your presses every year. From the fruits they will come to know you. And the day will come when they will call you and you will not be enough to go and serve them in the dioceses. I always envision great and wonderful things happening in the USA—many vocations, films, publications.... The time has come for you to cast, not a mere fishing line, but a huge net, in the United States."

Certainly the Founder, as a founder, was inspired to say these words, because in 1952, convents began to open one after another:

1944—*Youngstown, OH* (later closed when the convent in Cleveland was opened)
1952—*Alexandria, LA* (later closed when the convent was opened in Baton Rouge)
1953—*San Antonio, TX*, and *Boston*, MA (Book Center)
1956—*Boston*, MA (Provincial House and House of Formation);
San Diego CA; *Buffalo*, NY, and *Fitchburg*, MA (later closed)
1959—*Miami, FL*
1962—*Bridgeport, CT*
1963—*Bronx, NY*

1964—*Billerica, MA* (Retreat House)
1965—*Oakland, CA* (later closed when the convent was opened in San Francisco)
1966—*Cleveland, OH*
1968—*New Orleans, LA*
1969—*Philadelphia, PA*
1971—*San Francisco, CA*
1973—*St. Louis, MO*
1974—*Cincinnati, OH*, and *Honolulu, HI*
1975—*Anchorage, AK* (Mother Paula had always dreamed of Alaska, but had never thought that she could have gone that far to open a convent; and yet His Excellency, Most Rev. Joseph Ryan, then Archbishop of Anchorage, called us directly!)
1977—*Jersey City, NJ*; *Baton Rouge, LA*, and *Manhattan* (Book Center) (During 1976, something very special happened in the city of New York. His Eminence, Terence Cardinal Cooke visited our convent in Staten Island, and on his own initiative requested that a Book and Film Center be opened in Manhattan. With a smile he said that Mother Paula would never have thought that a Cardinal of New York would have asked her to open a Center in the heart of the city! How true is the Word of God: "Those who sow in tears will reap rejoicing.")
1979—*Chicago, IL* (Oh, how many times Mother Paula had tried Chicago, and now the center was opened at the late Cardinal Cody's personal invitation!)
1982—*Alexandria, VA*, at the gate of the nation's capital, Washington, D.C.

And how many more bishops would like to have the Daughters of St. Paul in their dioceses! Well, as our Founder had predicted, we are still too few to be able to reach all the states. But God is blessing us today with many vocations. When I came in 1949, I missed only one thing: the great groups of vocations we had in Rome. But today, at the time of our 50th anniversary of foundation in the United States, we have been given the grace of many vocations, good and fervent vocations who only want one thing: to live the authentic religious life, as Jesus did, and to bring Him to the people of today.

Our first novitiate house here in the States was in Derby, New York. There in the stable once used for horses, we began printing our books; the garage was also used for this purpose as well as for the storage of paper. When we did not have enough room, in the summertime we worked outside to prepare the packages for mailing. The greenhouse—cold as it was especially during the winter—was used for collating the holy Bible. But when our Founder and Mother Thecla came to visit

Continued on p. 69.

Fire-Tried Golden Years

In 1932, at twenty-four years of age, Sr. Paula Cordero left her native Italy to plant the congregation on American soil.

Today in 1982, after 50 golden years, she could repeat with our father St. Paul, "I have fought the good fight" (2 Tm. 4:7). Yes, she and her sisters prayed, trusting in grace, and soon victory over all difficulties was assured!

"There is cause for rejoicing here.
You may for a time have to suffer...many trials:
but this is so that your faith,
which is more precious
than the passing splendor of fire-tried gold,
may by its genuineness
lead to praise, glory and honor...."
—1 Peter 1:6, 7

Confident in the words of the Founder—"It is the will of God"—Mother Paula prayed earnestly to obtain permission to remain in the United States. She even dropped medals of Jesus the Divine Master, Mary Queen of Apostles, and St. Paul into the grating near the chancery's cellar windows, on the radiator behind Cardinal Hayes' throne in St. Patrick's Cathedral and into the sisters' mailbox at home, so that no letter of dismissal would ever arrive.

Later, in 1964, the Founder would write: "Your fidelity to the Congregation is one of the principal secrets of your good success."

1932—The second floor apartment on Glover Street. This was the first convent until another was found.

1934—The second convent of the Daughters of St. Paul, Byron Ave., New York. Mother Edvige, pictured in the center of the front row, was the community's first superior.

The works of the Lord were born in poverty, as He was born in poverty.

1938—Staten Island—the first house owned by the sisters

Here the Founder and Co-Foundress often visited the growing community.

The sisters always treasured this crucifix and picture of Mary, Queen of Apostles, which the Founder had given them upon their departure for America. Today both are kept in Boston in a small museum together with other mementos of the very beginnings.

The first chapel of the Daughters of St. Paul in the States

Statue of St. Paul which had "saved" the sisters and apostolate rooms in Rome during World War II. Brought first to Staten Island, it was moved to Boston after the novitiate was established there.

"I pray for your sanctity and for your health. The Lord gives to you the merit for each good work. May your initiatives flourish in the United States. Above all may the United States give saints to our congregation. I bless you."

—The Founder, 1940

Not new or elegant, but truly serviceable was the sisters' first car which they used to carry out their mission. A humorous, historical note: Mother Paula was the first sister to drive a car in New York City. The chancery suggested that she wear secular clothes instead of the religious habit, in order not to shock the people.

Always two-by-two they walked to homes, offices, factories and ghettos, to bring God's saving Word to all. At night they made the books they used for this diffusion.

They extended their charity to all they could.

During World War II permission was granted to the Italian prisoners to go in turn to the sisters' convent every Sunday for a day of spiritual and moral uplift.

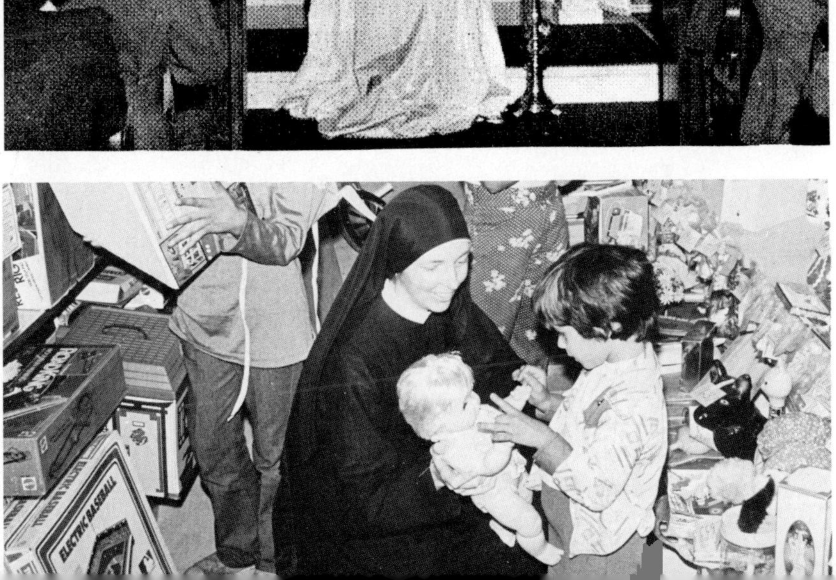

Thanks to many generous cooperators, an annual bazaar was and still is held to help support the Daughters of St. Paul in mission lands.

1949—Derby, N.Y.

The First Novitiate House—Another Humble Beginning

The Founder's words about the birth of the Pauline Family can literally be applied to this foundation: God was with them, "providing the help needed, always starting out in a stable." And in a former horse stable they did start again.

LEFT: Inconveniences were not lacking. The community had so few chairs, that at meal times these had to be carried from the school building, then back again before classes resumed.

Below left: The Daughters of St. Paul never hired gardeners. They considered recreation a relaxing and healthy change of occupation.

Above RIGHT: In the old greenhouse, the sisters gathered—by hand—the folded sheets of the Bible in numerical order...

...for the sewing machine (right). One of the sisters recalls: "Every night we diligently checked the windows near these machines—windows which ironically locked from the outside!"

Above far right: Another view of the bindery. The sisters often prayed for good weather, because when it rained, they had to put basins on top of the piles in order to catch the aftereffects of a leaky roof.

Far right: Packages of books were wrapped and tied by hand. On sunny days the sisters worked outside for lack of space in the stable.

Below right: What an inspiration it was to see Mother Paula working at the side of her sisters!

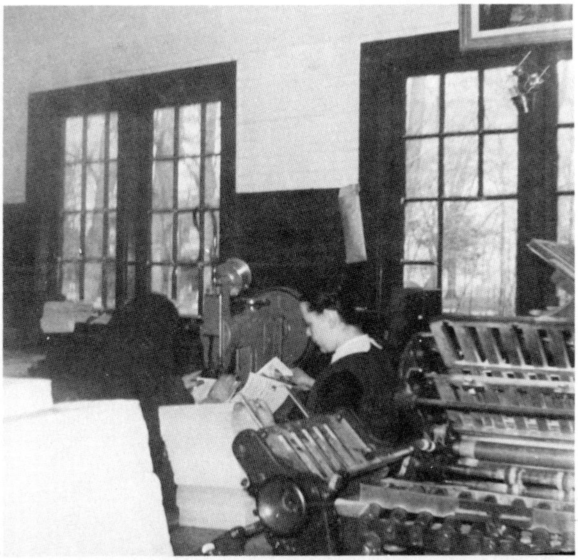

Even the chapel was small for the growing community.

Mother Paula reads the week's personal letter from Mother Thecla which she always shared with her daughters.

The Founder and Co-Foundress never spared sacrifices to visit their daughters. It was in their faith that in 1954 during their last visit to Derby they told Mother Paula that the time had come to do as St. Paul had done—to establish themselves in the largest cities and aim to open 25 convents and Book and Film Centers and to publish in one year 100 editions!

Just one year later the Founder asked of them still more faith: to open not 25 centers only, but 48—one in each state. He concluded:

"I pray the Lord to send you vocations...

...I always pray for you. I always think of beautiful and great things in the U.S.A.—vocations and film and press editions."

Continued from p. 59.
us on one occasion, they asked us to move the novitiate to a larger city, so as to be able to have our novices begin to exercise our mission of bringing people the Word of God at least once a week—the very mission that would later be theirs to fulfill every day.

So then, after many prayers and great trials, a door opened. His Excellency, Archbishop Richard J. Cushing of Boston invited us directly. Certainly he was inspired by God when he wrote to Mother Paula and said, "Your mission is great, and I want it in my archdiocese."

And so, in 1956, we moved our community from Derby to Boston. A large convent, which had been built in less than a year, was waiting, situated in Jamaica Plain, and we had a great reception planned by His Excellency, the Archbishop. When we finally came to our convent we could not believe our eyes! The building looked so large in comparison to the residence, stable, greenhouse, etc., of our property at Derby on Lake Erie.

Now this building in Jamaica Plain, Boston, was our new home. That arrival was an emotional moment. As soon as we entered the chapel the *Magnificat* was begun. It was played so beautifully on a new organ, but none of us from the community of Derby could join in the singing, for we were sobbing out of gratitude to God for having given us such a beautiful chapel, such a beautiful home. Above all, it was a large convent. So we thought, coming from a stable, until, little by little, we had to make additions. In fact, during the twenty-five years that we have been in Boston, we have built additions seven times. The convent has become like a little city, complete with our nearby burial chapel where four of our good sisters already rest.

During the homily of that first Mass in our new convent, Archbishop Cushing, who later became a Cardinal, said: "We extend to all of the members of the Daughters of St. Paul a hundred thousand welcomes to the Archdiocese of Boston. We offer them every opportunity to grow, to expand, and to do the works of their congregation without any restrictions whatsoever. We bless them and we give them our love and our prayerful mementos. May they always be as beautiful in the eyes of God as they are today."

Here in Boston we started our own high school for our pre-postulants, so that we could continue to accept girls still in high school. It is fully accredited by the Archdiocesan Department of Education. Then we started our college, St. Paul House of Studies, again with the faith of Mother Paula and the great understanding of Archbishop Cushing. Our higher studies for our postulants and sisters received the recognition of the Holy See as a Pontifical Catechetical Institute in 1981, with the recommendation of His Eminence, Humberto Cardinal Medeiros.

Besides being the center for the writing, printing and diffusion of our publications, the convent of Boston became not only the new spacious novitiate or house of formation, but the provincial house as well. From Boston our sisters are sent to the different convents mentioned before.

After the printing apostolate was well established, we began the film apostolate. In all we do, we keep in mind the entire mission given us by our Founder: to spread the Catholic Faith with the most modern media—press, films, radio and television.

We started by buying 16mm films to be rented from our centers. Today we produce them as well, having had our sisters trained for this apostolate.

Soon enough we also had the grace of beginning the apostolate of the radio. At present, twenty-four stations from coast to coast air a program a week each. Another is a shortwave station, reaching all of Europe, North Africa, and even part of the Soviet Union; an additional station is Radio Caymon, reaching the British West Indies, and portions of Central and South America.

Simultaneously with these steps came the mini-media—that is, filmstrips, cassettes, slides—all audio-visuals illustrating the Faith.

In explaining the growth of the U.S.A. province, Mother Paula gratefully acknowledges that progress has been due to the grace of God through the powerful intercession of St. Paul, and also, as she says to her sisters: "It was through your great cooperation that we have been able to accomplish so much in our great U.S.A., and now I will repeat again: you are worth a million, dearest! So please, I beg of you, pray, have faith, be docile to the grace of God, and try to be faithful Paulines all the way, as you have always been."

Although this vibrant woman of seventy-four never received any degree—due to her humility, faith and vision, she has had many honors: congratulatory letters from the President of the United States and from 146 American bishops on the occasion of her Golden Jubilee of religious profession; a citation from the Senate of the Commonwealth of Massachusetts; a flag that had been flown over the United States Capitol; a plaque from the Mayor of Anchorage, Alaska; an award bestowed at Boston's fifth annual Communicators' Mass in tribute to her fifty years "of dedicated service to God, the Church, her order and the media."

A brief profile of Mother Paula has been published in the *American Catholic Who's Who,* 1978-1979; in the *Dictionary of International Biography,* 1980; in the Encyclopedia *Contemporary Personalities,* 1981, and in the forthcoming *International Book of Honor.* Each of these volumes contains information on personalities distinguished for their achievements in our contemporary world.

In September, 1981, in preparation for the 1982 Golden Jubilee of the foundation of the Daughters of St. Paul in the United States, Mother Paula and a group of sisters were received by Pope John Paul II in a private audience.

Having heard of the celebration of their Golden Jubilee, soon after the pilgrimage and on his own initiative, His Holiness, John Paul II, very kindly honored the Daughters of St. Paul with a Papal Blessing personally signed.

Cardinals of the Roman Curia as well as the Apostolic Delegate and Cardinals, Archbishops and Bishops of the United States in great numbers, together with the Superior General of the Society of St. Paul and the Mother General in Rome, sent their very appreciated congratulatory messages for this same occasion.

Overwhelmed with gratitude, we Daughters of St. Paul renew our heartfelt fidelity to the Vicar of Christ and to all the members of the Hierarchy, and we promise to serve ever more fervently the universal and local Church with our mission of evangelization through the media of social communications.

In June, 1982, the Daughters of St. Paul of the United States solemnly celebrated the 50th anniversary of the American foundation.

Untiring and open to the signs of the times, Mother Paula instills through word and example the Pauline way of life—contemplation and apostolic action—into the ever-increasing numbers of pre-postulants, postulants, novices and professed sisters.

"America is my home. I love this great land and its wonderful people," she tells her sisters. "I thank God for calling me here to carry out our Pauline mission. I hope for the grace to leave even my body in this great nation....

"It took faith...yes, and I dare say, faith mixed with quite a few tears. But if I had to start all over again I would.... Yes, I would do it all over again. Only one thing would I wish to be different: I would demand of myself a greater faith, a greater love of God."

The present Provincial Superior, Sister Mary Domenica Vitello, the fourth Provincial, is taking her inspiration from the rich traditions of the past while looking ahead toward the future, with confidence in the words of the Founder: "Always onward! Do not stop to consider what you have done. Go ahead: The good to be done is much more."

St. Paul's motto was to strain ahead: "I strain forward; I do not look behind." And this is what we are trying to do.

Sr. C.B.

With Faith All Things Are Possible

Provincial House 1956

"In God's name I welcome you with my heart's full measure of love.

"Truly you have the spirit of St. Paul himself, because I believe if St. Paul, who was the greatest of all missionaries, were on earth today, he would utilize every modern means of communication for spreading the good tidings of great joy that our blessed Lord came upon this earth to preach, and for the preaching of which He also established His Church.

"You can never fully realize all the results that will follow as you go around from place to place distributing Catholic literature. You sow a seed and that seed in God's good time brings forth a harvest."

Richard Cardinal Cushing

First Chapel

"Oh, the beautiful mission you have in the United States! Have humility and faith in the Lord.

"From here (Rome) I blessed your new house, which you will fill with merit, vocations and works of apostolate."

—*The Founder to the Daughters of St. Paul in the United States, 1956*

In 1957, as this American Province was celebrating its 25th Anniversary, Mother Paula addressed these prophetic words to her sisters: "We are very few now at present, but if we are docile to the encouragement and to the words...of our Founder, we will reach the goal with the grace of God. And I'm sure that if we will be good and humble, pious, obedient, and zealous, and above all if we have faith, trust in God, we will multiply ourselves; and in another twenty-five years, God willing we will all be alive yet, and will say 'Remember....' Then this property may be full of buildings and we will go in many other places. We will thank our Lord then for the 50th Anniversary."

Provincial House 1982

"I think that the decisive moment has come for you to make rapid strides in every field."

—*The Founder, 1957*

17 Convents, 22 Catholic Book and Film Centers

" 'I strain forward!'
This is the Pauline spirit;
and I invoke upon you
light and strength
for an always more
decisive journey and
a greater reward—
an eternal one.

"I bless each
one of you.
I pray much for you.
Best wishes:
your 50th Anniversary
will find you many
in number and
in many convents."

—The Founder to the Daughters of St. Paul in the United States, 1957

Boston
Massachusetts

Staten Island
New York

New York
New York

Bronx
New York

Jersey City
New Jersey

Philadelphia
Pennsylvania

Buffalo
New York

Bridgeport
Connecticut

Alexandria
Virginia

Miami
Florida

Metairie
Louisiana

Baton Rouge
Louisiana

St. Louis
Missouri

Cincinnati
Ohio

Cleveland
Ohio

Chicago
Illinois

San Antonio
Texas

San Diego
California

San Francisco
California

"As we look back and then look to what the Daughters of St. Paul are today in the United States, we ask: How was all this possible? There is but one answer: 'The finger of God was here.' It was God who guided the work, blessed the efforts and granted this success.

Honolulu
Hawaii

Anchorage
Alaska

"What was the secret for the abundance of grace and help from God?

"1. *Fidelity to God* by doing His will and by having a great faith, a strong hope in His promises. It was faith that kept things going even in the most trying times;

"2. *Loyalty to the Founder's spirit*—The teachings of the Founder were followed very diligently and nothing was ever introduced that was not according to his directives. Whenever there was doubt, his advice was asked and followed.

"3. *Docility*—After the example of Mary, the sisters considered themselves as servants of the Lord and were ready to be His instruments of good.

"4. *Dedication*—The sisters had no other interest but the welfare of the Congregation in which they had consecrated their lives.

"The Daughters of St. Paul recognize that the credit of their success is not due only to their efforts, but they owe a great debt of gratitude to God who protected, assisted and guided them in every step and made their efforts successful."

—Rev. Father Stanislaus Crovella, SSP

"Here in America 'Alberione' Will Never Die...."

—Mother Paula

Outstanding among the publications of the Daughters of St. Paul are 40 currently translated books by their Founder, whose writings total 113 books and more than 5,000 articles.

His own sons and daughters especially, but also clergy, religious and laity, appreciate the value of his writings, which are theological and scriptural, yet at the same time, clear, practical and warm.

"Ever Onward, Daughters of St. Paul!"

— *The Founder*

"The Catholic Church, since it was founded by Christ our Lord to bear salvation to all men and thus is obliged to preach the Gospel, considers it one of its duties to announce the Good News of salvation also with the help of the media of social communication."

—***Decree on the Media of Social Communication***

Percentage of Catholics in the United States

TOTAL U.S. POPULATION — 266,504,825*

CATHOLIC POPULATION — 50,449,842 (22.05%)

NOT FORMALLY AFFILIATED WITH ANY RELIGION — 81,000,000 (40%)**

State	*Catholic Percentage*	*State*	*Catholic Percentage*	*State*	*Catholic Percentage*
Alaska	10.24	Louisiana	33.50	Ohio	22.01
Alabama	3.07	Maine	26.56	Oklahoma	4.21
Arizona	18.65	Maryland	17.45	Oregon	12.69
Arkansas	2.72	Massachusetts	39.60	Pennsylvania	30.94
California	22.09	Michigan	22.56	Rhode Island	64.97
Colorado	14.33	Minnesota	26.47	South Carolina	2.03
Connecticut	41.82	Mississippi	4.12	South Dakota	21.20
Delaware	13.73	Missouri	17.21	Tennessee	2.76
Florida	14.48	Montana	18.17	Texas	18.20
Georgia	3.19	Nebraska	21.28	Utah	4.09
Hawaii	20.88	Nevada	18.00	Vermont	30.52
Idaho	8.43	New Hampshire	36.52	Virginia	5.70
Illinois	31.76	New Jersey	38.84	Washington	9.82
Indiana	13.59	New Mexico	34.21	West Virginia	5.46
Iowa	19.25	New York	35.07	Wisconsin	33.40
Kansas	15.26	North Carolina	1.72	Wyoming	14.18
Kentucky	10.23	North Dakota	29.72		

* *1980 CENSUS*

** *National Catechetical Directory, p. 8, no. 14, 1979*

"How can they believe unless they have heard of him? And how can they hear unless there is someone to preach?... Scripture says, 'How beautiful are the feet of those who announce good news!' " (Rom. 10:14, 15)

"If St. Paul were living today, he would fly to the U.S.A. to bring Jesus Master, becoming an American with the Americans in virtue and in the apostolate." —*The Founder,* Sept., 1957

1960 witnessed the foundation of the ST. PAUL HOUSE OF STUDIES. In 1967, the building was dedicated by Rev. Msgr. Joseph Maguire (representing His Eminence, Richard Cardinal Cushing) and by His Excellency, Governor John A. Volpe.

"A complete education. Never remain in the school. Reach out into life! There is a whole work to be studied profoundly, but also to be simplified. Resemble the Divine Master, repeat His teaching, communicate it with His method.... Truly be *teachers!* The whole institute must be a magisterium!"
—*The Founder*

In 1981, the St. Paul House of Studies was elevated to the status of a PONTIFICAL CATECHETICAL INSTITUTE, by His Eminence, Silvio Cardinal Oddi, Prefect of the Sacred Congregation for the Clergy. His Eminence honored it with his visit on May 18 of the same year.

On the occasion of the 50th Anniversary, twenty-four Daughters of St. Paul received the catechetical diploma.

It is a joy for me to visit and bless the Catechetical Institute of the Sisters.. Daughters of St. Paul -, which I recently certified in Roma as Prefect of the Sacred Congregation for the Clergy
Boston. May 18, 1981 Silvio Card. Oddi

Always Traveling To Encourage

The visits of the Founder and Co-Foundress were never formal, but fatherly and motherly. They were always an occasion of growth for their daughters in their contemplative-active life: "I heartily bless all the apostolate you do with so much zeal....

"May you live the spirit of St. Paul! May the Daughters of St. Paul be multiplied! May the saints be many!"

—The Founder, 1966

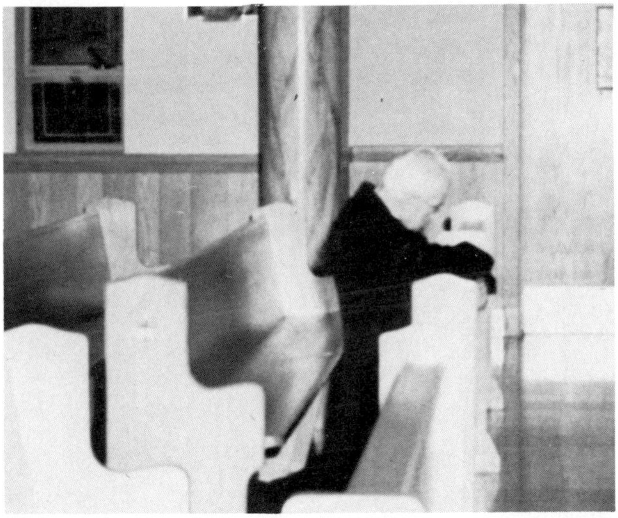

The Founder in the chapel of the Daughters of St. Paul in Boston.

"Forward—in your good apostolate, the religious life, vocations, the opening of convents, in the good formation of the postulants. Cultivate above all the interior life and intimate life with Jesus Master."
—The Founder, 1957

"I have neither gold nor silver nor gentleness, but I give you what I received from the Lord for you; it is for your sanctification and for the apostolate. Every blessing. Trust in God."
—The Founder, 1962

"Imitate Me as I Imitate Christ"

—1 Cor. 11:1

For the Daughters of St. Paul, their patron is a great saint and protector—the first in love for Christ, the Church and the whole world.

"We are to nourish ourselves on every phrase of the Gospel according to the spirit of St. Paul." ***—The Founder***

In June 1965, a famous Maltese reliquary, containing a fragment of St. Paul's arm-bone, was brought to Boston in anticipation of the nineteenth centenary of his martyrdom, and was loaned to the Daughters of St. Paul for a few hours.

Deeply grateful and enthused, Mother Paula and her sisters venerated the precious relic and carried it into the apostolate rooms to bless the machines with it.

United in Life and in Death

Like a signpost on the road to eternity stands the burial chapel of the Daughters of St. Paul where four sisters already rest. Clearly visible from the novitiate house, it calls us to pray for those who have gone before us and to "imitate their faith" (Heb. 13:7). On their part our deceased sisters pray for our sanctification and our mission.

FATHER FRANCIS BORRANO, the founder of the Society of St. Paul in the United States (1931), celebrates Mass for the departed sisters in the burial chapel.

"Come Apart...
and Rest a While"
—Mk. 6:31

St. Thecla's Retreat House provides a place for the sisters' annual retreats, monthly days of recollection, vacations and more.

The land was donated to the Daughters of St. Paul in 1964, by the late Cardinal Cushing, in memory of Mother Thecla.

During the annual retreats, Mass, as well as Benediction, was held outdoors until the new chapel was completed.

His Eminence, Humberto Cardinal Medeiros, dedicates the new building in 1980.

The superiors general of the Society of St. Paul, following in the footsteps of the Founder, visit the Daughters of St. Paul periodically. Like the Founder, they too spur them on in their fidelity to their charism.

FATHER LUIGI ZANONI, vicar to the Founder and his first successor as superior general of the Society of St. Paul

FATHER RENATO PERINO, present superior general

FATHER RAFFAELE TONNI, third superior general

His Eminence, Silvio Cardinal Oddi, Prefect of the Sacred Congregation for the Clergy

His Eminence, Agnelo Cardinal Rossi, Prefect of the Sacred Congregation for the Evangelization of Peoples

His Eminence, John Cardinal Krol, Archbishop of Philadelphia

Inspiring Visits

"Religious, even while showing a particular spirit of enterprise and foresight for the future, should be intensely loyal to the intention and spirit of their institute, in full obedience and adherence to the authority of the hierarchy."

—Mutual Relations Between Bishops and Religious, no. 34

His Eminence, Corrado Cardinal Ursi, Archbishop of Naples

His Eminence, Cardinal Colombo, Archbishop of Milan

John Cardinal Wright, former Prefect of the Sacred Congregation for the Clergy, on his last visit to the novitiate

His Eminence, Salvatore Cardinal Papalardo, archbishop of Palermo, Sicily

"The apostolate that you have is a very modern one, a very necessary one. And I think more and more that this will be apparent in the years ahead.... You are a joy to us—you are very much a glory to us. Keep up the great witness of faith and love seen in your own wonderful religious life." ***—Terence Cardinal Cooke***

His Eminence, Terence Cardinal Cooke, archbishop of New York, celebrates Mass in the book center of the Daughters of St. Paul and blesses it.

His Excellency, Bishop Joseph M. Pernicone, auxiliary bishop of New York

His Excellency, Archbishop Joseph T. Ryan, coadjutor to the Military Vicar, New York

As his predecessor, the late Cardinal Cushing, His Eminence, Humberto Cardinal Medeiros, has been more than a father to the Daughters of St. Paul in his archdiocese. While they strive to return his kindness by cooperating with him, in fidelity to their charism, they are spurred on in their mission by the hearty encouragement of their Shepherd:

"Your religious community has been faithful to their mission of evangelization with the media of social communication, and the Daughters of St. Paul have dedicated their lives and their apostolate to the spreading of the Good News of our risen Lord.

"The Daughters of St. Paul, alert to the advances in technology, have added to their printed media the most modern of communications means: filmstrips, slides, cassettes, films and records. In all of this, the Daughters of St. Paul have been faithful to the Apostolic Exhortation of His Holiness, Pope Paul VI, *On Evangelization in the Modern World,* in which he states that there is no doubt that the effort to proclaim the Gospel to the people of today is a service rendered to the Christian community and to the whole of mankind. In a very special way, the Daughters of St. Paul have fulfilled this commitment with dedication, with zeal and with a spirit of total commitment."

In keeping with Pauline tradition, His Eminence blesses a new printing press, readying it to multiply God's Word for millions.

As centers of light and truth, the St. Paul book centers are also blessed. The Cardinal officiates at the dedication of Boston's center on Tremont Street.

A new apostolic initiative and...a new blessing: the Daughters of St. Paul Bookmobile—a "book center on wheels."

"Let me assure you of my love for you and for your work and its precious place in the Church, especially in Boston."

—Humberto Cardinal Medeiros

Like Mother Thecla, her successors bring to their daughters God's measureless love. They urge them to work unceasingly to be faithful to the genuine spirit of their Founder and Co-Foundress.

"May we be faithful at all costs, with the kind of fidelity to which the Gospel invites us and which St. Paul so well understood, lived and exhorted others to live."

—Mother Ignatius

MOTHER IGNATIUS BALLA, *vicar to the Co-Foundress, Mother Thecla, and her first successor as superior general of the Daughters of St. Paul*

SISTER MARIA CEVOLANI, *present superior general*

"I am close to you and pray for all of you that the Lord may fill you with His blessings and be always with you. May the Lord grant me and all of you the grace to be always faithful."

—Sister Maria

Sister Maria with Father Perino, visiting the typography of the Daughters of St. Paul in Boston.

Mother Paula Cordero, pioneer sister of the American Province and first provincial

A devoted mother as well as a great leader, she writes weekly to her daughters to nourish their spirit and strengthen their unity:

"Let us love this great mission, this great apostolate—to bring Christ Truth to this poor humanity."

Sister Mary Celeste Carini, third provincial

Sister Concetta Belleggia, second provincial

Sister Mary Domenica Vitello, present provincial

A Woman of Vision

Shortly before becoming Pope Paul VI, His Eminence, Giovanni B. Cardinal Montini, visited the Daughters of Saint Paul in Boston.

Soon after, he honored them with the following letter:

"With a special prayer, I wish to return the respect and cordiality which you and your religious family showed me. May the Divine Goodness shower with richest fruits and spiritual satisfactions the apostolate of your Congregation, developed in the United States with so much courage and sacrifice. From my heart, renewing my sentiments of pleasure and best wishes, I send you my paternal blessing."

With His Eminence, Richard Cardinal Cushing

With His Eminence, Humberto Cardinal Medeiros

Mother Ignatius once called Mother Paula the "cornerstone of the edifice of our Congregation in the United States." Faithful and available to her major superiors, Mother Paula wins the same generous response from her own daughters and has been able to build this edifice, with the grace of God, upon the strong foundation of humility and faith.

Firm and maternal, with a heart that beats with the love of St. Paul himself, she perseveringly keeps to the spirit of the Founder and Co-Foundress and dynamically passes on to our U.S. Province all that builds our Pauline heritage.

With Mother Ignatius and the community, enjoying a restful moment

"Remain in your spirit; don't change yourselves, but draw the vocations to you with the Pauline spirit."

—The Founder

Who could ever count the trips by train and by plane that Mother Paula has made in these past fifty years to open convents and to visit her beloved daughters?

"When you love, nothing is hard, simply because you love."

—Mother Paula

With Sr. Mary Celeste, as they arrive in Honolulu to open a convent and book center there

Listening to His Excellency, Bishop Thomas V. Daily, Vicar General and Chancellor of the archdiocese of Boston, who graciously officiates at the various ceremonies of the community, such as entrance into the novitiate and religious investiture

Knowing the importance of well-prepared meals, Mother Paula teaches the young sisters how to cook. They enjoy learning from such an experienced teacher!

"There are some apostolates which remain buried, ignored by men. They will be revealed on judgment day. We think of the cook only when we go to eat, but the Lord thinks of her all the time."

—The Founder

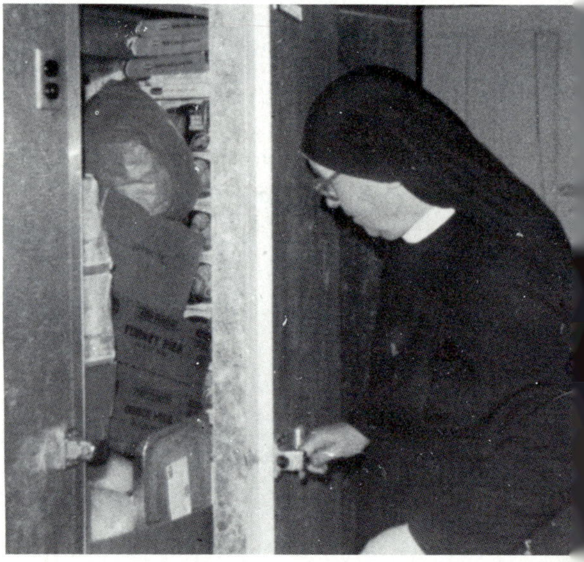

The bond of unity among the sisters of the various convents is strong and is shown even in the things they prepare for Boston's house of formation, which is full of young vocations. Whenever Mother Paula or the provincial superior comes for a visit, the sisters happily surprise them with their gifts—signs of their love and thoughtfulness.

July 3, 1977:

At a Mass marking her golden jubilee of profession, Mother Paula renews her vows—vows which she has truly lived in a heroic way.

On either side of her are Sr. Domenica Sabia and Sr. Mary Joan Baldino—silver jubilarians.

In recognition of her "sacred commitment to her apostolate of the media, through her faith in God, and through the love, loyalty and cooperation of her faithful daughters," Mother Paula was the awarded guest of honor at the annual Communicators' Mass (Saint Anthony's Shrine, Boston, Ma., Oct. 1981).

Mother Paula's favorite advice to her daughters:
"Be humble.
Be charitable.
Be faithful.
Be Paulines of great faith."

Christ-

Centered Spirituality

"You were born of the Eucharist. Your food is the Eucharist. Your spirituality is the Gospel lived in its entirety as explained by St. Paul. Your Mother and Model is Mary." *The Founder*

To live in Christ, in imitation of St. Paul, under the gaze of Mary, Queen of Apostles: this is the spiritual program of each Daughter of St. Paul. The Founder explains it in these words:

"We are to give our entire being to Jesus and live the whole Christ—this is our spirituality. And we are to live this spirituality under the protection of Mary, Queen of the Apostles, and of St. Paul Apostle, and in their spirit, for they are the ones who have interpreted and lived the Divine Master better.

"For us to become saints it is necessary to imitate Jesus, our Model. He is the Master, but we cannot do all that Jesus did—for example, perform miracles. Therefore we have a model we can imitate—St. Paul. We can imitate Jesus by following the example of St. Paul, by looking at what he did, and by doing the same, with Mary's help."

Jesus, the Divine Master

The entire spirituality of the Daughters of St. Paul is based primarily on the devotion to Jesus Master, Way, Truth and Life—an excellent and complete devotion. Christ the Truth enlightens minds. Christ the Way leads us to the Father. Christ the Life inflames our hearts to love Him entirely and to spread the love we have found. This devotion to Jesus Master—the Way, the Truth and the Life—includes all the devotions to the Person of Jesus Christ, the God-Man.

"You are not Daughters of a particular mystery of Christ," Fr. Alberione explains, "but of the whole Christ.

"Therefore go to Jesus Master with your whole being: mind, will, heart and body. Through the Holy Spirit, He will take full possession and then it will no longer be you who think, will, love and act, but rather Jesus: 'It is no longer I who live; it is Christ who lives in me.' "

The devotion to Jesus Way, Truth and Life so permeates the life of the Daughter of St. Paul that it touches every aspect of her interior life and her apostolic activity. Its aim is to bring the whole person to the whole Christ. Fr. Alberione explains how each of the daily "prayer-practices" could be carried out in this spirit so as to derive more abundant fruits for the sisters' sanctification and the effectiveness of their apostolate.

For example, about participation in the *Eucharistic Celebration* he states: "The Sacrifice of the Mass is offered every day, and in substance it is always the same. However for one who practices the devotion to Jesus Christ the Master, the Way and Truth and Life, it always offers some new lesson, some new way, and some new spiritual comfort. In the Liturgy of the Word we devoutly listen to the Father, who has revealed Himself to us especially in His Son, Christ the *Truth*, and we offer Him the homage of our mind, giving the full consent of our intellect and will. In the Eucharistic Liturgy, in union with Christ the *Way* who offers Himself to the Father, we offer ourselves, promising to follow Jesus, who is the sure Way to reach the Father, conforming our lives to Him who is our Model. In Communion Jesus is our *Life*. His divine life flows in us as lymph flows from the vine to the branch, and it vivifies us that we may bring forth lasting fruits of love of God and our brothers, whom we serve with the apostolate."

In addition to daily Mass and Communion, the Daughters of St. Paul make a half hour of meditation each morning, an Hour of Adoration before the Blessed Sacrament during the day, and a half hour of personal prayer added by the Founder after Vatican II. The Founder applied the same total approach to these practices.

In *meditation* "one contemplates a mystery, an episode of the life of Jesus Christ, or one of the eternal truths. The will is aroused to desire sanctity of life intensely, to follow Jesus. Finally, we pray for the grace of perseverance."

The distinctive sign of the Pauline spirituality is the daily *Hour of Adoration* spent before the Blessed Sacrament. "This Eucharistic Visit," says Fr. Alberione, "is the most privileged time of the day, the time in which the sister places herself in the presence of the Master.

"The Hour of Adoration is the practice which most directs and influences all our life and all our apostolate.

"It is the great means for overcoming immaturity and forming a personality in Christ.

"It is the secret of our transformation in Christ.

"The school of the Eucharistic Jesus is a perfect school—perfect on the part of Him who teaches, the very Son of God, the unique Master, He who descended from heaven to instruct humanity. 'When there is a God who teaches, it is easy to learn,' says St. Augustine.

"The school of Jesus is perfect because of the subject He teaches. And what does He teach? The divine knowledge which makes saints and which is necessary for all men.

"This school is also perfect due to its availability. Jesus has established His chair in each of your houses, and He wants you to approach Him and draw very close to Him.

"The school of Jesus is perfect, in addition, due to its perpetuity. 1900 years have gone by and Jesus has always continued to teach from the tabernacle, and He will do so until the end of the world.

"It is perfect due to its extension—it encompasses all regions of the earth.

"It is perfect due to its method of teaching. Jesus speaks to the heart; He enters sweetly, tenderly; He does not use high-sounding words, or thundering discourses.

"It is a perfect school due to the effects it produces.

"In the first part of the Hour of Adoration we adore Jesus Truth. We ask the Lord precisely to know natural and supernatural truths and to increase our faith. We ask to grow in the knowledge of the apostolate.

"In the second part of the Visit to the Most Blessed Sacrament, we honor Jesus Way, that is, Jesus sanctity. We must admire the example of Jesus and compare our life with His, in order to conform ours to His.

"In the third part, we honor Jesus Life, that is, the font of grace. He possesses all the treasures of grace. 'Ask and you will receive' (Jn. 16:24)."

The additional *half hour of personal prayer,* also before the Blessed Sacrament, is a time of private dialogue with the Divine Master, God, King, Spouse, Center and Life of every religious. In the silence of her heart He answers, inspires, corrects and purifies, helping her to grow in holiness.

For an ever greater union with God, there are daily periods of silence. The rosary, frequent aspirations recited throughout the day, and times of spiritual reading constitute other precious means of blending contemplation with action.

The daily practices culminate in times of deeper reflection in *monthly and annual retreats.*

The Founder continually reminds the Daughters of St. Paul of the importance of centering and rooting their lives in Christ, of reaching the point of configuration with Jesus Master.

"We must live—and this is not a small thing—the life of Jesus Christ in the most perfect manner possible.

"We must live Jesus Christ and make Him lived as He is—Way, Truth and Life."

Thus by living Christ in His totality, the Daughter of St. Paul is spurred on to be His witness to the world, making Him known, loved and imitated. Father Alberione writes:

"Configuration with the Divine Master cannot be reduced simply to prayer or to study or to some hymn. It empowers the whole person and extends itself to the entire apostolic life, because our apostolate is fruitful in the measure that it presents Jesus Christ, Way, Truth and Life.

"Our congregation has a mission. It must make Jesus Master, Way, Truth and Life known to the world, as He lives in the Eucharist, in the Gospel, in the Church, and also in the congregation, since it has the mission of teaching.

"In this regard much remains for us to do.... But as members of the congregation we have the duty of working so that devotion to the Divine Master will be propagated in the world. Herein lies salvation: 'to know you, the only true God, and Jesus Christ whom you have sent' (Jn. 17:3).

"There are various means for evangelizing, but the method is one: to give Jesus Christ, Way, Truth and Life, who must sanctify the whole person, all of society. Therefore, give the true Faith, liturgical piety, public and private Christian life.

"Give Jesus Christ, Way, Truth and Life, that is, as He is: totally. He is the Truth, so give clear doctrine. He is the Way, so give the world the virtues that teach the imitation of Jesus Christ. He is the Life, and life is drawn from Him, from the sacraments."

Mary, Queen of Apostles

Our Founder indicates that the surest and easiest way to configuration with Jesus Master is fervent devotion to Mary.

"Jesus Christ is the Master; He is the Apostle of the Father. We are to know Him always better. The journey to be made is unending: 'Be perfect just as your heavenly Father is perfect' (Mt. 5:48). Who will reach such a height? Who will reach the point of identifying herself with Christ? The way to reach this union is Mary. One who is more devoted to Mary will unite herself more intimately to Jesus Christ."

Since Jesus came to us through Mary, each Daughter of St. Paul strives to grow in knowledge, love and imitation of the Blessed Virgin, who is Mother, Teacher and Queen of the Apostles, and to make her known. Mary formed the first Apostles and joins the apostles of all times. She is the perfect disciple of Jesus Christ while she reigns at His side as Queen. The Daughters of St. Paul beg the Queen of Apostles to give them Jesus, Way, Truth and Life, and through them to give Him to souls.

"No greater wealth can be given to our poor, proud world than Jesus Christ," writes the Founder. "Mary gave the world grace in Jesus Christ. She continues to offer Him throughout the centuries.

Continued on p. 107.

"You belong to Christ, to Him alone! Penetrate as much as possible into Christ, into His thoughts, into His perfect adoration, into the praise He gives the Father—to the point of being really able to say: *Christ lives in me.*

"It is to this intimate communion with Jesus that you are called. You are called to be living tabernacles—bearing Jesus in the tabernacle of your heart. This is a fulfillment of that invocation to the Divine Master: 'May my presence be always sanctifying.' "

—The Founder

"Mary received from God the sublime mission of calling and forming apostles of all times and for every field."

—The Founder

"By nature Mary is essentially an apostle. She came to give Jesus, to bring life to souls, to be mediatrix and distributrix of grace. This is your vocation: to participate in Mary's apostolate."

—The Founder

"What is the spirit of St. Paul? It is this: he is the one who points out the Divine Master; he took the Gospel which he meditated profoundly and then he adapted it to the world, to the needs of the time and to the needs of the various nations. So must we apply the Gospel to our times and give the Gospel to the present world, with the means which progress presents to us as means capable of transmitting the doctrine of Jesus Christ. We must live in our time and make the world feel the effective presence of Jesus Christ."

—The Founder

Continued from p. 102.

"Mary is the apostle. Relative to us she is Queen because she calls us to participate in her apostolate, because she is greater than all apostles, and because she gathers and instructs all apostles. To them she gives graces and prepares the reward of glory."

Desiring to popularize this devotion to Mary, the Founder wrote a book entitled *Mary, Queen of Apostles.* His love for the Mother of God under this title is overwhelming, as can be seen from just a few excerpts from his writings:

—One who wants to be an apostle and does not let Mary enter his life deprives himself of an indispensable help.

—The apostle must be a saint in order to sanctify; wise in order to instruct; zealous in order to overcome the obstacles he meets. For all this, the apostle needs Mary.

—The Virgin will bless the apostle. She will console him in the sorrows and griefs of the apostolic life.

—With Mary everything is easier, everything is happier, everything is more fruitful, everything is holier. Let us consecrate ourselves and the means of our apostolate to her.

—The Virgin accomplished her first official act as Queen of Apostles during the nine days of retreat in preparation for Pentecost. From her the Apostles learned to pray, to persevere and to prepare themselves for the apostolate.

—The apostle must sanctify his mind in a faith that is always more lively; his will in a docility always more conformed to the will of God; his heart in a union always more intimate with the heart of Jesus. For all this the apostle needs Mary.

—Mary is Mother of apostolates; Mary is Mother of vocations; Mary is guide and help of apostolic souls.

—Mary Queen of Apostles will inspire vocations in the families consecrated to her.

—Mary Queen of Apostles will assist the vocations of the parishes and of the dioceses where her image is exposed.

—Mary Queen of Apostles will bless the families which will give a son or daughter to the Lord.

—Mary Queen of Apostles will smooth the way for those called to the apostolate during the period of their formation.

—Mary Queen of Apostles will form the souls of those called according to the model of Jesus, the first Apostle.

—Mary Queen of Apostles protects everyone who works with profound love for Jesus Christ and for the Church.

—Mary Queen of Apostles today offers greater graces to those who work in the more fruitful modern apostolates.

—Mary Queen of Apostles will sow comfort and joy in the work of the apostolate.

—Mary Queen of Apostles will bless every individual and social apostolate.

—Mary Queen of Apostles will assist her devotees in life and in death.

—Mary Queen of Apostles will free her devotees or shorten their purgatory.

—Mary Queen of Apostles will gather the true apostles around her throne of glory in heaven.

St. Paul the Apostle

Fr. Alberione considers St. Paul the founder, father and model of the Daughters of St. Paul. In St. Paul one finds the disciple who knows the Divine Master in His entirety, and who presents the whole Christ to us as He defined Himself: Way, Truth and Life. St. Paul's constant effort was to mirror Christ, and for love of Christ he spent himself even to the point of martyrdom. St. Paul's generous response throughout his life to God's call must become the sister's own so that with him she will become able to say, "Christ lives in me."

"St. Paul is our father," the Founder writes. "From him we must take our spirit, our mentality, our love for Jesus Christ and our love for souls. St. Paul's life was holy. So let our life be!

"Whoever draws close to St. Paul is gradually transformed and learns to live and pray as he did. Whoever loves St. Paul soon enlarges his heart, becomes generous and broad in his views. St. Paul no longer appears to him as a stern wielder of the sword, but rather as the most ardent and tender lover of Christ.

"The Pauline Family is St. Paul living today," Fr. Alberione says. And he asks his spiritual daughters:

"Are we truly living in the spirit of St. Paul? What is the spirit of St. Paul? It is this: he is the one who points out the Divine Master; he took the Gospel which he meditated profoundly and then he adapted it to the world, to the needs of his time and to the needs of the various nations. So must we apply the Gospel to our times and give the Gospel to the present world, with the means which progress presents to us as means capable of transmitting the thought, the doctrine of Jesus Christ. We must live in our time and make the world feel the effective presence of Jesus Christ.

"It is said: the devotion to St. Paul is not popular; it is a devotion of the learned, of the Fathers of the Church, of Bishops!...

"However, in the beginning of the Church it was a devotion of the people. The time has come that this devotion again take its place in the hearts of the Christian people.

"The diffusion of this devotion means to make St. Paul loved, to lead people to pray to him. The devotion to St. Paul is a great good for a soul, and also a great gift of the mercy of God. It is for this reason that it enters souls with difficulty.

"But once this devotion enters a soul, it grows steadily; it steals the heart, floods the spirit, transforms one's life and never diminishes but continues to grow. Make St. Paul known: his conversion, his work for souls, his mission, the graces God bestowed upon him.

"St. Paul is the knight of the Holy Spirit, the lover of the Father, the devotee of Mary.

"His life is most interesting. The story of the redemption of the Gentiles and of our redemption is edifying.

"Make St. Paul loved—because he loved us first, and he loves us with an inexpressible love; because in loving St. Paul, our heart is filled with love for Jesus Christ, and our life is directed to our heavenly fatherland.

"Make St. Paul be prayed to, because his power is equal to his love. He listens to us in all our needs, and God listens to him. He obtains many graces for us, the signs of gratitude to him increase daily, and books could not contain all the marvels of his goodness."

A Program of Life in Christ

"Remember always that the Pauline apostolate without the flame of interior life is sterile, and the interior life without the flame of the apostolate is an illusion." These words of the Founder echo in the heart of each Daughter of St. Paul.

They recall the warm recommendation of their Co-Foundress, Mother Thecla:

"We must imitate the life of Jesus and of the Apostles. First of all come the practices of piety. We must take good care of our interior life. We ourselves must be well nourished spiritually. To do good, that must be our greatest preoccupation. Let us do good to souls. After we have done good here on earth, a beautiful paradise awaits us hereafter.

"Let us be other Marys, bringing Jesus wherever we go."

The Pauline spirituality is the sustaining force of the dynamic apostolate of the Daughters of St. Paul—a spirituality that is vital...total...complete; a spirituality that is meant to transform all those who live it until they can say:

"The life I live now is not my own; Christ is living in me" (Gal. 2:20).

"Christ is my life,
Christ is my thought,
Christ is my desire,
Christ is my love,
my wish,
my speech.
My very actions are those of Christ.
I wish nothing else,
I delight in nothing else,
I do nothing else,
I think nothing else,
I speak of nothing other than Christ."

Sr. M.J.B.

The Formation of

a Daughter of St. Paul

"Let us lend our feet to the Gospel that it may run and extend itself...."

—*Mother Thecla*

The challenge is a great one. And no less great is the need for preparation in order to meet the challenge. This is the essential work of *formation:* to form a mind, will and heart anchored in Christ, founded firmly on the Gospel, animated by the spirit of the Apostle St. Paul. For this reason, the years of pre-postulancy, postulancy, and novitiate are aimed at the development of the whole person. Father Alberione liked to call this the transformation of the person into an apostle, after the example of Jesus Master, Way, Truth and Life. He wrote that "personality is perfect when one thinks, wills and lives in Jesus Christ completely, in an absolute manner, according to the doctrine and the life of perfection as lived by Jesus Christ.... The world needs Christ. The first great witness that we must give to men is to make His presence felt *in ourselves,* with the beauty of His spiritual values. Everything depends on Christ's life in us, on our enthusiasm, Christian optimism and fervor."

The sisters who print, who write, who cook, who diffuse the Word of God in homes and business areas, who train new members, who staff St. Paul Book and Film Centers—*all are to be religious first of all.*

The years of formation are truly happy years—the beginning of the total gift of oneself to God which culminates in religious profession.

Young girls who enter between the freshman and junior years of high school are "pre-postulants." These young candidates are introduced to religious life in the best way: by experiencing it. Perhaps this was most vividly expressed by an enthusiastic pre-postulant when she wrote the following:

"For the past three years, I have been living among some of the luckiest, or rather, most blessed, teenagers in America! Any girl who wants to be a Daughter of St. Paul doesn't have to wait until she completes high school and much less college.

"As a pre-postulant, I do not only attend high school at the convent, but actually live here, sharing the prayer-life and apostolate of the professed sisters.

"The formation we receive directs us spiritually so we can begin right away to reach the goal we have chosen for ourselves.

"We are welcomed into a community with sisters from many different cultures and backgrounds. Our family spirit is something we really treasure as Paulines.

"I love being a pre-postulant and I know I will always treasure the years I spent 'in blue' (the color of our pre-postulant habit). But pre-postulancy is only the beginning. We know from experience that pre-postulancy flies by and tomorrow we will be postulants, novices and professed sisters.

"Daily we thank God for the grace of being able to enter at a young age."

The pre-postulants are given a solid introduction to the Pauline religious life: spirituality and apostolate. They have the unique opportunity of continuing their education while beginning their formation. The St. Paul High School, which they attend, is fully approved by the Archdiocese of Boston and offers courses in preparation for higher studies.

The pre-postulants share in the joyful family spirit of the community. They integrate study with apostolic experience and participate in the mission of the congregation according to their age and experience.

Their enthusiasm knows no bounds when they have the opportunity to express their feelings about religious life:

"I entered the Daughters of St. Paul for many reasons, among which is the fact that they accept girls after 8th grade. I knew that I wanted to give God my whole being, and I wanted to do it right away!"

"I chose the Daughters of St. Paul because their religious life blends the contemplative and active lives. I entered soon after I visited because I could go to high school while beginning to live the religious life. My only regret is that I didn't come sooner!" (She entered at 16.)

Those girls who join the Daughters of St. Paul during their senior year of high school and up through the age of 26 go directly into the postulancy. The postulants attend the high school or St. Paul House of Studies, alternating study with prayer and apostolic experience. They enjoy (as do the pre-postulants) the privilege of daily Mass and meditation, as well as a full hour of Eucharistic Adoration. They share with the professed sisters in preparing the Word of God in the form of books, cassettes, films and the other media, and in bringing these to people. The postulants are deeply aware of how privileged they are to participate in the Pauline prayer life and mission. This love for our spirituality and apostolate is striking proof of the high ideals of many of our youth today.

"Our mission of giving God's Word through the media is the best answer to the needs of the present troubled world. This is why I entered this dynamic congregation at the age of 24 and after having finished my graduate studies. Now, I'm truly grateful that I responded to this Pauline vocation, because I'm able to use all my God-given potentials and my education in serving God and mankind through our most efficacious mission of evangelization."

"The spirit and mission of the Daughters of St. Paul are truly gifts from God. While studying in college I came to know the sisters and discovered that their apostolate really does reach out to all people, working to bring souls to Christ! At the same time the spiritual life is the core and strength of each Daughter of St. Paul. I thank God continually for having called me to be a religious sister and especially a Daughter of St. Paul."

Continued on p. 123.

PRE-POSTULANCY—

"Give the Lord your youth, your todays."
—*The Founder*

POSTULANCY

"A preparation for novitiate.
A great deal depends
on this preparation.
One might almost compare it to
the reception of Holy Communion
—the fruits depend greatly
on the preparation."

—*The Founder*

The Novitiate
is the school
of the Divine Master.

The holy habit is received by the novices in a simple ceremony the day before Profession.

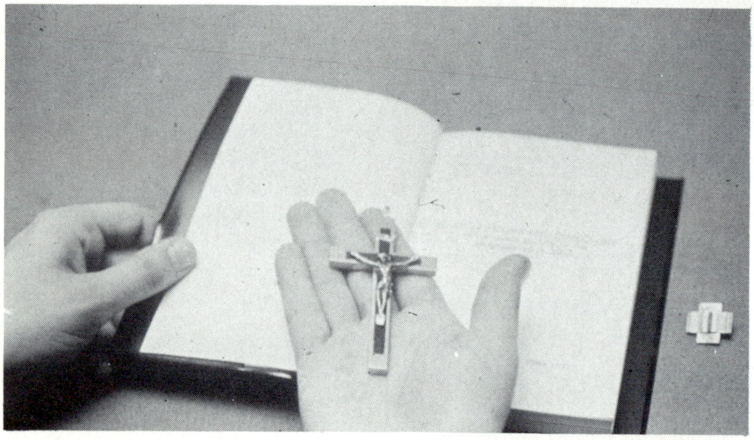

"In response to the love of Christ the Master, I... make the vows of chastity, poverty and obedience...."

Weekly conferences, given at the provincial house, are recorded and sent to each convent. The professed sisters greatly value this continuing formation.

"Let them live the way they were formed—it is the sure way."
—The Founder to Mother Paula, 1966

Each sister takes her place in the Pauline harvest field, ready to serve in every part of the vineyard.

Continued from p. 116.

"I entered the Daughters of St. Paul after attending college and working for several years. I saw people struggling to get better positions at their jobs or trying to better their social standing and I thought: 'What is all this effort and hard work for? Something that will eventually be meaningless.' I wanted to help people see beyond this life. This is what a Daughter of St. Paul does. With her mission, which is as vast as the world, she presents Jesus and His teachings to all people, while herself being filled with Him through the Pauline spirituality."

After postulancy, which lasts from ten months to two years, the candidate goes on to the novitiate. This two-year period is marked by more intense prayer, reflection, instruction and initiation into the essential demands of religious life. It builds on the experiences of postulancy, leading the novice to discover how she can faithfully live the requirements of the Pauline religious vocation in the context of a dynamic apostolate.

A very valuable part of the novice's formation is a three-month period of special apostolic experience, during which she shares more intimately the life of the professed sister, especially in the area of person-to-person contact to diffuse God's Word. Here, where the Gospel meets the world, she enjoys first-hand the privilege of being an instrument of God in touching the lives of others by bringing them His saving Truth.

Then the great and long-awaited day arrives: Profession. The novice consecrates her life to God by taking the three vows of chastity, poverty and obedience for one year. She will renew these vows annually for five consecutive years, and then, after a six-month preparation period, like a "second novitiate," she will make her Perpetual Profession.

By her consecration, the Pauline religious gives her personal response to God's special gift of love. Her sole concern is loving Him with an undivided heart, and loving everyone in Him. In her detachment from earthly goods, she is a sign to the world of the Gospel values of hope, joy in work, and the wisdom of storing up treasures for heaven. She strives to reproduce in herself the filial obedience of Jesus, so as to free herself interiorly for a total service to God and for the redemption of the world.

Each sister takes her place in the Pauline harvest field, ready to serve in every part of the vineyard. She knows that wherever she goes, she finds Jesus and souls, as well as a joyful community in which the beautiful family spirit is truly a source of strength and mutual love. Together the sisters experience the joy and satisfaction of reaching out to mankind in love and self-sacrifice, offering it the Truth that saves. And as the years go on, each sister will appreciate and feel always more deeply the gift of God that is her vocation and the vast horizons of a mission that never grows old. Sr. R.M.G.

Pauline Studies

The Founder of the Daughters of St. Paul taught that just as four properly functioning wheels make a vehicle stable, so four aspects of the Pauline way of life give stability to the congregation and to its apostolate. These four Pauline "wheels" are: piety, study, apostolate and poverty.

The first, *piety*, is essential for the living of the religious consecration and the carrying out of a true apostolate. Pauline *poverty*—which renounces the unnecessary, conserves the necessary and promotes the Pauline mission through hard work—safeguards the religious spirit and gives the apostolate a greater outreach. The *apostolate* itself was the Founder's first inspiration, and it remains the special purpose of the congregation.

The other "wheel" is *study*. Study is important because of the nature of the religious life. This supernatural way of life must be solidly grounded on Sacred Scripture and the principles of theology. Study is also important because of the nature of the Pauline apostolate. The *message* to be communicated must be firmly grasped by the communicator if it is to be properly conveyed. The nature of the *media* of communication must be sufficiently comprehended. And *mankind* must be understood—the people of today, who must be met on their own cultural levels, in this century of the knowledge explosion, by persons who understand the problems of our world here and now.

Study is the duty of every Daughter of St. Paul. Whether she attends formal courses or not, she is to deepen her knowledge of God and of mankind, of the religious life, and of the means of apostolate at her disposal, as well as the message she is to convey through the media. Therefore, "study" involves progress in writing, layout, printing, binding, recording, filming, displaying and offering the Word of God. "We must progress every day!" the Founder declared.

The formal studies of the Daughters of St. Paul of the U.S.A. are carried out: 1) in the Daughters of St. Paul High School, which belongs to the secondary school system of the Archdiocese of Boston; and 2) in the St. Paul House of Studies, a pontifical catechetical institute on the college level.

The Founder had always stressed the importance of carrying out one's academic studies *within the congregation*, whenever possible. With this goal in mind, Mother Paula had sent some of the first American postulants to complete their secondary schooling at Mother Cabrini High School in New York City and later to continue on to college at Fordham University. These sisters received their

"Our education is not simply instruction, or fostering of discipline, or preparation for a profession: It is formation of a Pauline mentality, of a Pauline will, of a truly Pauline spirit. It is the formation of a whole new being."

—*The Founder*

Winners of an essay contest sponsored by *Extension Magazine* are pictured here with His Eminence, Humberto Cardinal Medeiros. At the far right is first-prize winner, Pre-postulant Kathryn Hermes of the Daughters of St. Paul High School.

masters' degrees and became the first teachers in a private high school for Pauline pre-postulants and postulants. At first this high school was affiliated with Mother Cabrini High. Later, after the historic move to Boston, it became a private school in the archdiocesan school system.

The small size of classes in the Daughters of St. Paul High School enables teachers to help their students achieve high goals: these students *learn*, and learn with a *purpose*.

"Study should lead to union with God," writes the Founder. "Study should lead to the practice of virtue. Study should lead to apostolic action." The students of the Daughters of St. Paul High School are helped in every way to reach an enlightened, mature faith based on the teachings of the Magisterium of the Church, and then to proceed from this knowledge to develop a solid prayer-life and spirituality. This formation is always accompanied by awareness of the needs and signs of the times in city, nation and world. Once the students come to know God, His law of love, and the strengthening power of a vibrant, liturgical prayer life, then they will be able to more effectively reach out to their brothers and sisters through the Pauline apostolate.

Therefore, both theoretical and practical knowledge are imparted, so that there is a constant blending of what one ought to *know* with what one ought to *do* as a result of that knowledge. The educational process is directed to forming the "whole person."

The students are also given an active role in the actual production (and occasionally diffusion) of the Gospel message through all the media of communication. Each student is able to spend at least three hours a day in apostolic action.

In the fall of 1980, the province was afforded abundant evidence of the effectiveness of its high school program. The twenty-eight students of the Daughters of St. Paul High School entered an essay contest for secondary school students of the Boston Archdiocese, sponsored by *Extension Magazine*. One of the pre-postulants won first prize; six others, honorable mention. About one fourth of the awards given had gone to the D.S.P. High School! Using good research techniques, skillful writing and religious-apostolic knowledge, each of the students had written about a missionary on the American scene, his or her contributions to the growth of the Church, and the lessons that Catholics of the 1980's could learn from this missionary. The winner had written about one of her own sisters in religion.

The Pauline aspirants appreciate their high school for many reasons, as these comments show:

"I have learned so much here. I think this is true because, first of all, we are in the convent to become sisters, and our school is aimed at our future life—the religious life."

"St. Paul's High School was started with a lot of faith by our Mother Paula, the foundress of the Daughters of St. Paul in America. This high school is just wonderful. The classes are very informative and interesting. We learn not just for ourselves but to share with the world."

"Here we learn the true meaning of life. Our education is geared towards our vocation and our mission."

"St. Paul's High School is so good because of the concern of the teachers, the education and formation geared to religious life, the truth taught in its entirety. This high school is different, wonderfully different! We learn for life, not only for a day or two, but for eternity!"

"Our teachers are our own sisters. They are very helpful and understanding. We live with them, and so they understand us better. Our classes are aimed at our apostolate of bringing Christ to the world through the most modern means of social communication."

"The Daughters of St. Paul High School is a preparation for life. English and religion courses especially have taught me how to communicate the Word of God effectively. And this is so important, because who can reach as many souls as the Daughters of St. Paul with the media apostolate?"

"Our high school is really great because all the classes are interesting. Even subjects that are usually boring and hard become enjoyable."

"One good quality of our high school is that you are treated as an individual and not just a member of a class."

In 1960, Mother Paula took yet another step and established the St. Paul House of Studies, affiliated with the Catholic University of America.

1981 saw the fulfillment of a cherished dream. St. Paul House of Studies became a four-year pontifical catechetical institute, with authorization from the Holy See to grant a pontifical catechetical diploma for studies equivalent to those for a B.A., with a major in theology. The first graduates—those of the Jubilee Year, 1982—numbered twenty-four.

This catechetical institute was a dream-come-true because of the catechetical nature of the Pauline apostolate. As "loudspeakers" of the Pope and the Magisterium, the Daughters of St. Paul are to bring to the world the doctrine and moral code of the Church and lead mankind to the sacraments. They are to apply their spirituality to the apostolate and give Jesus, Way, Truth and Life, to all.

Writes the Founder:

"When the Daughter of St. Paul takes pen in hand and goes before the Divine Master, let her ask Him: 'What do You want me to say? What would You have done? What should I say to this group of people I am addressing?' Then she will feel a desire to write a catechism, but a catechism for an immense audience. How many thousands of copies will be printed!

"She will see in her mind's eye the many souls thirsting for truth and who, perhaps, do not even know they are thirsting for it. So she will make every effort to give them the supernatural, the spiritual."

So that this apostolate would give the pure wine of Catholic doctrine according to the Pauline spirit, the Founder had emphasized the necessity of establishing houses of studies in the various nations:

"The congregation must have its own houses of studies for the education of the sisters in the higher studies.

"The Daughters of St. Paul, in extent and depth but in the manner and form appropriate to their state, must devote particular care to the study of philosophical, theological and pedagogical subjects as the fundamental part of a solid formation for the apostolate. In their studies they shall strive ever to think more closely with the Church and shall filially obey its orders and directives. They shall pursue their studies in such a way that Jesus Christ, our Divine Master, the Way, the Truth, and the Life, is more intimately known and is formed fully in the mind, the will and the heart."

Because the apostolate of the Daughters of St. Paul involves fruitful contacts with persons of all races and creeds, social backgrounds and age levels, it calls for: a thorough grounding in theology, philosophy and catechetics; knowledge of the religious and cultural contributions of the various races and nations; a fundamental grasp of the principles of psychology and pedagogy; an understanding of modern man's mentality and needs; an acquaintance with foreign languages; and the skills needed for writing and speaking.

While seeking these general objectives, the St. Paul House of Studies also aims to form sisters capable of writing, translating, compiling and editing works in the fields of catechetics, Scripture, spirituality, Mariology, apologetics, Christian sociology, formation, vocational guidance, religious biographies and children's literature. The sisters must be trained, moreover, to speak to a variety of audiences on these subjects.

Through theoretical-practical courses on the various media of communications, the sisters are prepared to carry out the "technical stage" of their apostolate.

Continued on p. 135.

"In our studies the dominant principle must be this: *Learn for life!"* —*The Founder*

His Eminence, Silvio Cardinal Oddi, visited St. Paul House of Studies soon after he had elevated it to the status of a Pontifical Catechetical Institute.

"If you work well in the service of the Church, you will fulfill a magnificent apostolate. Be true daughters of St. Paul, that is, daughters of the Church." —The Founder

Continued from p. 131.

Another specific purpose of the House of Studies is to prepare sisters to establish and direct centers of information and of distribution of books, films, and audio-visuals, and to set up or furnish libraries in colleges, schools, institutions and parishes. Hence, in addition to a wide cultural background and understanding of modern tastes and needs, the Daughters of St. Paul must be prepared to evaluate contemporary works and to pass judgment on the propriety and suitability of various types of films and books for particular classes of viewers and readers.

Just as the pre-postulants appreciate the training they receive in the Daughters of St. Paul High School, so the postulants and professed sisters value the instruction that they are given in the St. Paul House of Studies, as well as the continual updating given to *all* the professed of the province. This instruction not only keeps them firm in the Faith; it also enables them to help those to whom they are sent—by giving a word of explanation, by offering a book or an audio-visual that will meet particular needs.

In the words of Father Alberione,

"Our education is not simply instruction, or fostering of discipline, or preparation for a profession:

"It is formation of a Pauline mentality, of a Pauline will, of a truly Pauline spirit. It is the formation of a whole new being."

The studies of the Daughters of St. Paul are intended to bring them to a deeper love of God, for "to know is to love," and to love God means to want others to love Him. "One love, Jesus Christ!" exclaimed the Founder. "One burning desire—to give Him to souls!"

Sr. M.A.H.

The Mission of the

Daughters of St. Paul
BASIC
CATECHISM
"What you hear in whispers,
proclaim from the rooftops"
-Mt. 10:27

The Daughters of St. Paul have as their specific mission *evangelization with the press, films, radio, television,* and all the inventions which human progress furnishes, and the needs and conditions of the times require.

Yes, they are *teachers,* but their classroom is as wide as the world.

Yes, they are *nurses,* but their healing is directed to the minds and hearts of all whom they reach with the Truth which comes from Jesus the Master.

Yes, they *help the poor*—the spiritually poor—by offering them the enriching Word of God.

The Daughters of St. Paul are called to preach the divine message from the rooftops!

"You will give the doctrine of the Church, Scripture and Tradition," said Father Alberione. "Seek the most effective and quickest means which human intelligence provides for the preaching of the Gospel.

"What are we to write? What are we to diffuse? We must fulfill our mission which is that of spreading faith, morality, and worship....

"The use of the press as a means of apostolate is in substance of divine institution. It is God who commanded to write.... Some divine truths reach the faithful by word of mouth; others through Scripture."

"Our apostolate is to produce Christians who know, love and follow Jesus."

—The Founder

The Sister Writer

"The *manuscript*, which is only a single copy, is prepared; the technical apostolate multiplies this copy by the thousands, by hundreds of thousands or more; according to the circumstances. The same for the film.... Writing, therefore, is putting our thoughts on paper or on film...." *The Founder*

Characteristic of that which should flow from the pen of a Daughter of St. Paul are works that are:

—Richly biblical
—Catechetical
—Pastoral
—Faithful to the Pope and the Magisterium.

"The mission of the Daughters of St. Paul is this: to diffuse the truth.... It is a mission that knows no boundaries. Its confines are those of the world. You are sent to the whole world to bring the Word of God."
—The Founder

Consecrated Technology

The technical phase is handled by the sisters themselves. The composition room, lithography, printing and binding departments prepare the Word of God in printed form.

The sisters who operate the large four-color printing machines that produce thousands of printed sheets daily rejoice that Christ's Truth radiates from those pages, which will become books to uplift mankind and bring all people to our Creator.

How did they learn their "skill"? The older sisters teach the younger ones!

Perhaps the most eye-catching phase is the book bindery, with its array of machines. They click and hum, and in the end—incredibly—a sturdy, durable, attractive book results.

Manuscripts are edited and sent to the composing room for typing and proofreading.

"Your books are very special. Our grandchildren are learning about God and learning to read and love books all at the same time. I am glad we discovered the Daughters of St. Paul. Thank you for helping children everywhere to love and honor God through your fine books.

"God bless you and your work."

E.H.
Memphis, Tennessee

In the lithography, page proofs are turned into negatives and then into plates for the offset presses.

"Your printing machines are pulpits from which the Word of God is preached."
—The Founder

Sections of books are sewn together, glued, trimmed, and made into hardback or paperback books.

Piles of books are wheeled on skids into the shipping department.

What Do They Publish?

SCRIPTURE

"The Gospel is always up-to-date.
The Church is always young!
Give people the doctrine that saves!
Imbue all thought and human knowledge with the Gospel.
The Gospel is the salvation of the world."
—The Founder

The Holy Bible

Translated from the original languages, the edition contains the complete text of *The Holy Bible* with footnotes.

To encourage fuller understanding and appreciation, this Bible also contains:

*the complete text of the *Dogmatic Constitution on Divine Revelation*
*an invaluable index of pertinent Bible themes
*17 full-color Bible maps
*family record pages.

CONTEMPORARY NEW TESTAMENT SERIES:

To know the Bible
To love the Bible
To live the Bible!

22 BOOKLETS Plus Indexes and Study Guides. The texts contain *The New American Bible*—complete and unabridged, with footnotes and cross references; clear, up-to-date articles by noted biblical scholars on the history and physical description of the New Testament regions and cities; origins of the various books of the New Testament; discussions of authors' styles and purposes; explanations of special passages or doctrinal problems; answers to questions frequently asked; word meanings; glossary of persons, places and terms. Full-color photographs of artistic masterpieces and biblical sites and scenes as they look today are further enriched by in-depth explanatory captions of great educational value.

BOOKS THAT EXPLAIN THE BIBLE

The Vatican II Sunday Missal

*Complete
*Up-to-date
*Perpetual

A B C CYCLES

★ Imprimatur by His Eminence, Humberto Cardinal Medeiros, Archbishop of Boston, Mass.
★ Special introduction to each liturgical season from His Holiness, Pope Paul VI.
★ General introductions to every Mass and biblical introductions to each Reading written in accord with contemporary Scripture scholarship by His Excellency, Most Reverend John F. Whealon, STD, SSL, DD, Archbishop of Hartford, Connecticut.
★ New American Bible translation of all Scripture texts.
★ Nine special sections explaining motivation and practice of the Catholic Faith today also by His Excellency, Most Reverend John F. Whealon, STD, SSL, DD.

The Vatican II Weekday Missal in only ONE volume

CONTENTS

* **Complete texts** of the revised Roman Missal of:
  * all weekday Masses
  * Proper of Saints and Commons
  * Ritual Masses
  * Masses and Prayers for Various Needs and Occasions
  * Votive Masses
  * Masses for the Dead
* **Order of Mass,** conveniently placed near center of missal, printed in red and black
* **Scripture texts** from the New American Bible
* **Optional texts** clearly indicated
* **Liturgical Calendar,** giving exact page number for Weekday Masses up to 1999
* **Brief profiles of each saint, daily meditations and biblical introductions** to each Reading of the Weekday Masses, written in accord with contemporary Scripture scholarship by His Excellency, Most Reverend John F. Whealon, STD, SSL, DD, Archbishop of Hartford, Connecticut

The ONE volume edition of CHRISTIAN PRAYER: The Liturgy of the Hours

It contains:
* Morning Prayer (complete)
* Daytime Prayer (complete)
* Evening Prayer (complete)
* Night Prayer (complete)
* Office of the Dead (complete)
* Office of Readings (4-week Psalter) with a selection of biblical and non-biblical readings

"The Daughters of St. Paul have at all times been faithful and loyal workers under the guidance of the bishops. They are a consolation to the bishops.

"My knowledge of the spirit and vigor of the Daughters of St. Paul goes back to their pioneer Cleveland days. Our collaboration has seen the *Vatican II Sunday Missal*, the *Vatican II Daily Missal*, and the one volume *Liturgy of the Hours*—so I speak from experience.

"It is gratifying to see the Daughters of St. Paul increasing in numbers and works. May they and their apostolate flourish, for the advancement of the Lord's Church."

Most Reverend John F. Whealon
Archbishop of Hartford

CATECHETICAL MATERIAL

ST. PAUL WAY, TRUTH AND LIFE RELIGION SERIES

Student textbooks, activity books, teacher's manuals and parents' guides for every grade—for parochial schools and CCD programs.

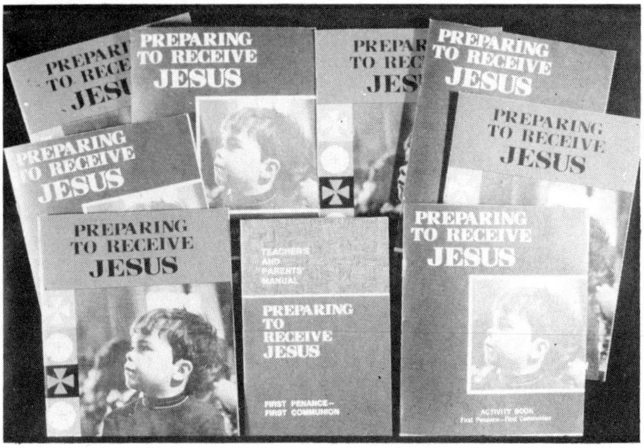

"The fundamental work of the apostolate of the press is the catechism: print books for catechists and catechism students; provide posters and holy pictures; give young people books which will form their character for life." —THE FOUNDER

Written illustrated, printed, bound and distributed by the Daughters of St. Paul.

Imprimatur by
His Eminence
Humberto Cardinal Medeiros
Archbishop of Boston

Classroom tested by the Sister-authors who teach religion in Boston parishes.

THE DIVINE MASTER HIGH SCHOOL SERIES FOR PAROCHIAL SCHOOLS AND CCD PROGRAMS

"Your series is excellent on every score—artwork, type, format, content, reliance on Scripture, Vatican documents and lastly Catechetical Directory. The Teacher's Guide is a masterpiece and the supplementary audio-visual aid help is most complete. It is the total program with total quality across the board."

Father Tom Golden
Church of St. Francis Xavier
De Pere, Wis.

"At the heart of catechesis we find...a Person...Jesus, who is 'the way, and the truth, and the life.' "

—Pope John Paul II, "Catechesi Tradendae"

Three Monthly Magazines

the family

"Born" in 1952, this 32-page magazine is printed monthly. Its articles are faith-filled, lively, practical and optimistic.

Short stories, feature articles on topics of current interest and "inspiration," words of the Pope, Family Catechetics, a series on Christian doctrine, articles on the spiritual life, a Bible puzzle, the Letter of the Month, recipes and homemaking tips add enjoyment and appeal.

Dear Sisters,

Thank you for your beautiful magazine—truly inspiring! I look forward with great anticipation to future editions.

M.L.
San Diego, CA

STRAIN FORWARD

The monthly magazine for priests, religious and lay people desirous of deepening their prayer life is called *Strain Forward.* In the spirit of St. Paul who strained ahead, always with the finish line in view, this magazine, featuring liturgical reflections, words of the Pope, and meditations, nourishes and reinforces its readers in their quest towards personal fidelity and union with Christ.

Dear Sisters,

Your magazine is such a source of comfort and encouragement to those of us who are trying to lead the religious life according to the Vatican directives. Each copy is read by so many sisters.

Erie, PA

MY FRIEND

My *Friend,* the only Catholic magazine in America for children, is the latest of the magazines published by the Daughters of St. Paul. With 32 pages of learning and fun, its particular audience is children ages 6-12. Each issue contains: Bible stories, lives of saints, contests, projects, science and many other features which keep the youngsters involved. The numerous letters of appreciation which arrive daily, attest to its popularity with the children.

Dear My *Friend,*

I just love to read your magazine. I can never wait to get a new one every month. I like to read the cartoons, and do the puzzles. When I get a new magazine I turn right to the "Between Friends" section, that's my favorite part of the magazine.

Allison Van Osten
Age 10

OTHER ST. PAUL EDITIONS

Papal Teachings

Papal Books
by Pope John XXIII, Pope Paul VI
Pope John Paul I, Pope John Paul II

Prayerbooks

Religious Instruction for All Ages

Mariology

Spirituality

Sociology

Parenthood

Education

Formation

Biographies of Saints
and Heroes of God

Psychology

Children's Books

BOOKS AND PAMPHLETS

Audio-Visuals for the Age of Media

Film, radio, television, slide/sound programs, filmstrips, records, cassettes—unlimited media opportunities!

Little by little, sound, animation and duplicating studios have been added to the Jamaica Plain novitiate, and the Daughters of St. Paul produce:

films ☆ radio programs ☆ filmstrips ☆ slide/sound programs ☆ records ☆ cassettes

Their goal?

A Daughter of St. Paul radio station for the 50th anniversary of the congregation's foundation in the U.S.A.

"I think immediately of the great possibilities offered by the means of social communication ...television, radio, the press, records, tape recordings—the whole series of audio-visual means. The achievements in these spheres are such as to encourage the greatest hope."

POPE JOHN PAUL II

"I always envision great and wonderful things happening in the U.S.A.—many vocations, films, publications.... The time has come for you to cast, not a mere fishing line, but a huge net, in the United States."

—The Founder

16mm Film Production

EDUCATION

Books, Books, Books—
How To Make a Book

ANIMATION

Grandpa O'Shea Tells a Story

God's Rules for Me

Joey

Learning About Jesus

The Wonderful World God Gave Us

The Star of the King

DOCUMENTARY

Freedom's Challenge

ENRICHMENT

Christmas Looking!

Besides diffusing for purchase or rental the films produced by the sisters, the St. Paul Catholic Book and Film Centers also rent films produced by the Society of St. Paul—for example, biblical films—and films from other producers.

Radio

Radio Programs Produced by the Daughters of St. Paul Are Being Broadcast From Coast to Coast and Beyond...

Media's importance cannot be minimized. It has the capacity to present the *true* image, the *total* message of the Church, and it should not be used for anything less worthy than that.

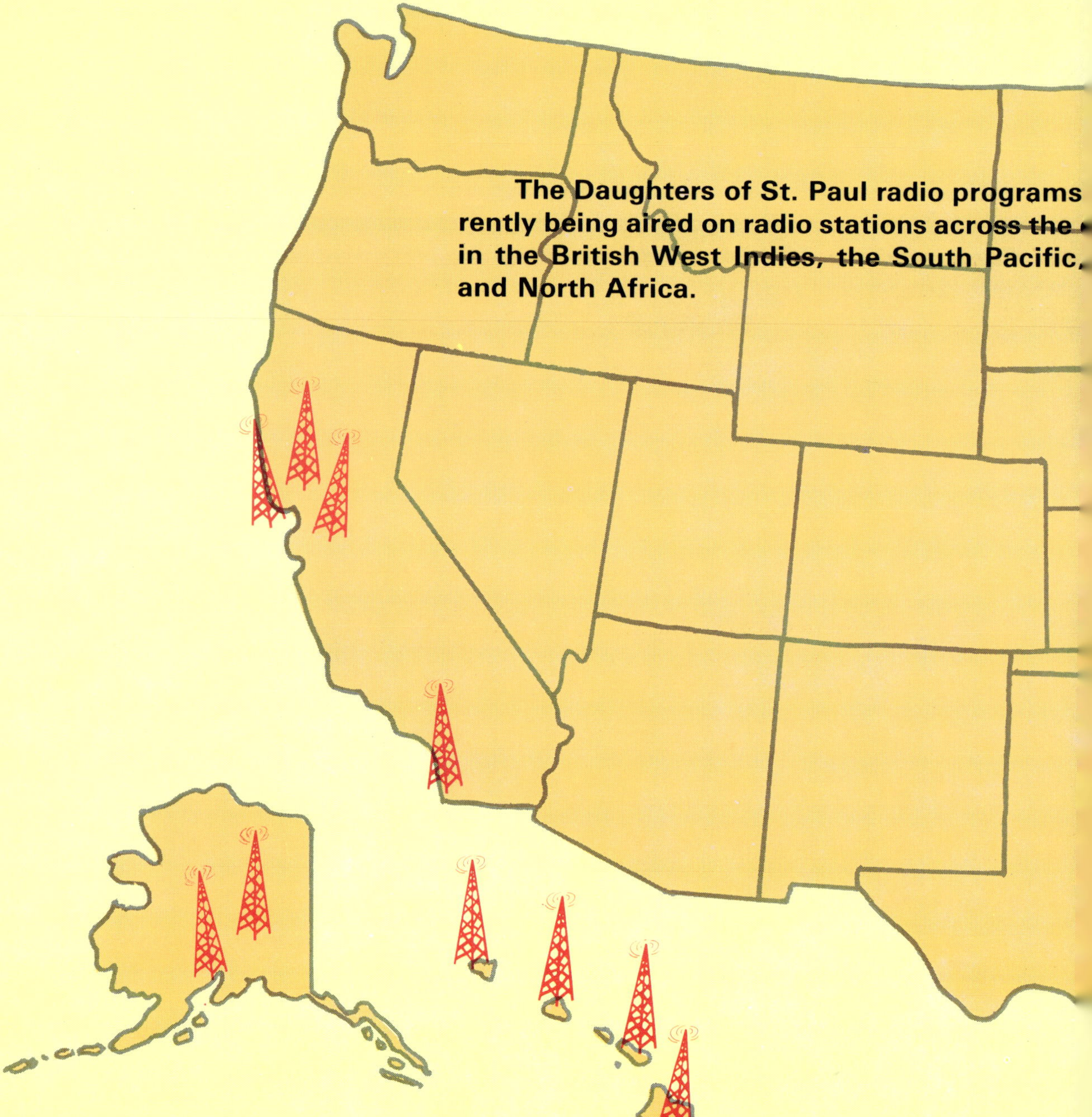

In this media age, we realize that the Church is in dialogue with the world. She listens; she hears the cries and laments; she offers solutions to the problems. As her Founder before her, she "has the words of eternal life" (cf. Jn. 6:68). Just as great missionaries of all times, such as *Paul the Apostle* and Francis Xavier, traversed land and sea to bring this precious redeeming message, so Catholic journalists, producers and technicians can reach millions today with the pen, printing press, television productions and films. This *is* the age of media.

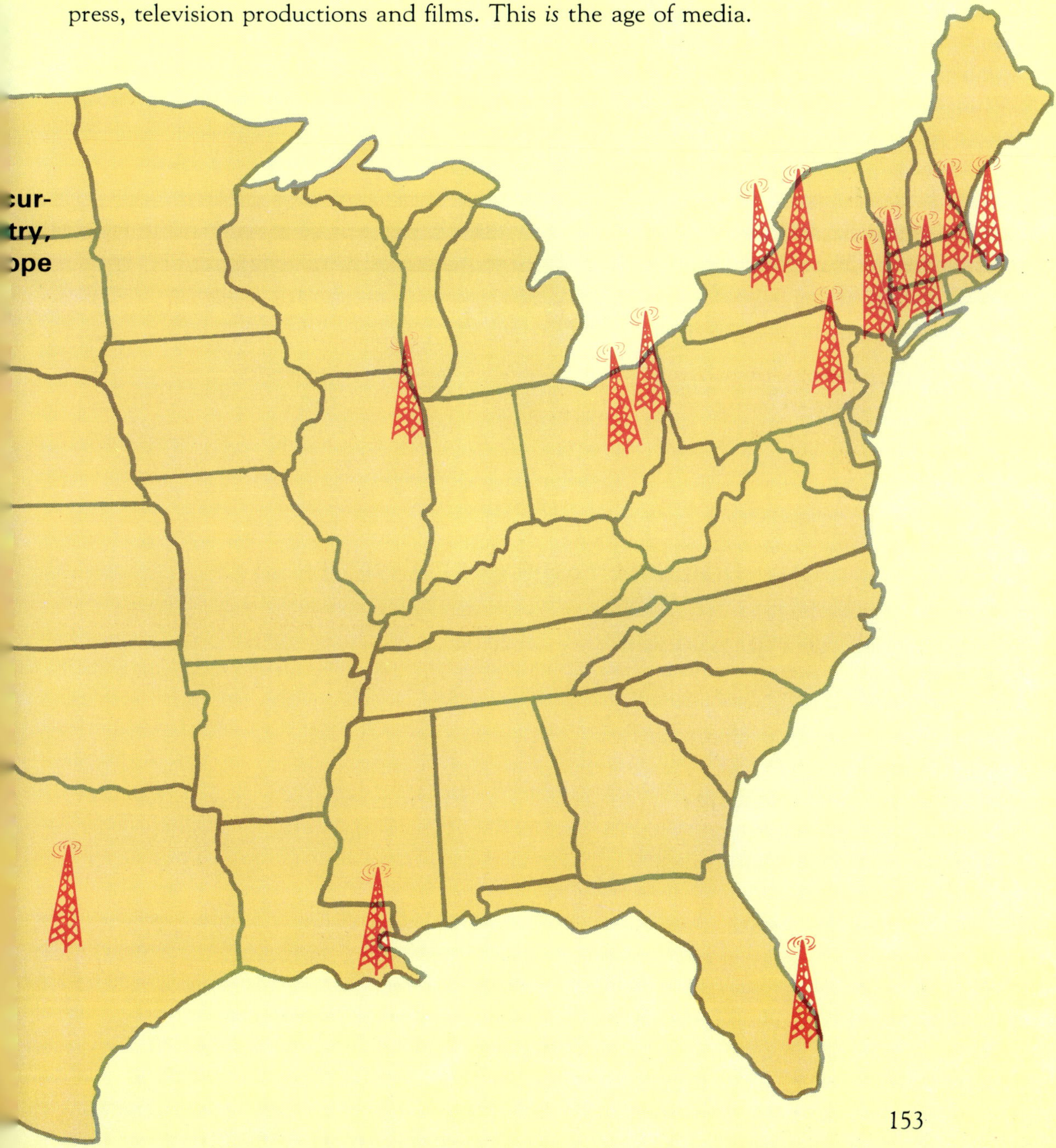

Slide-Sound Programs and/or Filmstrip-Cassette Programs

BIBLICAL SERIES
Old and New Testament in 18 parts

CATECHETICAL PROGRAMS

CASSETTES

Listening to the Bible

Reverently proclaimed by
Rev. Frederick Ryan, M. Div.

* **The Entire New Testament**
* **The Entire Books of Psalms, Ecclesiastes and Wisdom**
* **The Entire Books of Job, Proverbs, Song of Songs and Sirach (Ecclesiasticus)**
* **The Entire Prophetic Books**

BIBLE THEMES ON CASSETTE

FOR SPIRITUAL GROWTH

Five series of cassettes by Rev. John A. Hardon, S.J.

Cassettes on the Sacred Heart by Rev. Francis Larkin, SS.CC.

The Holy Rosary Cassettes
Available in 7 languages

Fathers of the Church Series
by Rev. Donald Wuerl

CASSETTE READERS

SONGS AND HYMNS ON CASSETTE AND RECORD

Diffusing the Word of God

"When a beautiful book comes out, they do not speak much of the author, or of the printer, or of the propagator, rather, they say the Pauline Family has published that book....

"The author, the printer, and the propagator are profoundly united.

"Diffusion is the principal and indispensable part. If we do not bring doctrine, souls remain in their ignorance, and how will they be saved? Hence, the substantial part of your mission is truly diffusion." *The Founder*

Daily the Daughters of St. Paul diffuse the Word of God in the form of books, magazines or audio-visuals in the following three ways:

* from *home*—their shipping department, staffed by the sisters
* from *book centers*, operated by the sisters
* through *personal visitations*

From Home—the Shipping Department

Each day the U.S. mail truck is filled with packages of books and audio-visuals that are being sent throughout the United States and abroad.

Through St. Paul Catholic Book and Film Centers

17 CONVENTS
22 BOOK CENTERS

"Our book centers are centers of apostolate. Indication of this is the Gospel with the statue of St. Paul. They are not stores, but service to the faithful; not selling, but apostolate for offerings; they do not have customers, but cooperators; not for business, but centers of light and warmth in Jesus Christ. The aim is not to dominate, but to serve the Church and souls; not to make money, but to benefit souls. Lay apostles and clergy must find in them collaboration, light and direction for their ministry. The book center is a TEMPLE. The clerk is the PREACHER. The counter is a PULPIT of truth. IT IS THE EDITING HOUSE OF GOD. Light, sanctity, joy in Jesus Christ and Christian life are the fruits sought."

—The Founder

"A center such as this responds to the hungers of mankind, of the human family. The hunger for truth, the hunger for spiritual consolation, for the grace and love of God, the hunger that is so deep that it needs to be satisfied. Here we have this wonderful effort and I am happy that our sisters, the Daughters of St. Paul, are the ones who are the instruments and channels of grace and service to us. I am sure that their work is the work of the Holy Spirit. They have such a beautiful way. Just to see them, to be near them, to come in contact with the sisters—that in itself will be such an encouragement."

His Eminence
Terence Cardinal Cooke
Archbishop of New York

A young priest, only recently ordained, told us his vocation started with a visit to our *San Diego* book center. He had been very confused and was on the verge of abandoning his Catholic Faith. In the book center he found books that not only saved and nourished his faith, but inspired him to follow his vocation to the priesthood.

Film Purchase and Rental
Through the St. Paul Catholic Book and Film Center

"The split between the Gospel and culture is, without a doubt, the drama of our time.... Every effort must be made to ensure a full evangelization of culture, or more correctly, of cultures." *Pope Paul VI*

"The apostolate of the film, for what concerns the rental of the films, requires much wisdom.... It is necessary to invoke the light of the Holy Spirit."
—The Founder

Films with a Message

The Haitian Baptist Church in *Boston* has periodically booked films for its youth group. When returning one of our newer films entitled, *Neighbor* (a modern day version of the Good Samaritan), we asked if they enjoyed it. We were answered with an enthusiastic "Oh, yes, Sister! The film was so good that we'll be back to rent it again and others very soon. We need films like these to keep close to Christ in these troubled times."

The Decision

A junior college student walked into our *Jersey City*, New Jersey St. Paul Catholic Book and Film Center with a big smile on his face. "Remember me, Sister? A friend of mine brought me into your center about four months ago to get me familiar with some Catholic literature. I told you I had been searching for the true Faith and you helped me select the books that would benefit me the most. Now, Sister, I've come back to tell you of my great happiness.... Next month, for the first time at our college, a baptismal ceremony is going to take place—and it will be mine! The books I got from you were instrumental in leading to my final decision. Thank you, Sisters!"

"The Church is the editing house of God, and you are the postmistresses who go from house to house distributing the divine Good News to men; or you are the ones who remain in the post office of God—which is the book center—awaiting souls to whom you hand the Good News." *The Founder*

Through Personal Visitations

The third means of bringing the Message to the people is defined and explained by the Founder as personal diffusion. This involves taking the Word of God directly to individuals—to everyone—in their homes, in factories, offices, stores, on the docks at the piers, in city buildings, and markets—wherever they may live or work.

Pairs of Daughters of St. Paul carry bags filled with "spiritual food" for the minds and souls of people. They meet, on a personal basis, an average of 17,000 persons across the United States every day, and offer them the opportunity of choosing the Word of God in the form of a book or audio-visual.

The sisters also make their books available to public and school libraries, rectories, schools, hospitals and prisons.

SOME EXAMPLES OF THE FRUITS OF OUR MISSION

No Real Obstacles!

A sister writes: "Last week we were visiting shop owners and employees in a cluster of stores in a small industrial section here in *Buffalo.* We approached one building that almost looked abandoned. The windows were boarded up; the door was hanging off the hinges and the wooden walls cried for paint. The only signs of life were the two chained dogs that lunged and jumped.

"We squeezed in through the broken door and found ourselves in a machine shop where three men welded pieces of metal.

"The boss was especially interested in *The Family* magazine and books on the Faith. Somewhere along the way he had given up the practice of his Catholic religion. 'Am I too late?' he asked the sisters.

" 'Do you think I can go back to church?'

" 'Will one of the books you left teach me again how to go to confession? I've forgotten so many things, you know.'

"'Yes,' we answered to the last two questions. And with each 'yes' a deeper serenity lit his face.

" 'Thank God you came,' he said half out loud, half to himself, as sister and I slid through the narrow passageway out into the muddy yard. Again the dogs barked, but we hardly noticed. We were too busy being overjoyed that a man had found his God again through our mission."

Visitations to the People Are Accomplished in a Variety of Ways...

Visits to families

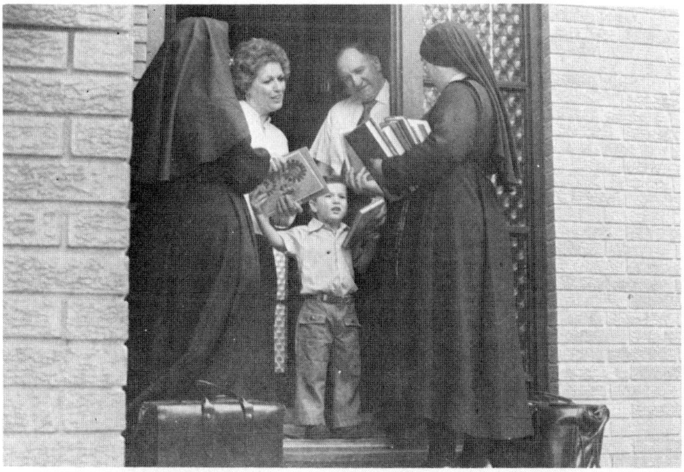

Parish displays after Saturday evening and Sunday Masses

Visits to libraries and schools

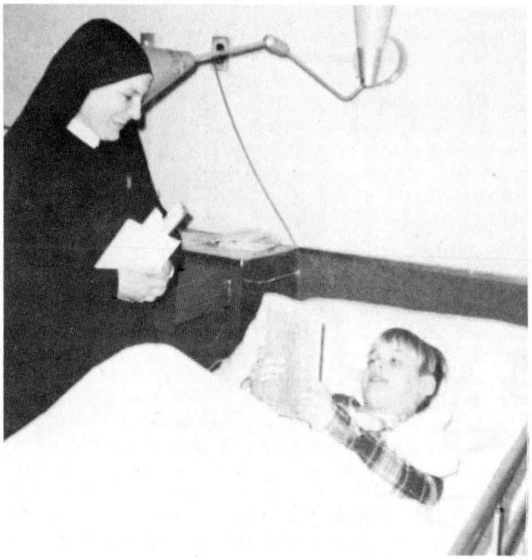

Visits to hospitals and homes for the elderly

Visits to prisons

Displays at congresses and conventions

Visits to individuals in the business areas

**Jesus said to the Apostles:
"The gift you have
received, give as
a gift."**

—Matthew 10:8

Catechetical workshop given by the sisters

Visits to rectories

Letter of Encouragement

From *San Francisco* a gentleman wrote:

"Dear Sisters,

"I am sorry I missed you this time when you were in the area. The first time I heard of your order was last year, when you stopped by our business office. Since then I have enjoyed *The Family* magazine very much. To know of your works makes me feel so good. At times I think the average Catholic is too complacent. It is a shame.... But with an outreach such as yours, the Good News does touch more and more people.

"May you have the joy of the Spirit in your wonderful endeavors.

"Please accept the enclosed offering for whatever use you see fit.

"Thank you for your hard work. May God richly bless you." G.T.

From New York to Miami God Followed Him

The sisters in *Miami* tell this inspiring story: "Eighteen years ago a man stood leaning against the doorpost of his little store on 29th Street in New York City when two Daughters of St. Paul passed by. He was troubled and disturbed. The sisters greeted him and then asked: 'Is something the matter?'

" 'Yes,' he confided, 'my little daughter is in the hospital and is not expected to live through the night. The doctors can't stop her hemorrhaging.'

" 'We'll pray for her today,' the sisters assured him, 'and we'll light a candle for her when we go home.'

"The sisters of New York did not know about the 'last chapter' of that story which we have just found out. A few days ago, we met the same man. He is now a manager at a large car dealer's firm right here in Miami. When he saw us coming through the front door, he recognized the religious habit, and beamed. He said: 'Sisters, your prayers were answered eighteen years ago. My daughter recovered.' We were puzzled. 'Oh, I know it wasn't the two of you,' he added, 'but it was your sisters. You were there when I needed a kind word and a prayer. I'll never forget it. Now, come into my office. I want to see your books!' "

That Book Changed My Life

A sister relates: "A woman came up to the counter in our book center in *Grand Central Station*. 'Sister,' she announced, 'I need 10 copies of *Creed of a Catholic.*' As sister got them, she continued: 'Two of your sisters came in one day to the office where I work, and I selected *Creed of a Catholic.*

" 'Well, that book changed my life. I was a fallen-away Catholic, and had not been to the sacraments for years. Not only have I returned to the practice of the Faith, but several other members of my family have also returned. Now I need these 10 copies to give to other people I know.' "

Motivation

The sisters from *Staten Island*, New York, tell this incident: "A bright nine-year-old girl was given four books on lives of the saints—three men saints and one woman saint from the *Encounter Book Series*. She avidly read the stories. One evening, before going to bed, she whispered in her mother's ear: 'Mom, I want to become a saint.' "

Thank You for Being Here

"A mother and teenage daughter entered our *Cincinnati* book center," the sisters recall. "She looked around and began to pile books at the counter. The woman was especially interested in heaven and purgatory. We showed her several books on those topics and others. She took all that we suggested. Her face glowed as she said softly, 'Sisters, I knew I could count on your book center here. I have eight children. One of them was just killed in an accident and these books are going to help me and the rest of my family to accept God's will. Thank you for being here.' "

Good Reading Straightened Out My Life!

A sister recalls: "It was one of my first times to serve the people in the *Philadelphia* book center. A gentleman came in, chose a book, and brought it to the counter. As he picked up his package, he casually remarked, 'I enjoy coming here to obtain good books for myself as well as for my friends. If it were not for these books, who knows where I would be today!' He indicated that his life had been marked by many problems, but good reading had helped him straighten things out."

"From your book centers you direct souls, you enlighten them, you guide them." **—The Founder**

Eternal Secrets

The sisters in *Baton Rouge*, Louisiana, relate: " 'Oh, Sisters, I was waiting for you to come,' a man called out as we entered his small sports shop.

"We remembered that last year he had taken the *Queen of Apostles. Prayerbook* for his wife, so we asked, 'Did your wife like the book that you took for her?'

" 'Yes, Sister, you don't know how much Ethel loved to say the prayers in the book. That's why I wanted to thank you. You see,' he paused, 'Ethel died two months ago; it was cancer. You know, that prayerbook was her biggest comfort. She used to say that it helped her even more than the medicine. I'm so grateful to you, Sisters, for coming to my shop.'

"This made us remember the Founder's words, 'We will only know in eternity how much good our books were able to do.' "

Backbone!

From a CCD teacher:

"The book *Morality Today* became the backbone of my entire session. This book is superbly written and to the point. To the author (a Daughter of St. Paul) go many thanks and gratitude from fifty young people and their teacher, a humble hairdresser."

R.J.P.
Weston, CT

Ecumenism

"One afternoon while visiting a business area in *San Antonio*," write the sisters, "we walked down a side street in the hope of finding more stores to visit. When we reached the end of the block, we realized that the only place remaining was a neat parish house connected with a small, colonial-style Episcopal church. We rang the bell. The secretary of the minister greeted us with not a little surprise.

" 'Wait here for a moment, Sisters, and the pastor will see you,' she said kindly.

"A few minutes later, an Episcopalian clergyman invited us into the office. 'How can I help you, Sisters?'

"We explained our mission and the pastor replied that he was very pleased we had stopped in. He began to question us about the number of postulants and novices we have, and the nature of our apostolate.

" 'You are doing a wonderful work,' he said in sincere admiration.

"Then he began to tell us about his work in his new parish, and we could see how dedicated he was to his parishioners. In the meantime, he selected: *Reading the*

Bible, Bible Stories for Young Readers, I Learn About Jesus, Morality Today, and twenty-five copies of *Biblical Way of the Cross* for use during the Fridays of Lent.

"After we left, Sister and I remarked to each other that for so many we are the only contact with the Church. What a privilege and a grace to represent the Church and perhaps in a small way help to bring about the desire of Jesus: *That they may be one.*"

From a religious brother:

"Your community reflects the apostolate in an exceptional way. How nice to see the sisters in their habits and in the center of the city. So many lay people have remarked about your total dedication; they become encouraged by such example."

R.E.L.

A Great Renewal

"While visiting with the Word of God and taking a parish census, we encouraged a man who had been away from the sacraments for fourteen years to make a good confession. He responded to grace and made his peace with God.

"A woman in the same parish had been away from the sacraments for nineteen years, but returned after we made an appointment with the priest for her.

"The pastor of that large parish told us: 'You are carrying on a great mission in my parish. I called a priest to come to preach a mission, and you might say that he *saved the saved,* those who have already been coming to church. But you, Sisters, continue to bring in the lost sheep. Look at these cards that you gave us,' he said. 'They are all marriage cases in the process of being rectified. And the sick calls to be taken care of are many.' "

Rewarding, indeed, are such results of apostolic labors in the Pauline mission.

Taxi Driver's Request

A sister in our *Chicago* book center writes: "A young man came in and asked for the book, *The Practice of Humility.* He wanted two copies. I gave them to him and couldn't help asking: 'Are you familiar with this book because you saw it in our window display last week?' 'No, Sister,' he responded. 'Yesterday someone left a copy in the back of my cab. I read it last night and it did me so much good. I want an extra one to keep on hand and I want one to give as a gift to a friend. We cab drivers certainly do need the virtue of humility!' I smiled and told him that I was reading the book, too."

Mark's Legacy

The sisters from the *Bronx* write: "While we were making our usual apostolic visits, we came upon a family whose son had just died the week before. Mark had been sixteen years old, and the members of his family were deeply impressed, not only because of his death, but because of the memory of how he had lived. Since this family knew the Daughters of St. Paul and our mission, they wanted to share with us one of the reasons why Mark's life had been the way it was.

"They showed us Mark's room as he had left it. His rosary was hanging from the headboard of his bed and on his desk was a very large pile of books written and printed by the Daughters of St. Paul. Most of the books were on the lives of the saints: *Ahead of the Crowd* (St. Dominic Savio); *57 Stories of Saints for Boys and Girls*; *Faces of Courage*. We then began to understand *why* Mark had been so good; he had read inspiring books that had led him to practice virtue. He also had prayed every day to the Blessed Mother, who had helped him to make the right choices."

"You are the light of the world. A city set on a hill cannot be hidden. Men do not light a lamp and then put it under a bushel basket. They set it on a stand where it gives light to all in the house. In the same way, your light must shine before men so that they may see goodness in your acts and give praise to your heavenly Father."

—Matthew 5:14-16

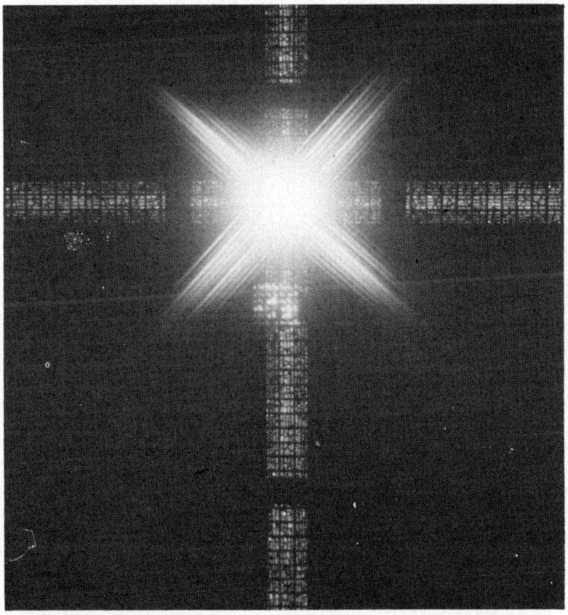

Good Reading Fosters Vocations

As the Daughters of St. Paul were exhibiting books and audio-visuals at a teachers' convention, a sister from another religious community came up and said: "You know, Sisters, whenever I see you Daughters of St. Paul, I have to smile. I always say I owe my religious vocation to you. Your sisters used to visit my home

"It was not you who
chose me,
it was I who chose you
to go forth and bear fruit.
Your fruit must endure."
—John 15:16

The Arlington, Virginia Archdiocesan Bookmobile is made available to the Daughters of St. Paul for distributing St. Paul Editions in Virginia and the Washington, D.C. area.

"Where are men going? Mankind is continually renewed on the face of the earth. It is like a large river flowing into eternity."
—The Founder

Continued from p. 165.

every year in Perth Amboy, *New Jersey*, and each time, Mom would get me a big pile of books. Then I would read and read and read. I was not called to be a Daughter of St. Paul, but I always say I owe my religious vocation to the Daughters of St. Paul because you nourished me with good literature."

He Found Courage

Another sister recalls: "We were visiting with our books in *Honolulu*. In one shop, there was a young man who didn't want any books, but was glad to accept the leaflets we gave him. Some days later, he came into our book center to ask for more leaflets. Explaining that he was an alcoholic and a drug addict, he said that the leaflets had encouraged him to try to fight his problems. After that, he came in again and got some books. He began to come in regularly, and one day told us that he had gone back to Mass. Yet, he felt he still did not have the courage to go to Confession. We encouraged him and promised our prayers.

"Some time later, he came in again, radiant with joy. He happily announced that he had just gone to Confession and had received Communion. He felt like a new person. 'I am so grateful to you, Sisters,' he told us. 'It was only through the great work you do—printing and distributing the Word of God—that I was able to rebuild my shattered life.' "

Books Are Reinforcement

As part of his adult religious education program, one pastor selects a different book each month for 80 of his parishioners who attend classes. He varies the subject matter to provide spiritual reading, lives of saints, religious instruction, and books that follow and explain the liturgical seasons. Sometimes the people are so interested that Father needs to obtain even more copies. Among their favorites: *Spiritual Life in the Bible*, *Mary of Nazareth*, and *Paschal Mystery and Christian Living*.

Anxious To Learn

"One day while visiting with our books in a doctor's office," the sisters in *Virginia* recall, "we met an eight-year-old boy who was waiting for someone. We noticed that he was focusing intently on a small pamphlet. We went a little closer and found out that the pamphlet was *Basic Prayers*, printed by the Daughters of St. Paul, so we asked him where he had gotten it. With a big smile he told us that he had received the pamphlet from Sister at school and that he knew the Daughters of St. Paul had printed it because the sister who teaches them told the children all about us. Then he added, 'Sisters, I'm trying to learn every prayer in this book. It is taking time, but I really want to learn *all* my prayers!' "

Marvel in a Prison

Our sisters in *New Orleans*, Louisiana, received the following letter from a prisoner:

"Last summer some holy soul at your place sent us a whole box of good books. I am still feeling the warmth of your charity, which lets us know we are not forgotten. Since then, something marvelous has happened. The apostolate—dead here for years—has flowered to a point that I'm in wonder at the profound graces being lavished upon us. Martin was the first catechumen in years. Now Steve has joined us. Steve brought young Tommy, an earnest seeker of Truth. And somehow Jaime entered the group. Even a guard sat in on one of our impromptu sessions as a participant! It's all breathtaking!" M.M.

(in prison for 19 years)

Pro-Life

The sisters from *Bridgeport* write: "Two girls abruptly walked into our book center one day. As we soon learned, they were on their way to an abortion clinic. One of them was resolved to have an abortion, but her friend was trying to dissuade her.

" 'Sisters, do you have something to convince my friend of the evil of abortion?' We immediately gave a pamphlet on abortion to the other girl, and tried to say a few words to make her reconsider her decision. But the girl remained undecided.

"The next day, the phone rang. A timid voice said, 'Sisters, I am the girl who came in yesterday. I read the pamphlet on abortion and I changed my mind. I am going to have my baby.'

"What gratitude to God we felt, to think that through the power of our mission, another life had been saved."

A Surprise

The sisters write from *St. Louis*: "Some months ago, we were visiting with our books in Belleville, Illinois. Just before the time to return home, we stopped in our last office for the day. A receptionist greeted us kindly. She looked through the books with interest and chose some titles for herself. She explained that she was not Catholic, and had never been baptized in any religion, but wanted to know more about God. Before leaving, we said to her: 'Maybe next year when we come back, you'll have a surprise for us!'

"Not long after, she came into our St. Louis book center and got more books. 'Sisters,' she said, 'I'm taking instructions to become a Catholic! When I met you that day, your words really struck me. At first I wondered what you meant about the surprise. Then it dawned on me, and as I thought about it, I wanted to know more about the Catholic Faith.'

"Three of us were present at her recent Baptism. She wrote a letter to us in which she said: '...You have helped me find the most beautiful road in life.' "

Transformation

Another sister recalls this story: "A young soldier told us how reading had transformed his fiancée. Though they were seriously thinking of marriage, he was disturbed by her immature attitude. The superficial magazines she read, centering on fashions and social life, were the source of these ideas. She often said she wanted to enjoy life first, and seemed interested only in having a good time. She even talked of getting her own maid after marriage so she wouldn't have to do housework.

"The soldier finally thought of an idea. He often bought her little gifts, and he began to slip in books on formation and family life published by the Daughters of St. Paul. He also subscribed her to a good Catholic magazine. Little by little, as she read these, her attitude matured. She gave up reading the superficial magazines. When they married, her outlook was completely transformed. She was rereading the formation books and looking forward to a happy family life."

God's Gifts for an Eskimo Village

The sisters from *Alaska* say: "Two of us Daughters of St. Paul walked through the streets of a small village located in a remote area of Alaska. As Christ's apostles, what were we bringing to the Eskimos? His Word—presented in the form of a book, a magazine, slide or cassette.

"Families welcomed us warmly. Our knock at each door usually evoked a 'Come in.' On entering, we were met by four, five, six or more Eskimo children of varying ages, and, of course, Mother and Father. Each house usually consisted of one large room, with smaller rooms partitioned off by curtains. On the walls, pictures of our Lord, the Blessed Mother and some saints displayed the devotion of these good people. Their names also revealed the solid training received from the

missionaries. Everyone had a beautiful saint's name like Margaret, John, Paul, Angela, and there were many 'Marys.' One man with eleven children was named Charles Borromeo.

"We Pauline missionaries found the ideal situation to be when Mother and Father were home together. It was impressive to see the cooperation between husband and wife. They would look through the books individually; then at a certain point, they would talk back and forth quietly in Eskimo. They took a large selection of our editions as a result of their mutual dialogue. What one wanted, the other nodded in agreement. It was a similar experience in nearly every home we visited.

"Back at our mission post, a man approached us. 'Could I see the things you've got?' We showed him our literature. He chose many titles, including a subscription to *The Family* magazine. From the address he gave, we noted he was from a distant village, so we asked, 'How did you find out we were here?'

" 'I was on my way back from a fishing trip; the friend I stayed with told me. So, as long as I was still nearby, I wanted to see you before going home.'

"How eager souls are to receive God's Word! Jesus said, 'Blessed are they who hunger and thirst for holiness; they shall have their fill' (Mt. 5:6).

"Yes, how hungry mankind is for that joy which God alone can give! They will search for it until they possess it. But who is there to serve Truth to God's people? Who is there to bring Jesus Christ, the true Joy of all hearts? St. Paul asked the Romans:

" 'And how can they believe unless they have heard of him? And how can they hear unless there is someone to preach? And how can men preach unless they are sent? Scripture says, "How beautiful are the feet of those who announce the good news!" ' (Rom. 10:14-15)

"Yes, as our Founder once said, each step we take is counted in heaven—even footsteps in icy Alaska—and will be rewarded a hundredfold!"

"Blessed Are the Walkers of God..."

From the heart of the Reverend Founder, almost like a canticle, came the *Beatitudes of the Daughters of St. Paul:*

"Blessed are the footsteps of her who proclaims the Gospel, the Good News of peace.

Blessed are the handmaids of the Church, for they possess the heart of this Mother.

Blessed are the walkers of God, who in the mystic silence of the convent study the ways of the world, and on the morrow walk them to reach souls.

Blessed are these angels of the Lord, who seek out those who have lost or never found the path of the Church.

Blessed are the postmistresses of God, who bring to every family His Gospel of love.

Blessed are these cooperators with the zealous efforts of priests; silently they preach Jesus Christ, the Way, the Truth and the Life.

Blessed is the sweet fragrance of the lily, the rose and the violet, which they leave behind wherever they pass.

Blessed are the imitators of Mary, who present Jesus to the shepherds, to the Magi, to the Temple, to the disciples, to the world.

Blessed are the Daughters of St. Paul, who possess the heart of their Father, who give their Father's word, who with their Father—suffering, praying, working—accomplish the work assigned them by God."

St. Paul Cooperators

The aim of the St. Paul Cooperator is to work for his own sanctification and to cooperate in the achievement of the aims of the Pauline Family—spreading the Catholic Faith through the apostolate of the editions: press, motion pictures, radio, television, records, cassettes, etc.

To reach the aim of this sanctification, the St. Paul Cooperator instructs himself in the Christian faith and lives as a good Christian according to his state in life; he practices the Pauline piety as far as possible by frequent reception of the sacraments, adoration before the Blessed Sacrament, devotion to the Blessed Virgin, meditation and examination of conscience.

We cordially invite to become members of St. Paul Cooperators all those who are apostolic-minded, of all age levels, and in all walks and professions of life. To those who become members is given the noble privilege of helping to carry out Christ's mandate to: "Go, teach all nations."

WAYS OF COOPERATION

St. Paul Cooperators foster and promote the apostolic works and mission activities of the Daughters of St. Paul in the following ways:

Prayer

1. Pray for the Congregation's initiatives, apostolic works, activities and undertakings. One can offer a Communion, a Mass, a visit to the Blessed Sacrament, recitation of the rosary each week, etc., or one of the prayers to St. Paul.
2. Pray for and foster vocations to the mission of the Daughters of St. Paul.

Works

1. Aid in the spreading of our holy Faith through the diffusion of books, magazines, pamphlets and leaflets.
2. Obtain subscriptions and renewals to their magazine *The Family* and other Pauline periodicals.
3. Help to found Catholic libraries in homes, parishes, schools, colleges and universities.
4. Aid by submitting manuscripts and publicizing the mission of the Daughters of St. Paul and their publications.

5. By word and deed, influence others to refrain from attending morally harmful movies, help to increase the demand for good films, promote the knowledge and diffusion of "St. Paul Films."

6. Advocate better television and radio programs.

7. Diffuse and publicize St. Paul catechetical aids: catechisms and teacher's guides, posters, filmstrips, slides, cassettes, records, etc.

8. Promote the observance of World Communications Day (Sunday after the Ascension) and Catholic Press Month (February), as well as Gospel Days or Bible Sundays.

9. Make sacrifices for the mission of the Daughters of St. Paul and for the success of their apostolic works at home and abroad.

Offerings

1. Contribute weekly, monthly, or yearly donations to meet the financial needs of the congregation, such as expenses for printing the Word of God, opening convents, helping their mission, etc.

2. Contribute to the support of the monthly upkeep of needy postulants or for a religious investiture.

3. Remember the Daughters of St. Paul in wills.

4. Enlist others to become members of St. Paul Cooperators.

SPIRITUAL ADVANTAGES

From the first moment of their inscription, the St. Paul Cooperators participate perpetually in the fruit of 2,400 Masses celebrated in the Temple of Mary, Queen of Apostles in Rome, by the Fathers of the Society of St. Paul. The Cooperators are eligible to obtain the many plenary indulgences granted to the Daughters of St. Paul, and members of the entire Pauline Family, by the Holy See.

Daily the Pauline Family recites the following prayer for the Cooperators: "We ask You, O Lord, for Your Name's sake, to reward our benefactors with eternal life. Amen."

The Cooperators are in the prayers of the community, during life and after death.

RECOMMENDED DAILY PRAYERS

Prayer to St. Paul

O St. Paul, most glorious Apostle of the Gentiles, with so much zeal you spent yourself to destroy in Ephesus those writings which you knew would have perverted the minds of the faithful. Now, too, look upon us kindly. You see how an unbelieving press, without hindrance, seeks to snatch from our hearts the precious treasure of faith and good morals. Enlighten, we beg you, O holy Apostle, the minds of many writers, so that they may cease bringing ruin to souls through their teachings and perverse insinuations. Move their hearts to detest the evil they do to the elect flock of Jesus Christ. Obtain for us the grace to be always docile to the voice of the Supreme Pontiff and never read perverse writings. Rather, may we seek to read, and as much as we are able, to distribute those writings whose salutary contents will help all to promote the greater glory of God, the exaltation of His Church, and the salvation of souls. Amen.

Novena to St. Paul

For nine days, say the following prayers: Our Father, Hail Mary, Glory Be.

Antiphon: O St. Paul, the Apostle, preacher of truth and Doctor of the Gentiles, intercede for us to God, who chose you.

V. You are a vessel of election, O St. Paul the Apostle.

R. Preacher of truth to the whole world.

Prayer: O God, you have instructed many nations through the preaching of the blessed Apostle Paul. Let the power of his intercession with You help us who venerate his memory this day.

Enrollment

A minimum offering of $10.00 is required to be enrolled among the St. Paul Cooperators. The enrollment is individual.

Please send your name and address, and the name and address of each person to be enrolled, and include the offering for the enrollment. A receipt card will be sent to you along with the *St. Paul Cooperators Manual of Prayers.*

Our

Pauline Pilgrimage

As St. Paul said many years ago, "God makes all things work together for the good of those who love him" (Rom. 8:28). We have to agree with our patron and father that God shows His love in many ways. One example of this is indelibly impressed upon our hearts and minds. And the impression is renewed every time we remember our Pauline Pilgrimage to Rome in preparation for the celebration of our 50th Anniversary.

We "pilgrims" numbered forty-six Daughters of St. Paul, from all of our convents in the United States.

It was a dream come true as we boarded the plane in the evening of August 30, 1981. We were heading for the city of the Pope, the heart of Christendom, the core of our congregation. There early Christianity had budded, and the blood of martyrs had been the seed of the Church's growth. In Italy, God had inspired our Founder to initiate the Pauline Family, and his sacrifice had been the seed which God had blessed with abundant growth.

It was with all this in mind that we set out not for a trip, but for a *pilgrimage.*

We were warmly greeted by our Pauline community in Rome. Our Reverend Mother General, not in Italy at the time, was expected back during the course of our visit. We eagerly awaited her return.

Our pilgrimage days were full. Sights, sounds, new experiences—but the pervading character was a profound sense of prayer and great awe at seeing so many holy places.

Our first outing in Rome brought us to the Queen of Apostles Temple, which our Founder had built in thanksgiving to Mary for the safety of the Pauline Family during World War II.

On the same grounds is the house of the Society of St. Paul where our Founder lived a number of years and where he ended his prayerful, active life.

We saw the "bureau-like" altar on which he celebrated Mass during his last illness, and we marveled at the simple poverty so evident in the surroundings. When Pope Paul VI went to visit the Founder shortly before his death, the Pope had exclaimed, "Only this? And so poor!"

The Three Fountains

This church, also called the Church of the Pillar of St. Paul, contains the pillar upon which the Apostle laid his head for execution. And, along the side, are the three altars built above the three fountains which sprang up miraculously when St. Paul's head touched the ground in these three places. Here we renewed our resolve to carry out our mission with the same zeal as our Father had.

St. Paul's Basilica

St. Paul's Outside the Walls is one of Rome's four major basilicas. And to us, Daughters of St. Paul, it is "our Father's mansion." The sentiments we felt could never be fully expressed.

Basilica of St. John Lateran and the Holy Stairs

The cathedral church of the Pope himself—St. John Lateran. Inside this imposing sanctuary are large, dynamic white marble statues of the Apostles—including certainly our father St. Paul.

Across the street from St. John Lateran is the Shrine of the Holy Stairs. Over these stairs Jesus walked after His scourging and crowning with thorns. As the many other pilgrims there, we scaled them on our knees, devoutly praying on each step.

A Day Never To Be Forgotten

Although our first two days in Rome were memorable, the climax was yet to come.

When we returned to the General Motherhouse, we were given the news for which we had prayed. The Vatican had called: "The Pope expects you to be present for his Mass tomorrow morning at 8 o'clock." His Holiness also wanted us to read the First Reading and the Responsorial Psalm and to sing the hymns in English. The Mass would be in English!

On the morning of September 2nd, we were at Castel Gandolfo at 7:15 a.m. A Swiss Guard came out: "You are a little early, Sisters," he smiled. A uniformed commander of the Swiss Guard remarked also: "How beautiful your habits are! Do you wear them all the time or only for this occasion?"

"Oh no! We wear the habit all the time!" He was happy with our answer.

The papal photographer also arrived early. Finally at twenty to eight, we were led to the private papal chapel. We had only been kneeling a couple of minutes when the Holy Father simply walked into the chapel. When a very audible gasp came from us, the Holy Father raised his finger to his lips, and with a twinkle in his eyes and a tiny smile, he motioned us to silence. His Holiness wore a very simple white cassock without the usual elbow-length cape or cincture. He knelt, preparing for Holy Mass. Then he rose and stepped up to the altar to vest. The Holy Father stood facing us in his green vestments; his eyes studied our group one by one. What fervor and devotion during this Mass and Communion!

During the Holy Father's thanksgiving after Mass we were led to a private audience hall next door. When the Pope entered, we clapped, beside ourselves with joy. The Holy Father began greeting us individually and gave each of us a special rosary. As the Holy Father circulated among us, we sang a song written in his honor for the occasion. The song expressed our love for the Vicar of Christ, our desire to live our Founder's spirit and to serve the Church through our specific apostolate. As the Holy Father passed, we were also able to give him a short message. One sister said, "We all love you, Holy Father, and we pray for you." He answered, "Thank you very much, because I need it." Another said, "Please pray for us, Holy Father, that we may always be faithful." The Pope nodded emphatically and, raising his right hand, gestured, saying, "You must *always* be faithful!"

Then His Holiness admonished the photographer: "A good picture!" As we were waiting, while the photographer arranged for the picture, we had a beautiful dialogue with the Pope. The Holy Father began:

The Pope: **You are from Boston?**

Sisters: Yes!

Sr. Paula: Your Holiness, we are from all over the States. We have sisters from Alaska here, Hawaii, San Francisco....

The Pope: **Alaska? Anchorage?**

Sisters: Yes.

The Pope: **Anchorage. Very nice.**

Sr. Paula: We have sixteen convents and there are one or two sisters from each.

The Pope: **Sixteen?**

Sr. Paula: Sixteen convents.

The Pope: **And here you are having a reunion?**

Sr. Paula: We came to Rome, to Italy, to make a pilgrimage.

The Pope: **Pilgrimage? I see. Yes.**

Sr. Paula: Next year, Your Holiness, we celebrate the 50th Anniversary of our foundation in the United States.

The Pope: **Fifty?**

Sr. Paula: Yes, Your Holiness.

(At these words, the Pope gave Sister Paula a special blessing, tracing a cross on her forehead with his thumb and then placing his hand on her head.)

The Pope: **Ah, yes. Fifty years of your....**
Sr. Paula: Of our establishment. We arrived in New York.
The Pope: **Very nice, and you are doing good things.... You are publishing—you are publishing also—Oohh!... I saw the books you sent me yesterday!**
Sr. Paula: We have three [printing] machines, and one we call the machine of the Pope.
The Pope: **One machine is the machine of the Pope!**
Sr. Paula: We always have books....
The Pope: **For me!** (Taking a card from Sr. Paula) **I must take this. This is for me?**
Sr. Paula: Oh, yes!
The Pope: **And you are from Boston?**
Sr. Paula: Yes.
The Pope: **My best greetings to the Cardinal. You know Cardinal Medeiros?**
Sr. Paula: Oh, and how.
Sisters: Yes!
The Pope: **And you know Monsignor Sypek?**
Sisters: Yes! Yes!
The Pope: **Also to him!**
Sr. Paula: He comes to teach in our college.
The Pope: **He is teaching in your college. Very nice.**
Sr. Paula: So we are sure that we have a solid teacher.
The Pope: **God bless you!**
Sr. Paula: We are *very* grateful, Your Holiness!
The Pope: **I bless all your sacred objects....**
All: Thank you, Holy Father. Deo Gratias.

After the group picture was taken, the Holy Father began moving towards the door. We started a special song, "We love you...," and as we finished, he answered, "I love you, too."

For a short period of time we went to wait for the Angelus message among the various groups of pilgrims crowded in the inner courtyard of Castel Gandolfo. At about three minutes to twelve, the Holy Father appeared on the balcony and thunderous applause rocked the air. In his message the Holy Father encouraged us all to reason not by man's standards, but by God's. Then he began addressing the various language groups. We held our breath. Did we dare hope His Holiness would still mention us after our beautiful privilege of Mass and a private audience with him that morning?

The Holy Father continued in English, welcoming all English-speaking pilgrims thus:

"I am happy to greet all the English-speaking visitors and pilgrims who are present here today. To you and to your families at home, I cordially impart my apostolic blessing.

"My special welcome goes to the Daughters of St. Paul from Boston. May God sustain you in your generous service of the Gospel, in the great task of helping to spread Christian doctrine. I am very grateful to you for your devoted collaboration in publishing and diffusing papal teaching. I pray that through your apostolate 'the word of the Lord may speed on and triumph' (2 Thes. 3:1)."

He closed with his usual greeting: *"Praised be Jesus Christ!"*

We answered as one voice: *"May He always be praised!"* The Holy Father's response was one of pleasant surprise, accompanied by an approving "Good!"

Afterwards, as we rode to our nearby Queen of Apostles Hospital in Albano, it was hard for us to explain the grateful sentiments which filled our hearts. We will never forget that day, for which we will always be thankful to God!

Piedmont—Land of Our Pauline Birth

On September 3rd, we were up bright and early and off to the north by 7:15 a.m. It was about a twelve-hour drive up the coast of Italy, through beautiful fields and rolling hills.

We stopped in Pisa to see the famed Leaning Tower, then resumed our journey.

Soon our bus began climbing the foothills of the Alps. As we neared Genoa, the home of Christopher Columbus, we began driving *through* the mountains: 76 tunnels in all!

Finally, toward 7:30 p.m., we spotted the first sign for Alba—the cradle of our congregation. At about 8:00, we drove up to the Motherhouse with its complex of buildings, several of which were built of the bricks made by the first members of the Pauline Family.

Tired but happy, we rejoiced at the thought of staying in the very house in which Mother Thecla, our Co-Foundress, and others of the first Paulines had prayed and worked and struggled through difficult years in the beginning of our congregation. More than bricks had been fashioned by them: a Family had been molded by their faith, love, courage and zeal. And we were grateful to be part of that worldwide Family, and to be able to see with our own eyes where it had all begun.

On Friday, September 4th, we attended Mass in the Church of St. Paul, constructed under our Founder's direction.

Behind the main altar is the "Glory of St. Paul," a huge white marble carving of St. Paul, surrounded by saints and devotees. Above St. Paul and to the left is the Divine Master with an angel offering Him the emblem of the Pauline Family.

The side altars all have beautiful paintings and statues pertaining to Pauline spirituality.

While in Alba, we also visited the building which houses *Famiglia Cristiana*, the largest Catholic weekly magazine in the world. It is published by the Society of St. Paul.

On the way to the Cathedral of Alba, we passed by the Church of Saint Damian, where Mother Thecla gave her famous "yes" to God and to Father Alberione, and where Canon Chiesa (the Founder's spiritual director) had been pastor for thirty-two years. It is a small, inconspicuous church in Alba.

In the Cathedral, we prayed together at the altar where our Founder made his four hours of adoration on the night that divided the 19th and 20th centuries.... Here he was first inspired to found our congregation.

Within walking distance is the Seminary of Alba, where the Founder studied and later was professor and spiritual director. The worn stairs he once used daily are still there, as well as his classroom for Church History and Pastoral Theology. The beautiful little chapel where he was ordained a deacon and where he later gave daily meditations is just down the hall.

In the afternoon, we were off for Castagnito, the birthplace of Mother Thecla Merlo. It is a small village perched on a hilltop.

We prayed in her parish church, St. John the Baptist, and there we saw her baptismal and confirmation records. We sang the Creed at the baptismal font which gave spiritual life to our spiritual mother.

Just down the hill, at no. 19, was the original Merlo home, a small white house with a hay loft adjoining the second floor. What humble beginnings for so great a woman of God!

"The Glory of St. Paul," sculptured over the altar dedicated to him. He is surrounded by his disciples and admirers, and to all he points out the Divine Master.

The pressroom of Famiglia Cristiana

The main altar in the Cathedral of Alba

On Saturday we drove to Turin. There we visited the Shrine of Our Lady of Consolata, where the Founder so often prayed in his younger years.

At the Cathedral of Turin, we prayed before the large reliquary containing the Holy Shroud of our Savior.

Next we saw the Salesian Motherhouse and the Church of Mary, Help of Christians. Here Sts. John Bosco, Dominic Savio, and Maria Mazzarella are buried in ornately decorated side altars.

The famous "Little House of Divine Providence" was our next stop. It is truly a city within the city of Turin. Block after block of buildings serve the needs of sick, elderly, or handicapped people and include two complete hospitals!

We prayed at the tomb of St. Joseph Cottolengo in the church there. He lived just prior to Father Alberione, who admired him greatly.

Sunday dawned bright and beautiful as we drove to Priocca, Mother Paula's birthplace. In the beauty of this small town in northern Italy, with its great-hearted and faith-filled people, we recognized the surroundings that had helped 17-year-old Adele Cordero (now Mother Paula) to listen to the voice of God. Her decision to say yes to her Pauline vocation was the first link in the chain of graces that we thank God for after fifty years in the U.S.A.

Monday, September 7th, was a day of retracing the Founder's steps as a youngster. We were impressed at the utter poverty of his birthplace in Fossano. Because of his family's lack of material goods, the Alberiones were confined to one rented room in a small house. Now, however, no matter what farmer you ask, he will be able to tell you immediately where the Alberiones had lived!

On the way home to Alba, we stopped at the Shrine of Our Lady of Moretta. It was here, in 1914, that the Founder was asked to preach during the Mass on the feast of Our Lady of Moretta. Bishop Re was there, along with many priests and influential persons. During this time, Father Alberione was struggling to gain permission to found the Daughters of St. Paul, but had met with much opposition.

His sermon was one of ardent praise of Mary—so much so that when he descended from the pulpit, Bishop Re was standing there and embraced him, saying, "My dearest James, go ahead and do all that you plan." We saw this very pulpit and prayed to be as fervently devoted to the Queen of Apostles as our Founder was.

On Tuesday, September 8th, we left the Motherhouse for the last time. We knew we would miss Piedmont and this place hallowed by our Founder and Co-Foundress. But although we were leaving physically, the memories engraved on our minds and hearts would be present always.

Venice, St. Mark's Square

Assisting at the Mass of His Eminence, Silvio Cardinal Oddi, in the Lithuanian Chapel beneath St. Peter's Basilica. The sisters are wearing the summer habit.

Our next stop was Milan. We were awestruck at the magnificent Gothic cathedral there, which appeared as "lacework in stone." Our tour also included the office complex for *Famiglia Cristiana* and the radio and TV studios operated by the Society of St. Paul.

Venice and Padua

Venice, the city of canals, was more picturesque than we had imagined. As our oversized "water taxi" dodged between gondolas down the Grand Canal, we headed for St. Mark's Square. We arrived just in time for the ringing of the Angelus bells. They tolled their welcome, and we remembered in prayer the three recent Popes who had once been Patriarchs of Venice: St. Pius X, John XXIII, and John Paul I.

From Venice we went to Padua and the shrine of the great wonder-worker, St. Anthony, and then we headed back to Rome.

The Eternal City

On Friday, September 11th, we had the privilege of participating at the Mass offered by His Eminence Cardinal Oddi in one of the chapels in the crypt of St. Peter's Basilica. Later in the morning we met with His Eminence in the office of the Sacred Congregation for the Clergy. His was a heartfelt welcome to Rome: "My dear Daughters of St. Paul:

"It is a great joy for me to welcome you today to the Eternal City, to the city of Sts. Peter and Paul, to the city of the Holy Father, and to be able to thus reciprocate the warm welcome you gave me in Boston a few months ago.

"For the majority of you, this is your first visit to Rome, and I have asked myself why you have wanted to come. It was not difficult to discover many answers. You have wanted to come to Rome because you are Roman Catholics. You have wanted to visit the tombs of Peter, the first Pope, and of Paul, the Apostle of the Gentiles. You have wanted to express in a tangible manner your loyalty to the Successor of St. Peter, Pope John Paul II, who in these troubled times is fearlessly and surely guiding the Bark of Peter through the troubled waters. Your desire to profess your personal allegiance to the Pope has already been rewarded, for you all have had the happiness of meeting him personally last week and receiving his apostolic blessing.

"You have wanted to visit Rome because you are religious who are consecrated, or preparing to be consecrated, to a life of loving service to Christ and to

St. Peter's Basilica

Bell tower of basilica in Pompeii

Statue of St. Benedict in the courtyard of Montecassino

His Church. You have wanted to visit Rome to confirm and to strengthen your religious vocation to that life by visiting the Colisseum, the catacombs and other tombs of the martyrs by which you will be inspired to total loyalty to Christ despite the allure and the pressures of the world around you.

"You have wanted to visit Rome as Daughters of St. Paul, for your patron is buried here; your Mother General lives here and your Motherhouse is not far away—by American standards, just around the corner—in Alba. From this visit you will absorb more deeply and understand more clearly the charism of your Founders and the spirit of your institute.

"You have wanted to visit Rome as cultured women, for you know the major role this city has played in the development of western civilization, which, with all its weaknesses, is still of enormous importance in the world in which we live.

"Welcome, my dear sisters, to Rome!

"As we read over today's first letter of Paul to Timothy: '...the grace of our Lord has been granted me in overflowing measure, along with the faith and love which are in Christ Jesus' (1 Tm. 1:14), it seemed to me to have been chosen precisely for our meeting here today, for it touches the heart of your vocation to the religious life: divine love. Love, and you will rightly be called daughters of the Most High. Love as your heavenly Father loves. Your work is to love men, women and children by bringing them the Word of God, in print, on film, on radio, on television. But you must not be satisfied merely to produce and distribute the instruments by which knowledge of God's love is brought to men, you must make that love take flesh and blood in your own persons, so that when people see you they will see Christ's love, as it were, walking. That is why, of course, you wear a religious habit, as a visible witness of your consecration to divine love, helping other men and women to surrender to it as you have. And that is why, also, you must strive more and more every day to put on Christ, as your patron sought to do, so that you no longer live of yourselves but Christ lives in you.

"May God shower all of you with the joy that only love of Him can bring and may Jesus, His Blessed Mother be with you always to guide and to strengthen your perseverance in your glorious vocation of Daughters of St. Paul."

Pompeii, Naples and Montecassino

On Saturday, September 12th, we were again heading toward a sanctuary of our Blessed Mother. We attended Mass at the Shrine of Our Lady of Pompeii, so near to the famed Mount Vesuvius.

Entrance to Montecassino

Basilica of St. Francis, Assisi

Mamertine Prison

Afterwards, we went to Naples and enjoyed the beauty of this world-renowned seaport. Mother Paula recalled that it was from Naples that she had departed for the United States nearly fifty years before.

On the way back to Rome we had one more stop—Montecassino, home of St. Benedict. The word painted on the entrance described it all—*Pax*, peace.

Assisi

Assisi is a town which looks like it came right out of a movie on medieval Italy. We visited all the classic places in Franciscan history, including the Portiuncula, St. Damian's and the Basilicas of St. Francis and St. Clare. The whole town breathes the spirit of St. Francis' love of God and Lady Poverty.

Fittingly enough, we ended our pilgrimage the way we had started it—with St. Paul. Crowded together in the small, low-ceilinged cell of the Mamertine Prison, where Sts. Peter and Paul were held for a time, we assisted at Mass and prayed with all our hearts to become like St. Paul, our father.

We also visited a number of Pauline communities and, as had happened throughout our pilgrimage, we felt "right at home" because of the warm reception we received everywhere.

Among our most cherished memories are the times spent with our Mother General, Sister Maria, whose return to Rome was a highlight of our pilgrimage.

We came back to the U.S.A. happier than ever to be Daughters of St. Paul, daughters of the Church and heralds of her teaching. And our hearts will always be grateful for this gift of God through the goodness of our dearest superiors.

Sr. J.P.F.

Congratulatory Messages

From the American Hierarchy

CARDINALS

Carberry, John Cardinal
Cooke, Terence Cardinal
Dearden, John Cardinal
Krol, John Cardinal
Manning, Timothy Cardinal
Medeiros, Humberto Cardinal
Oddi, Silvio Cardinal
Pironio, Edward Cardinal

ARCHBISHOPS

Bernardin, Most Rev. Joseph L.
Byrne, Most Rev. James J.
Hannan, Most Rev. Philip M.
Hickey, Most Rev. James A.
Laghi, Most Rev. Pio
Lipscomb, Most Rev. Oscar H.
McCarthy, Most Rev. Edward A.
McDonough, Most Rev. Thomas J.
Martinez, Most Rev. E.
May, Most Rev. John L.
Mayer, Most Rev. Augustine, O.S.B.
Power, Most Rev. Cornelius M.
Quinn, Most Rev. John R.
Roach, Most Rev. John R.
Sheehan, Most Rev. Daniel E.
Sulyk, Most Rev. Stephen
Tawil, Most Rev. Joseph
Whealon, Most Rev. John F.

BISHOPS

Ahern, Most Rev. Patrick V.
Anderson, Most Rev. Paul F.
Angell, Most Rev. Kenneth A.
Begley, Most Rev. Michael J.
Benincasa, Most Rev. Pius A.
Bevilacqua, Most Rev. Anthony J.
Bosco, Most Rev. Anthony G.
Boudreaux, Most Rev. Warren L.
Brunini, Most Rev. Joseph B.
Brzana, Most Rev. Stanislaus J.
Caillouet, Most Rev. L. Abel
Carroll, Most Rev. Mark K.
Connare, Most Rev. William G.
Cronin, Most Rev. Daniel A.
Crowley, Most Rev. Joseph R.
Cummins, Most Rev. John S.
Curtis, Most Rev. Walter W.
Daily, Most Rev. Thomas V.
D'Antonio, Most Rev. Nicholas
Dolinay, Most Rev. Thomas V.
Dougherty, Most Rev. John J.
Dozier, Most Rev. Carroll T.
Driscoll, Most Rev. Justin A.
Drury, Most Rev. Thomas J.
Dudick, Most Rev. Michael J.
DuMaine, Most Rev. Pierre
Elko, Most Rev. Nicholas T.
Fiorenza, Most Rev. Joseph A.
Fitzpatrick, Most Rev. John J.
Flavin, Most Rev. Glennon P.
Forst, Most Rev. Marion F.
Franz, Most Rev. John B.
Franzetta, Most Rev. Benedict C.
Frey, Most Rev. Gerard L.
Friend, Most Rev. William B.
Gallagher, Most Rev. Raymond J.
Ganter, Most Rev. Bernard J.
Garmendia, Most Rev. Francisco
Gaughan, Most Rev. Norbert F.
Gelineau, Most Rev. Louis E.
Gendron, Most Rev. Odore J.
Gracida, Most Rev. Rene H.
Graham, Most Rev. John J.
Grellinger, Most Rev. John B.
Greteman, Most Rev. Frank H.
Guilfoyle, Most Rev. George H.
Hacker, Most Rev. Hilary B.
Harper, Most Rev. Edward J., C.SS.R.
Harris, Most Rev. Vincent M.

Hart, Most Rev. Daniel A.
Hastrich, Most Rev. Jerome J.
Helmsing, Most Rev. Charles H.
Hoffman, Most Rev. James R.
Hogan, Most Rev. James J.
Hubbard, Most Rev. Howard J.
Hughes, Most Rev. Alfred C.
Hurley, Most Rev. Mark J.
Johnson, Most Rev. William R.
Joyce, Most Rev. Robert F.
Kellenberg, Most Rev. Walter P.
Kenny, Most Rev. Michael H.
Kucera, Most Rev. Daniel W.
Law, Most Rev. Bernard F.
Lessard, Most Rev. Raymond W.
Lohmuller, Most Rev. Martin N.
Losten, Most Rev. Basil H.
Lyke, Most Rev. James P.
Lyons, Most Rev. Thomas W.
McCormick, Most Rev. J. Carroll
McDowell, Most Rev. John B.
McFarland, Most Rev. Norman F.
McKinney, Most Rev. Joseph C.
McLaughlin, Most Rev. Bernard J.
McNicholas, Most Rev. Joseph A.
McShea, Most Rev. Joseph
Maher, Most Rev. Leo T.
Mahony, Most Rev. Roger
Maloney, Most Rev. Charles G.
Marconi, Most Rev. Dominic A.
Marshall, Most Rev. John A.
Newell, Most Rev. Hubert M.
Niedergeses, Most Rev. James D.
O'Connor, Most Rev. John J.
O'Leary, Most Rev. Edward C.
Oliver, Most Rev. Fremiot T.
Ott, Most Rev. Stanley J.
Paschang, Most Rev. John L.
Pilla, Most Rev. Anthony M.
Proulx, Most Rev. Amedee
Quinn, Most Rev. Francis A.
Reilly, Most Rev. Daniel P.
Riley, Most Rev. Lawrence J.
Roman, Most Rev. Agustin A.
Russell, Most Rev. John J.
Scanlan, Most Rev. John J.
Schad, Most Rev. James L.
Schladweiler, Most Rev. Alphonse J.
Schmitt, Most Rev. Mark F.
Schoenherr, Most Rev. Walter J.
Schuster, Most Rev. Eldon B.
Sklba, Most Rev. Richard J.
Stafford, Most Rev. J. Francis
Sullivan, Most Rev. James S.
Sullivan, Most Rev. Joseph V.
Swanstrom, Most Rev. Edward E.
Symons, Most Rev. J. Keith
Tafoya, Most Rev. Arthur N.
Unterkoefler, Most Rev. Ernest L.
Vath, Most Rev. Joseph G.
Vonesh, Most Rev. Raymond J.
Walsh, Most Rev. Nicolas E.
Welsh, Most Rev. Lawrence H.
Welsh, Most Rev. Thomas J.
Zayek, Most Rev. Francis M.

MARIA REGINA MATER

December 7, 1981

My dear Mother Paula,

I am sure that as you look back over the years, particularly to the day you arrived in New York City in 1932, to establish the Apostolate of the Daughters of Saint Paul in the United States of America, you never dreamed of all that would happen in the subsequent years. In January of 1982, the Community will be celebrating its Golden Jubilee of Foundation in our blessed country.

God entrusted to you, through your Founder, Father Alberione and your Co-foundress, Mother Thecla Merlo, the heavy responsibility of coming to America with a younger companion in a mission which is truly a mission of Faith. With confidence in God and trust in our Blessed Mother and with perserverance and the spirit of holiness, you began what is today a Congregation here in the United States of which we are so proud.

May I offer, Mother Paula, my heartfelt congratulations to you and to Mother Domenica, your Provincial, and to the entire Congregation, my prayers and the assurance of my thankfulness and the gratitude of so many thousands of souls who have come closer to God, and have learned their Faith more deeply and have been inspired to practice it through the Apostolate of the Daughters of Saint Paul.

I remember well when you came to Saint Louis with the purpose of opening a mission here. To me it was a comfort and a consolation to welcome you wholeheartedly and prayerfully. The Archdiocese of Saint Louis are debtors to the Daughters of Saint Paul for it was the opening of the new center here in Saint Louis which has been a source of inspiration, comfort and consolation to all of us. I rejoice in the fact that it was a privilege of mine to welcome the Daughters to the "Gateway to the West", and you know how much the priests and laity of the Archdiocese extended to you the warm hand of welcome.

We are so proud of what the Daughters have done in the years that they have been with us. They continue to grow and to be loved by the faithful and they are a great asset to the Church of Saint Louis.

I offer to you, dear Mother Paula, my humble prayers and shall celebrate the Holy Sacrifice of the Mass for all of your intentions in gratitude to you and your companions for what you have accomplished in the Name of the Lord, not only here in Saint Louis, but in fifteen States in the United States, and the establishment of twenty two centers. How proud you must be to see that the Province of the United States of the Daughters of Saint Paul has 154 Professed Sisters, 25 Novices and 40 Postulants.

With my humble blessing and prayers and commending you to the loving care of Our Lady, whom you love so much, and I ask God the Father, the Son and the Holy Spirit to bless you with all the graces you need and for which you pray. May They be your joy and constant help as the Daughters of Saint Paul recall God's blessing to them over these fifty golden years.

Ad multos annos, Gloriosque annos!

Most devotedly and prayerfully yours in Our Lady,

† John J. Cardinal Carberry

John Joseph Cardinal Carberry
Retired Archbishop of Saint Louis

Mother Mary Paula, D.S.P.
50 Saint Paul's Avenue
Jamaica Plain
Boston, Ma., 02130

452 Madison Avenue
New York, New York 10022

January 1982

Dear Mother Paula,

I extend to you and to all the Community of the Daughters of St. Paul my heartfelt congratulations on the Golden Jubilee of your Foundation in the United States of America.

In the providence of Almighty God, through the inspiration of the Holy Spirit, you accepted the mission given to you by Father James Alberione and Mother Thecla Merlo in 1932. With courage and perseverence, the pioneers overcame many obstacles and have seen your Congregation become a source of many blessings for God's people in America.

With you, I offer gratitude to our Heavenly Father above all for the beautiful example of your Religious Life, for your adherence to the vows of Poverty, Chastity and Obedience, and for your lives of constant prayer and loving service.

I am filled with gratitude and admiration for all your Community has been to the Church in America in communicating the eternal truth of God to millions of our brothers and sisters in His one human family. The Good News of Jesus Christ is heard and seen and believed by so many each day because of your untiring and consistent efforts.

As I offer the Holy Sacrifice of the Mass at St. Patrick's Cathedral, I will remember you and your Community, especially asking the Lord to bless you with vocations and to strengthen you in your most special apostolate.

With prayerful good wishes, I am

Devotedly yours in Christ,

+ Terence Cardinal Cooke

Archbishop of New York

Mother Paula Cordero
Daughters of St. Paul
50 St. Paul's Avenue
Jamaica Plain
Boston, MA. 02130

SERVIO IN EVANGELIO

1234 WASHINGTON BLVD.
DETROIT, MICHIGAN 48226

November 20, 1981

Dear Sister Domenica:

Very properly, the members of the Congregation of the Daughters of St. Paul are preparing to celebrate the Golden Jubilee of work in the United States. Because it is so memorable an occasion, it is well worthy of grateful remembrance.

Through these years, your community has pursued with dedication your commitment to this special apostolate. What had great importance even at the time you began your work, is of even greater significance in our time. The use of the media for the spread of the Gospel message is both a challenge and opportunity. Your own community has recognized this and is applying its energies to this important field of evangelization.

On this Jubilee occasion, I offer you my personal congratulations!

I pray your work may continue to be blessed in our midst.

Cordially yours in Christ,

+John Card. Dearden
Former Archbishop of Detroit

Sister Mary Domenica, D.S.P.
Provincial, Daughters of St. Paul
50 St. Paul's Avenue
Jamaica Plain
Boston, Massachusetts 02130

Archdiocese of Philadelphia
222 N. 17th Street
Philadelphia, Pa. 19103

Office of the Cardinal

October 28, 1981

Sister Mary Domenica, D.S.P.
Provincial
Daughters of Saint Paul
50 Saint Paul's Avenue
Jamaica Plain
Boston, Massachusetts 02130

Dear Sister:

It is with sincere pleasure and profound gratitude to Almighty God that I extend to you and all of the Daughters of Saint Paul my congratulations and best wishes on this Golden Jubilee. For fifty years the Church in the United States has been blessed by the presence of the congregation of the Daughters of Saint Paul. This blessing has taken place within the framework of your community's mission so wisely stated by your founder Reverend James Alberione: "Become the voice of the Church, of the Pope, of the episcopate, of the clergy. That same voice is then to be multiplied and reinforced by you as if by an amplifier, so as to reach everyone."

One cannot help but recall the intertwining of the lives of the Daughters of Saint Paul in America with the life of Mother Paula Cordero. How courageous she was as a young religious to travel to a new country with literally nothing as her own except a tremendous love for and faith in the Christ to whom she had espoused herself. What a tremendous lesson she gives us all in the great things God accomplishes in those who open their hearts to Him. On this special anniversary, our affection and admiration reach out to Mother Paula, thanking her for bringing Christ among us.

It is interesting, also, to note that in a time when many communities of Religious Women are experiencing a dearth of vocations, the congregation of the Daughters of Saint Paul are enjoying an unprecedented growth. Within the Province of the United States, there are, today, 154 Professed Sisters, 25 Novices and 40 Postulants. Faithful to the teachings of the Church particularly as they are stated in the documents of the Second Vatican Council, the Daughters of Saint Paul have prayed and worked for the true renewal for which that same council calls.

As you recall with fondness the joys of these golden years, be sure to look ahead as well. See in the days to come countless opportunities to continue the good work God has begun in you: The glory of God and the salvation of souls through evangelization with the media of social communications. In this way, you will continue the mission envisioned by your founder, a solid spiritual life which blends contemplation with action.

Asking the Missionary Paul to guide and inspire your efforts, entrusting your Community to the mother of the Word Incarnate and invoking the blessing of Almighty God on the Daughters of Saint Paul, I remain

Devotedly yours in Christ,

John Cardinal Krol
Archbishop of Philadelphia

ARCHDIOCESE OF LOS ANGELES
1531 WEST NINTH STREET
LOS ANGELES, CALIFORNIA 90015
388-8101

November 2nd, 1981

Sister Mary Domenica, D.S.P.
Provincial
Daughters of St. Paul
50 St. Paul's Avenue
Jamaica Plain, Boston, Ma. 02130

Dear Sister Mary Domenica:

It is indeed a joy of great moment to felicitate the Daughters of St. Paul on the Golden Jubilee of their apostolate in the United States.

The incredible growth in membership and the authenticity of the message of evangelization are certainly evidences of God's benediction on this favored Community.

May He continue to bless its membership, its apostolate, and continue to enrich the Church in the United States through them.

Very sincerely yours,

Timothy Cardinal Manning

Timothy Cardinal Manning
Archbishop of Los Angeles

Archdiocese of Cincinnati

Office of
The Archbishop
100 East Eighth Street
Cincinnati, Ohio 45202
513/421-3131

November 2, 1981

Dear Mother Paula:

I am writing to extend congratulations from all the people of the Archdiocese of Cincinnati to you and the Daughters of St. Paul on the Golden Jubilee of the Foundation of the Congregation in the United States.

For fifty years the people of our country have benefited from your efforts in evangelization. I am confident that these years are just the beginning of a long history of service to the Church in this area.

I am especially thankful for the work that the Daughters of St. Paul are doing in the Archdiocese of Cincinnati. Your presence among us has certainly brought great blessings upon the Archdiocese.

With cordial good wishes, I remain

Sincerely yours in Christ,

+Joseph L. Bernardin

Most Reverend Joseph L. Bernardin
Archbishop of Cincinnati

Mother Paula, D.S.P.
Daughters of St. Paul
50 St. Paul's Avenue
Jamaica Plain, Boston, MA 02130

P.O. BOX 479
DUBUQUE IOWA 52001

November 2, 1981

Sister Mary Domenica, D.S.P.
Provincial
Daughters of St. Paul
50 St. Pauls Avenue
Jamacia Plain
Boston, Massachusetts

Dear Sister Mary Domenica:

It is indeed a source of great joy for me to express my hearty congratulations to you and to the Daughters of St. Paul in this country and in the world on your coming Golden Jubilee of foundation in the United States!

I join with you in thanking God for the blessings of the past fifty years and asking Him to bless you abundantly as you start the next fifty years of apostolate in communicating the message of the Gospel. It has been my privilege to have had some experience of the excellent work that the Daughters of St. Paul have done in the past. I have been impressed and encourage by it.

It seems to me that your apostolate is all of the more necessary in these days when the media of social communication are being used for less worthy projects than that of spreading the Good News of Jesus.

Asking Our Blessed Lady's powerful intercession for the Daughters of St. Paul in the United States, may I close with my blessing: "Benedictio..." etc.

Sincerely yours in Christ,

+James J. Byrne

Most Rev. James J. Byrne
Archbishop of Dubuque.

ARCHDIOCESE OF NEW ORLEANS

7887 WALMSLEY AVENUE

NEW ORLEANS, LOUISIANA 70125

OFFICE OF THE ARCHBISHOP

October 31, 1981

Mother Paula Cordero, D.S.P.,
Daughters of St. Paul
50 St. Paul's Avenue
Jamaica Plain,
Boston, Massachusetts 02130

Dear Mother Paula:

On behalf of all the people of God of this Archdiocese and especially on my part I wish to express our heartiest congratulations on the Golden Jubilee celebration of the Foundation of the Daughters of St. Paul in the United States. The apostolate of the Daughters of St. Paul has been of enormous value not only to those who have been served by them but by all those who have secured their publications.

The Daughters of St. Paul certainly deserve their name. In conformity with the example of their Patron they have proclaimed the Word of God in season and out of season to the whole world. They have not only been very zealous in publishing catechisms, speeches and encyclicals of the Holy Fathers but also in presenting the material in an attractive way. They have sought successfully by the broad spectrum of their publications to be all things to all mankind.

May the good God Who inspired you to come to this Country continue to bless you abundantly for your immense work in His Name.

With assurance of my prayers and best wishes, I remain,

Sincerely yours in Christ,

Philip M. Hannan

Archbishop of New Orleans

ARCHDIOCESE OF WASHINGTON
1721 RHODE ISLAND AVENUE, N.W.
WASHINGTON, D.C. 20036

November 9, 1981

OFFICE OF THE
ARCHBISHOP

Mother Paula Cordero
Daughters of St. Paul
50 St. Paul's Avenue
Jamaica Plain, Boston, MA 02130

Dear Mother Paula,

I am pleased to congratulate you and your Sisters on the forthcoming Golden Jubilee of the Foundation of the Congregation of the Daughters of St. Paul in the United States of America.

I appreciate so much the many printed materials which you make available together with the other audio-visual items and radio programs.

I recall from my years of service in Cleveland that your Sisters served the local Church very well, and made available to us all many excellent materials. I recall also the great kindness of the Sisters and a visit with yourself shortly after 1974.

I pray that God continue to bless your community with vocations and give you much joy and wisdom in the service of the Church.

With kindest personal regards, I am

Sincerely in Christ,

+Jm A. Hickey

Archbishop of Washington.

THE CATHOLIC CENTER
Archdiocese of Mobile
400 Government St., P. O. Box 1966, Mobile, Alabama 36633, (205) 433-2241

December 8, 1981

Mother Paula Cordero, D.S.P.
50 St. Paul's Avenue
Jamaica Plain
Boston, Massachusetts 02130

Dear Mother Paula:

It is with a deep sense of joy and gratitude that I write to congratulate you on the forthcoming Golden Jubilee of the Foundation of the Congregation of the Daughters of St. Paul in the United States of America.

The remarkable growth of your community, and the abundant ministry to which it addresses itself with such zeal and enthusiasm is a sign that God's spirit is truly with you in so many ways in your work.

The richness of our Catholic history in the United States has been enhanced by your media outreach in so many ways so that for our times and in keeping with the means of technology available through our culture you have become a channel for God's Word and the embodiment of His Presence.

May God bless and prosper you and your Sisters in the golden years ahead and grant you every success and happiness.

Faithfully in Christ,

+ Oscar H. Lipscomb

Most Rev. Oscar H. Lipscomb
Archbishop of Mobile

THE ARCHDIOCESE OF MIAMI
FROM THE RISING TO THE SETTING OF THE SUN IS THE NAME OF THE LORD TO BE PRAISED

OFFICE OF THE ARCHBISHOP

November 20, 1981

Sister Mary Domenica, D.S.P.
Provincial
Daughters of St. Paul
60 St. Paul's Avenue
Jamaica Plain, Massachusetts 02130

Dear Sister Mary Domenica and Religious of the Congregation of the Daughters of St. Paul:

Greetings and congratulations as you celebrate your Golden Jubilee, fifty years of proclaiming and witnessing to the Word of Our Lord Jesus Christ. I want to express a heartfelt thank you to you and to all the Sisters, but, most of all to the Sisters who have served through the years in the Archdiocese of Miami. Your presence has made the difference in our community. In this age where we are challenged to be evangelized and to evangelize, your ministry stands in the midst of the Church's needs and tends to it.

I pray that God may continue to bless the Community of the Daughters of St. Paul. Ad Multos Annos.

Devotedly yours in the Lord,

Edward A. McCarthy
Archbishop of Miami

6301 BISCAYNE BOULEVARD • MIAMI, FLORIDA 33138 • TELEPHONE (305) 757-6241

ARCHDIOCESE OF LOUISVILLE
212 EAST COLLEGE STREET • P.O. BOX 1073 • LOUISVILLE, KENTUCKY 40201

OFFICE of the ARCHBISHOP

November 9, 1981

Dear Mother Paula:

It is an honor for me to extend to you and the members of your Congregation congratulations upon the attainment of the 50th Jubilee of the foundation of the Congregation of the Daughters of St. Paul in the United States of America.

In retrospect, you and your Community have done so much in the past 50 years in behalf of the extension of the Church, especially in the field of evangelization. Through your publications, the St. Paul Catholic Book and Film Centers in 15 states have become articulate instruments of the Church in bringing to so many the contents of our Holy Faith.

It is my hope and prayer that Almighty God will continue to bless abundantly your work and enable you to go forward in growth, hope and prayer.

With prayers and best wishes and renewed thanks for all of your efforts, I am

Devotedly yours in Christ,

+ Thomas J. McDonough

Most Reverend Thomas J. McDonough
Archbishop
Apostolic Administrator

Mother Paula, D.S.P.
Daughters of St. Paul
50 St. Paul's Avenue
Jamaica Plain
Boston, Massachusetts 02130

THE CATHOLIC CENTER
Archdiocese of St. Louis

Mother Paula, D.S.P.
Daughters of St. Paul
50 St. Paul's Avenue
Jamaica Plain
Boston, Massachusetts 02130

Dear Mother Paula,

It is a great joy for me to send you this word of heartiest congratulations for a half century of service to the people of our country by the Daughters of St. Paul. It is a particular joy to be able to salute you personally for having established the work of your community on our shores. Surely it has been a beautiful and fruitful work for the Lord and His people in the United States.

Here in St. Louis we are especially blessed in having your St. Paul Catholic Book and Film Center in our Archdiocese. Only the Lord knows how many people have been reached through your publications, your audio-visual productions and your religious life in our midst. We will always be in your debt.

Assuring you of our prayers for many more years of service to the Lord and His people,

Gratefully in Christ,

John L. May

Most Reverend John L. May
Archbishop of Saint Louis

4445 Lindell Boulevard St. Louis, Missouri 63108 314 • 533-1887

ARCHDIOCESE OF PORTLAND IN OREGON

THE CHANCERY OFFICE
2838 EAST BURNSIDE, P. O. BOX 351
PORTLAND, OREGON 97207

January 19, 1982

Sister Mary Domenica, D.S.P.
Provincial, Daughters of St. Paul
50 St. Paul's Ave.
Jamaica Plain
Boston, Massachusetts 02130

Dear Sister Mary Domenica:

While I have had your request for a brief contribution to your Golden Jubilee Album on my desk for several months - and I see now the deadline is upon us - I am only now preparing my response. Forgive my tardiness. The last couple months have been very busy ones. If it is too late for inclusion in your anniversary album, at least you will know my high regard for the ministry of evangelization you perform so well.

> Faithful to their Founder and Co-Founder, the Daughters of St. Paul for fifty golden years have been bringing the Gospel of Christ to the people of the United States. Through leaflet and pamphlet, through book and magazine, through movies, filmstrips and audio tapes, the Word has been sent to the four corners of this land to teach, to uplift, to inspire, to save.
>
> The Church in America has been blessed with the presence and the zeal of these twentieth century apostles, who are using the most advanced communication techniques to spread from their headquarters in Boston the News of the greatest importance "to every middlesex, village and farm," like Paul Revere did two hundred years ago. And the Church in America is most grateful.

May you and your work prosper, Sister Mary Domenica, and Daughters of St. Paul.

Sincerely and gratefully yours in Christ,

+Cornelius M. Power
Archbishop of Portland
in Oregon

Archdiocese of San Francisco
CHANCERY OFFICE
445 CHURCH STREET
SAN FRANCISCO, CALIFORNIA 94114
(Area Code 415) 863-5112

November 3, 1981

Mother Paula
Daughters of St. Paul
50 St. Paul's Avenue
Jamaica Plain
Boston, MA 02130

Dear Mother Paula:

I would like to take the occasion of this letter to congratulate you and your congregation as you celebrate your Golden Jubilee in 1982. I feel very fortunate to have a community of your sisters in the Archdiocese of San Francisco and wish to thank your entire community for your tireless efforts to propagate the teaching of the Church.

Since the Second Vatican Council, the laity of the Church have become increasingly informed and want to know what the true teaching of the Church is. The Daughters of St. Paul thus provide a singular service in making publications of the Holy Father and bishops so readily available at such a reasonable price.

Praying that God will continue to bless your efforts in this important service of evangelization and teaching, I am

Devotedly yours in Christ,

+John R. Quinn

Archbishop of San Francisco

ARCHDIOCESE OF SAINT PAUL AND MINNEAPOLIS

226 Summit Avenue

Office of the Archbishop Saint Paul, Minnesota 55102

November 4, 1981

Daughters of St. Paul
50 St. Paul's Avenue
Jamaica Plain
Boston, Massachusetts 02130

My Dear Daughters of St. Paul,

On this happy occasion of the golden jubilee of your foundation in the United States of America I congratulate you. Your apostolate of evangelization through the media of social communication is a valued and significant contribution to the life and growth of the Catholic Church in our country. I encourage you to continue your dedication to this specific mission of spreading God's Word by means of press, radio, films and television.

The mandate of your founder that you "become the voice of the Church" and then multiply and reinforce that voice "so as to reach everyone" was indeed farsighted and courageous in those early decades of our twentieth century. It is clear that the Church of our day must make increasingly effective use of all the media available to us in order to reach all the people of our world with the message of salvation. May your part in this essential work of evangelization be blessed by God.

To Mother Paula, to you, Sister Domenica, and to all your sisters I impart my pastoral blessing and my good wishes.

Sincerely yours in Christ,

+ John R. Roach

Most Reverend John R. Roach, D.D.
Archbishop of Saint Paul and Minneapolis

ARCHDIOCESE OF OMAHA

Chancery Office

100 North 62nd Street
Omaha, Nebraska 68132

October 27, 1981

Mother Paula
Daughters of St. Paul
50 St. Paul's Avenue, Jamaica Plain
Boston, MA02130

Dear Mother Paula:

It was a happy day for the Church of the United States when 50 years ago you and your companion brought the Daughters of St. Paul to our land. God has blessed your work, and I am confident that your ministry has strengthened the faith of our Catholic people. We are a missionary church and the message is spread by communication. This has been your work and you have been most successful with it.

I congratulate you and the Congregation of the Daughters of St. Paul as you celebrate the golden jubilee of your establishment in the United States. May God continue to shower his blessings upon you! May you continue to grow and illumine our land with the Good News of Christ, Our Blessed Lord!

Asking God's blessings on all the members of your Congregation, I am

Sincerely yours,

+Daniel E. Sheehan

Daniel E. Sheehan
Archbishop of Omaha

УКРАЇНСЬКИЙ КАТОЛИЦЬКИЙ
МИТРОПОЛИЧИЙ ОРДИНАРІЯТ
У ФІЛЯДЕЛЬФІЇ
Злучені Стейти Америки

UKRAINIAN CATHOLIC ARCHDIOCESE
815 North Franklin Street
PHILADELPHIA, PENNSYLVANIA 19123
United States of America

Reverend Sister Mary Domenica
Daughters of St. Paul
50 St. Paul's Avenue
Jamaica Plain
Boston, Massachusetts 02130

Dear Sister Mary Domenica:

The Second Vatican Council states that "the unity and brotherhood of man are the chief aims of all communications(PCISC no.8); and that "communication is more than the expression of ideas and the indication of emotion. At its most profound level, it is the giving of self in love(PCISC no. 11).

The Daughters of St. Paul have given of themselves in love through their apostolate. Yours has been FIFTY fruitful years of evangelization in the United States; FIFTY fruitful years of multiplying and amplifying the Word of God - the voice of the Church; FIFTY fruitful years of aiding and strenghtening the People of God in their faith and love of the Way and the Truth.

I am pleased to join my brother Bishops and all thePeople of God in extending to the Daughters of St. Paul and especially to Mother Paula, my heartfelt congratulations and prayerful good wishes on this joyous occasion.

AD MULTOS ANNOS!

Sincerely yours in Christ,

+ Stephen Sulyk

Most Reverend Stephen Sulyk, D.D.
Archbishop-Metropolitan

DIOCESE OF NEWTON
Melkite-Greek Catholic
19 Dartmouth Street
Newton, Massachusetts 02165

28 October, 1981
Saint Anastasia

The Sister Mary Domenica, D.S.P.
Provincial
Missionary Sisters of the Media of Communications
50 Saint Paul's Avenue
Boston, Massachusetts 02130

Reverend dear Sister Mary Domenica:

I was very impressed on reading your letter of October 20, 1981, describing the extraordinary activities of the Missionary "Daughters of Saint Paul" over the past half century here in the United States of America. Through your "Good Press" and the dissemination of your numerous publications: books, pamphlets, magazines, audio-casettes, and so forth, you have been spreading the Word of God and the teachings of the Church on the largest possible scale.

I should like to take this opportunity to congratulate you and your Congregation on your Golden Jubilee and to thank you for the collection of Papal addresses you kindly sent me.

With my prayerful good wishes for the continued progress and success of the beautiful work you are doing, I remain

Devotedly yours in Christ our God,

+ Joseph Tawil

Archbishop Joseph Tawil
Eparch of Newton

VOX CLAMANTIS IN DESERTO

Archdiocese of Hartford
134 Farmington Avenue
Hartford, Connecticut 06105

November 5, 1981

Archbishop's Office

Mother Paula, D.S.P.

Dear Mother Paula:

I am looking forward with anticipation to the formal celebration, next June 27, of the Golden Jubilee of Foundation of the Daughters of St. Paul in the United States of America.

There are two facets of this celebration that deserve special emphasis. First is the powerful, continuing influence for good accomplished by the Daughters through the printed, film and electronic media. The Sower, by these media, has broadcast the Good News.

Second is the way in which the Daughters of St. Paul have kept the spirit of their founder and a pattern of religious and community life that attracts vocations. For this we thank God.

St. Paul, whose feast we shortly celebrate, once looked across the waters to the west, to Europe, as the follow field awaiting God's Word. Similarly you, a half century ago, looked westward to the nation across the Atlantic, to the United States of America. Today we thank God for five decades of zealous missionary work and leadership for the kingdom.

May God bless you, keep you in health and holiness, and foster this apostolic work.

Devotedly yours in Christ,

Most Reverend John F. Whealon
Archbishop of Hartford

Patrick Ahern

December 6, 1981

Dear Mother Paula:

I wish to express heartfelt congratulations to you and your companions on the Golden Jubilee of the Founding of the Daughters of St. Paul.

I read with interest the record of achievements your Community has compiled during the past fifty years, the huge number of religious publications which has poured forth from your Centers and the vast amount of personal visits and other contacts your Sisters have been able to make during this time. It has been an eventful half century and there can be no doubt of God's blessing on your work. How many graces have come to all of you, and through you been channeled to others.

I am especially pleased to note the large number of young women you are attracting and I ask God to continue to bless you with many vocations.

I trust you will not think me provincial for taking pleasure in the fact that your Community was founded in New York.

Thank you for all that you have done and are doing for the Church.

Sincerely,

+ Patrick Ahern

Most Reverend
Patrick V. Ahern

Mother Paula, D.S.P.
Daughters of St. Paul
50 St. Paul's Avenue
Jamaica Plain
Boston, Massachusetts 02130

DIOCESE OF DULUTH
BISHOP'S OFFICE

215 WEST FOURTH STREET DULUTH, MINNESOTA 55806

November 6, 1981

Mother Paula Cordero
Daughters of St. Paul
50 St. Paul's Avenue
Jamaica Plain,
Boston, Mass 02130

Dear Mother Paula,

Congratulations on the Golden Jubilee of the Foundation of the Congregation of the Daughters of St. Paul in the United States of America.

I suppose your jubilee has some special meaning to me because I grew up and was ordained a priest for the Boston area before moving to the midwest. Let me take this opportunity to congratulate you and your sisters for the great ministry they have performed for the Church in America, especially in the field of the printed word.

Hoping that you will have a beautiful celebration later in the year and asking God to continue to bless you in your work of evangelization, I remain

Sincerely yours in Christ,

Paul F. Anderson

+ Paul F. Anderson
Bishop of Duluth

DIOCESE OF PROVIDENCE

CATHEDRAL SQUARE
PROVIDENCE, RHODE ISLAND
02903

OFFICE OF THE
AUXILIARY BISHOP

January, 1982

Dear Sisters,

On the occasion of the Golden Jubilee of the foundation of the Congregation of the Daughters of St. Paul in the United States of America, it gives me great pleasure to send you this message of prayerful congratulations.

Since the founding of the Congregation in 1932, you have persevered in your mission of spreading the Gospel message of Jesus Christ through "Evangelization with the Media of Social Communication". May your work continue to flourish and may the choicest of God's blessings always guide the endeavors of your Congregation.

Assuring you of my continued prayers for the success of your good work, I am,

Sincerely yours in Christ,

+ Kenneth A. Angell

Auxiliary Bishop of Providence

Office of the Bishop
Diocese of Charlotte
Post Office Box 3776
Charlotte, N. C. 28203

November 3, 1981

Daughters of St. Paul
50 St. Paul's Avenue
Jamaica Plain
Boston, MA 02130

Attn: Mother Paula

Dear Reverend Mother:

I would like to congratulate the Daughters of St. Paul on the occasion of their Golden Jubilee!

Your Community has been of tremendous help through the years by way of providing an assortment of materials - books and periodicals, both in the area of spiritual reading and educational materials.

May the Holy Spirit continue to provide vocations to young women interested in the great evangelical work of the Daughters of St. Paul.

Wishing you and your Community God's blessings, I am

Sincerely in Christ,

Most Reverend Michael J. Begley,
Bishop of Charlotte

ST. ALOYSIUS RECTORY
157 Cleveland Drive
Buffalo, N. Y. 14215

December 15, 1981

Mother Paula Cordero
Daughters of St. Paul
50 St. Paul's Ave.
Jamaica Plain, Boston, Ma. 02130

Dear Mother Paula:

I was very pleased to hear of the forthcoming Golden Jubilee of the Foundation of the Congregation of the Daughters of St. Paul in the United States of America.

God has certainly blessed your zealous efforts throughout this half century. First of all, from two noble Sisters (you and your companion) you have multiplied to 154 professed Sisters; 25 Novices and 40 Postulants - quite a number in these trying days of few vocations. Secondly, from a humble start in New York, after much hard work and perseverance, you now have 22 flourshing Centers in 15 states.

The Daughters of St. Paul are certainly achieving there aim of Evangelization with the media of social communication - by the millions of books and pamphlets they have produced in the field of Sacred Scripture, catechetics, liturgy, papal teachings, Mariology, spirituality, sociology and children books.

Your three monthly magazines and your hundred of thousands of audiovisuals in the aforementioned field have effectively assisted so many millions of persons.

Dear Mother Paula: As we join the Daughters of St. Paul in thanking God for His countless Blessings of the past fifty years, we beg Him to continue to shower His choicest graces and favors upon you, your dedicated Sisters, and upon your very zealous and effective work of spreading the gospel through the media of social communication.

Sincerely yours in Christ,

+Pius A. Benincasa

+Pius A. Benincasa
Auxiliary Bishop of Buffalo

ROMAN CATHOLIC DIOCESE OF BROOKLYN
POST OFFICE BOX C
BROOKLYN, NEW YORK 11202

OFFICE OF THE CHANCELLOR
75 GREENE AVENUE

December 17, 1981

Reverend Mother Paula, D.S.P.
Daughters of St. Paul
50 St. Paul's Avenue
Jamaica Plain, Boston, MA. 02130

Dear Mother Paula:

May I take this occasion to thank you for the great apostolate that you are so successfully conducting for the Glory of God and the Salvation of Souls through Evangelization. I express my congratulations on the occasion of the 50th Anniversary of the foundation of the Congregation of the Daughters of St. Paul in the United States of America. Your work of Evangelization through the media of social communication has proved to be a great contribution to the mission of the Church in this country. I have always found your publications in conformity with the Magisterium of the Church and full of spiritual treasures.

With prayerful best wishes, I remain

Sincerely yours in Christ,

+Anthony J. Bevilacqua

Anthony J. Bevilacqua
Auxiliary Bishop - Chancellor

OFFICE OF THE VICAR GENERAL — CHANCELLOR

DIOCESE OF PITTSBURGH

111 BOULEVARD OF ALLIES
PITTSBURGH, PENNSYLVANIA 15222
(412) 456-3131

December 23, 1981

Dear Mother Paula:

The growth and vigor of the Daughters of St. Paul must be interpreted as a sign of God's blessing on the holy work you do. How many people have met Jesus Christ through the printed word film and radio.

How comforting it is to a bishop to know that there are such devoted heralds of the Word seeking to preach and to teach and doing it so successfully.

I ask God's blessing on your community and your work.

Wishing you peace and joy as we await His Coming, I am

Sincerely yours in Christ,

+ Anthony G. Bosco

+ Most Reverend Anthony G. Bosco
Vicar General - Chancellor
Auxiliary Bishop of Pittsburgh

Mother Paula Cordero, D.S.P.
50 St. Paul's Avenue
Jamaica Plain
Boston, Massachusetts 02130

Diocese of Houma – Thibodaux

1220 Aycock Street
Post Office Box 9077
Houma, Louisiana 70361

Phone (504) 868-7720

December 11, 1981

Daughters of St. Paul
50 St. Paul's Avenue
Jamaica Plain
Boston, MA 02130

Reverend and Dear Sisters:

I am pleased to join my voice to that of the multitude of your friends and admirers as you prepare to celebrate the Golden Jubilee of the Foundation of your Congregation of the Daughters of St. Paul in the United States of America.

Your devotion to the cause of Christ, your sacrificial concern for the care of His people and the numerous book and film centers which you have established are among the more visible works that you have contributed to the Church in these United States.

Your influence for good in the country is further evidenced by the number of vocations that you have attracted in recent years.

For these reasons and for others best known to yourself I send you congratulations and best wishes as you celebrate your Golden Jubilee and look forward to long years of service in the days ahead. God bless you all and prosper you in His service.

Respectfully and sincerely
yours in Christ,

Warren L. Boudreaux
Bishop of Houma-Thibodaux

CATHOLIC DIOCESE OF JACKSON
P. O. BOX 2248
JACKSON, MISSISSIPPI 39205

237 E. Amite Street
601 969-1880

GOD AND NEIGHBOR

OFFICE OF THE BISHOP

January 4, 1982

Sister Mary Domenica, D.S.P.
Provincial
Daughters of St. Paul
50 St. Paul's Avenue
Jamaica Plain
Boston, MA 02130

Dear Sister Mary Domenica:

Heartiest congratulations, best wishes and prayers on the occasion of your Golden Jubilee of the foundation of the Daughters of St. Paul in our country. You are doing a wonderful job and I am sure that Almighty God will continue to give the increase to your zealous labors in the years ahead.

Evidently the Holy Spirit is moving mightily in your congregation as evidenced from the many vocations you have received. Yours is a wonderful apostolate and will bring a growth and closeness to our Divine Saviour through your many activities.

May 1982 - in a special way - bring you many spiritual and material blessings.

Cordially in Christ,

+ Joseph B. Brunini

Joseph B. Brunini
Bishop of Jackson

624 WASHINGTON STREET
OGDENSBURG, NEW YORK 13669

October 29, 1981

Sister Mary Domenica, D.S.P.
Provincial
Daughters of St. Paul
50 St. Paul's Avenue
Jamaica Plain
Boston, Massachusetts 02130

Dear Sister Mary Domenica:

Many congratulations to you and to all the Daughters of St. Paul on the 50 years of service which you will be celebrating in 1982.

The brief history of your community indicates how wonderfully you have been blessed and how much you have contributed to the spread of the word of God in our country and the welfare of the Church. I am happy to note that in these days of vocation shortages you have so many novices and postulants.

May Our Lord Jesus Christ, with the intercession of Mary and of St. Paul, your special patron, bless you abundantly in the years ahead so that you may continue your apostolate in the spirit of St. Paul.

With repeated congratulations and best wishes, I am

Fraternally yours in Christ,

+ Stanislaus J. Brzana

Most Rev. Stanislaus J. Brzana, S.T.D.
Bishop of Ogdensburg

NATIONAL VOTIVE SHRINE OF OUR LADY OF PROMPT SUCCOR
PATRONESS OF THE STATE OF LOUISIANA
MOST REV. L. ABEL CAILLOUET,
Former Auxiliary Bishop of New Orleans,
Rector

2705 STATE STREET TELEPHONE (504) 866-6612 NEW ORLEANS, LOUISIANA 70118

November 5,1981

Sister Mary Domenica,D.S.P., Provincial,
Daughters of St.Paul,
50 St.Paul's Avenue,Jamaica Plain,Boston,MA.02130

Dear Sister Mary Domenica:

Heartfelt congratulations to you,to the Sisters of the Province and particularly to Mother Paula Cordero,chosen by the saintly Founder and Co-Foundress of the Daughters of St.Paul to bring their blessed presence among us in the United States!

What a wonderful growth in spreading the Word of God through the communications media,placed at the service of Evangelization,during this half century! Behind the scenes of this apostolate,and accentuating it as clearly blessed by Our Divine Lord and His Apostle to the Gentiles, are the difficulties,the frustrations,the 'benign' silence that tried the courageous Faith of the Sisters during these fifty years - all the more precious and golden by that very fact.

Total loyalty and fidelity to the Chair of Peter in the person of its Successor to him,has been the hallmark of the Daughters of Saint Paul and continues to be such during these trying days and years when many - even bearing the name Catholic - are disloyal to the Pope and turn a deaf ear to his magisterial teaching.

Congratulations dear Sisters,worthy Daughters of Saint Paul. May years without number find your apostolate flourishing among children,youth,adults,unto a "profound persuasion about revealed truth" leading to "a practical and constant exercise of the Catholic Faith."

Faithfully yours in Christ Our Lord,

+L. Abel Caillouet

(Most Rev.) L.Abel Caillouet
Auxiliary Bishop of New Orleans (ret.)

Most Reverend Mark K. Carroll
3600 EAST HARRY STREET
Wichita, Kansas 67218

October 27, 1981

The Daughters of St. Paul
50 St. Paul's Avenue
Boston, Mass. 02130

My dear Daughters,

It is a great pleasure for me to send you loving greetings and fervent congratulations as the Daughters of St. Paul pause to thank God for the fifty years of graces and blessings and marking your Golden Anniversary here in the United States of America.

I am very familiar with the magnificent work that the Daughters have accomplished in telecasting in every possible way the good news of the Lord Jesus Christ. You dear Sisters have pooled your talents and resources and have made the United States shine with a crown of glorious achievement. May God continue to grant you the spiritual and financial prosperity that has enabled you to bring the precious word of Christ to so many localities. May your great faith, hope and love and your labors for the propagation of the faith continue unabated and successful as you will now wait in anticipation for a Diamond Jubilee in the early part of the next century.

God bless each one of you Daughters individually and give you His Fatherly love.

Yours devotedly in Christ,

+ Mark K. Carroll

+Mark K. Carroll

Bishop's House MAPLEWOOD TERRACE
GREENSBURG, PA. 15601

November 2, 1981

Sister Mary Domenica, D.S.P.
Provincial
Daughters of Saint Paul
50 Saint Paul's Avenue
Jamaica Plain
Boston, Massachusetts 02130

Dear Sister Mary Domenica:

It gives me pleasure to join with the Bishops of this country in saluting you and your Sisters on the occasion of your Golden Jubilee here in this country. I know we consider your coming to the United States one of the blessings to the Church here in this past half century.

Father Alberione and Mother Thecla Merlo made a wise move in sending Sister Paula Cordero to establish your apostolate in this country. Spreading from New York these fifty years have witnessed your establishing twenty-two centers from coast to coast, and even beyond in Hawaii.

The Lord has truly blessed your work in the United States Province. With 154 professed Sisters, 25 novices and 40 postulants you are rendering a genuine service in the field of social communications. You are telling the "good news" to many estranged from the Church, and many others totally unaware of its mission. One of these years I sincerely hope you will be able to make a foundation within our own Diocese.

Asking the Lord's choicest blessings on you and all your Sisters in the coming year of Jubilee, I am

Devotedly yours in Christ,

Bishop of Greensburg

DIOCESE OF FALL RIVER
47 Underwood Street
Fall River, Massachusetts 02720

617-675-1311

Office of
THE BISHOP

October 30, 1981

Mother Paula, D.S.P.
Superior General
Daughters of Saint Paul

Dear Mother Paula,

On the significant occasion of the Fiftieth Anniversary of the Foundation of the Congregation of the Daughters of Saint Paul in the United States of America, as Bishop of Fall River, I have the pleasure of extending heartfelt congratulations and good wishes.

I pray that Almighty God will continue to endow you and the members of the Congregation with a full measure of His most choice blessings for many fruitful years to come.

Reiterating my congratulations on this significant anniversary and extending prayerful good wishes to one and all, I have the pleasure to remain

Faithfully yours in Christ,

+ Daniel A. Cronin

Bishop of Fall River

1701 Miami Street
South Bend, Indiana 46613

Most Rev. Joseph R. Crowley, D.D., V.G.
Auxiliary Bishop of Fort Wayne-South Bend

Sister M. Paula
Daughters of St. Paul
50 St. Paul's Avenue
Jamaica Plain
Boston, Massachusetts 02130

Dear Sister Paula:

I'm deeply indebted to you for the books which you sent me at Christmastime; they're another example of the great work that the Daughters of St. Paul are doing for the Church in the United States and throughout the world.

As you look back on your 50 years of work in the United States, you must be grateful to God for the wonderful opportunities given you to communicate His word. The Church in the United States must also be grateful to you for your work in this apostolate.

Praying God to continue blessing you and again thanking you, I am

Sincerely and gratefully in Christ,

Joseph R. Crowley
Auxiliary Bishop of Fort Wayne-South Bend

through christ our lord

DIOCESE OF OAKLAND

2900 LAKESHORE AVENUE • OAKLAND, CALIFORNIA, 94610 • 415/893-4711

October 30, 1981

Sister Mary Domenica, D.S.P.
Daughters of St. Paul
50 St. Paul's Avenue
Jamaica Plain
Boston, MA 02130

Dear Sister:

Congratulations on the Golden Jubilee. The Sisters served in the diocese here under Bishop Begin. He was very appreciative of their apostolate. May I add the continuance of good wishes.

May the Lord bless the celebration and the work ahead.

Sincerely,

+ John S. Cummins

John S. Cummins
Bishop of Oakland

Office of the Bishop
238 Jewett Avenue
Bridgeport, Connecticut 06606

November 18, 1981

Rev. Mother Paula, D.S.P.
Daughters of St. Paul
50 St. Paul's Avenue
Jamaica Plain
Boston, MA 02130

Dear Reverend Mother Paula:

It is with great joy that I write to congratulate you on the occasion of the Golden Jubilee of the Foundation of the Congregation of the Daughters of St. Paul in the United States of America. I am well aware of the work that the Daughters of St. Paul have done throughout the Church in publication of Catholic materials and with their dedication to the apostolate of Evangelization in the American Church.

The Diocese of Bridgeport is especially blessed with the St. Paul Catholic Book Center which is located in Bridgeport, Connecticut and I always found the Sisters willing to be of assistance to myself personally and to the priests and people of our Diocese.

On this the occasion of the Golden Jubilee of the Daughters of St. Paul, please accept my prayerful best wishes and congratulations and the assurance of my prayers that God will continue to bless your Congregation.

With all best wishes, I remain

Sincerely yours in Christ,

+ Walter W. Curtis

Most Rev. Walter W. Curtis, STD
Bishop of Bridgeport

CHANCERY
ARCHDIOCESE OF BOSTON
2121 COMMONWEALTH AVENUE
BRIGHTON, MASSACHUSETTS 02135

OFFICE OF THE CHANCELLOR

February 16, 1982

Sister Mary Domenica
Daughters of St. Paul
50 St. Paul Avenue
Jamaica Plain, MA 02130

Dear Sister Mary Domenica:

It is a real privilege for me to respond to your invitation to write concerning the Golden Jubilee of Foundation of the Daughters of St. Paul in the United States.

There is no doubt that the Church in the United States has been blessed by the presence of the Daughters of St. Paul. The Foundress of the Community in the United States, Mother Paula Cordero, and all of her Sisters have taken to heart the command of the Lord Jesus Christ to the apostles and their successors to "teach all nations" and to be "the light of the world", to announce the Good News in all places at all times. Indeed the Sisters have shown themselves to be imitators of the Lord Jesus Christ as the "perfect Communicator" and have promoted every means of social communication to preach the gospel to every creature. In this, the Daughters of St. Paul are an exemplary image of what the Church in action should be. Therefore, as a religious community, they are an inspiration to bishops, priests, deacons, religious and faithful to "use effectively and at once the means of social communications zealousy availing themselves of them for apostolic purposes".

For the past several years it has been the privilege of the priests who staff the Archdiocesan Chancery here in Boston to serve many of the spiritual needs of the Daughters of St. Paul at the Motherhouse in Jamaica Plain, Massachusetts. If our small contribution has been helpful to the Daughters and enable them to enhance their religious lives and Community, it has been most worthwhile and salutary for us. To have the Community as a pastoral responsibility enables us to receive much more than we give because of the inspiration of their lives.

My dear Sister, please convey my best wishes and congratulations to Mother Paula and to all the Daughters of St. Paul and assure them of a most sincere remembrance in prayer and at the altar on their 50th Anniversary in the United States.

With best personal regards, I am

Sincerely in Christ,

+Thomas V. Daily

Most Rev. Thomas V. Daily
Auxiliary Bishop of Boston
Chancellor

ANNUNCIATION CHURCH
Corner Marais and Mandeville Streets
New Orleans, Louisiana 70117

Ave Maria!

Nov. 13, 1981

Sister Mary Domonica, D.S.P.
50 St. Paul's Ave.
Jamaica Plain
Boston, MA. 02130

Beloved Sister Mary Domenica,

Thank you for your informative letter of Oct. 20, 1981.
You asked for a small favor. I comply with the following:

"It is truly mind-boggling the way the Holy Spirit has used the Congregation of the Daughters of St. Paul as an instrument of integral evangelization in the vast field of the media of social communication.
Your productivity is due, I am sure, to your community spirit of contemplative prayer, study and personal sacrifices. Obviously, I cannot discount the intercessary power of your Patron-Models St. Paul the Apostle and your Founders.
May this same Holy Spirit and Patrons continue to inspire and assist you in the astounding output of authentic religious material so staunchly faithful to the Magisterium of the Holy See.

You have my pastoral blessing on your GOLDEN JUBILEE and for a constant increase of vocations!

With Admiration in Jesus, Mary and St. Paul,

+ Nicholas D'Antonio

Nicholas D'Antonio,. O.F.M.

CHRIST IS AMONG US

Dear Sister Mary Domenica:

Just a note of thanks for your kind remembrance of me with "To the Church in America" publication.

Having been stationed in Bridgeport, Connecticut for fifteen years I know of your zeal in the areas of evangelization. I appreciate your orthodoxy of faith in the face of some trying situations.

May the Spirit of Jesus Christ continue to dwell in your midst! Your apostolate is in my prayers daily.

Fraternally in Christ,

Most Reverend Thomas V. Dolinay

CUI SERVIRE REGNARE

SETON HALL UNIVERSITY
SOUTH ORANGE, N.J. 07079

November 4, 1981

Daughters of St. Paul
50 St. Paul's Avenue
Jamaica Plain
Boston, Massachusetts 02130

Dear Mother Paula:

I have learned from Sister Mary Domenica of the forthcoming Golden Jubilee of the Foundation of the Congregation of the Daughters of St. Paul in the United States of America. I would be remiss if I did not extend my congratulations on this milestone in the apostolate of the Daughters of St. Paul.

I pray God's blessing on the Congregation in the apostolate of Evangelization with the Media of Social Communications, press, radio, films and TV. I beg His blessing on those who planted, those who watered, and praise God who gave the increase.

I extend my episcopal blessing to all.

Sincerely yours in Christ,

+John J. Dougherty

+John J. Dougherty
Auxiliary Bishop of Newark

DIOCESE OF MEMPHIS
1325 Jefferson Avenue
Memphis, Tennessee 38104
(901) 725-6761

OFFICE OF THE BISHOP

Mailing address:
P. O. Box 41679
Memphis, TN 38104 1679

November 4, 1981

Sister Mary Domenica, D.S.P.
Provincial, Daughters of St. Paul
50 St. Paul's Avenue
Jamaica Plain
Boston, MA 02130

Dear Sister:

Congratulations to the Daughters of St. Paul on your Golden Jubilee. It is an anniversary to be celebrated with great pride, the fact that you have endured many hardships during the years and yet so much has been accomplished, the publishing of your books, magazines and the great work you are doing in the field of the media. I enjoy your publications and look forward to them.

With best wishes to you for the next fifty years in the service of our Lord, I remain

Sincerely in Christ,

Carroll T. Dozier, D.D.
Bishop of Memphis

THE DIOCESE OF FARGO
1310 BROADWAY
BOX 1750
FARGO, NORTH DAKOTA 58107

CHANCERY

October 26, 1981

Sister Mary Domenica, D.S.P.
Daughters of St. Paul
50 St. Paul's Avenue
Jamaica Plain
Boston, Massachusetts 02130

Dear Sister Mary Domenica:

Many thanks for your gracious message of October 20, 1981 and I thank you with all my heart for these insights in particular. I express gratitude for your sending me the copy of our Holy Father's message to the Church in America.

Again my thanks, my prayers and special remembrance at the Altar of the Lord.

With every best wish, I remain

Sincerely yours in Christ,

+ Justin A. Driscoll

Most Reverend Justin A. Driscoll
Bishop of Fargo

DIOCESE OF CORPUS CHRISTI
620 LIPAN STREET
CORPUS CHRISTI, TEXAS
78401
882-6191

January, 1982

Sister Mary Domenica, D.S.P.
Provincial - Daughters of Saint Paul
50 St. Paul's Avenue
Jamaica Plain, Boston, Massachusetts 02130

Dear Sister Mary Domenica:

When the late Founder of the Daughters of St. Paul, Father James Alberione, together with the saintly Co-Foundress, Mother Thecla Merlo, set out to establish an Apostolate that would be embraced by the members of the Community, it is certain that many concerned persons shook their heads in disbelief. It never dawned on them that the program of Social Communication, as we know it today with satellites and instant video transmission, would be the order of the day in this century. Radio was in its infancy in the early twenties - television was unheard of at least among the ordinary people.

With what great insight, then, had these two servants of God been blest when they began their works of evangelization by means of the printing press, transportation and talented writers who would hold firmly to the sana doctrine! But they began and they succeeded.

Early in this blessed year of 1982, you are celebrating the Golden Anniversary of your beginnings in the United States. These were beginnings based on faith, on love and on deep devotion. The, then, 24 year old Sister Paula and her still younger companion journey to our shores from sunny Italy to establish what today is recognized as the Social Communication program using the press, film, radio and television as a means of evangelization.

During the late Vatican Council days, it was my privilege to meet and talk with Father Alberione and Mother Thecla. I was very impressed with their deep spirituality and their loyalty to the Holy See. As you celebrate your Golden Jubilee of service among us, please accept my sincere congratulations and an assurance of prayers for the continued success of your Apostolate.

Cordially yours in Christ,

+Thomas J. Drury

+Most Reverend Thomas J. Drury
Bishop of Corpus Christi

BYZANTINE CATHOLIC
DIOCESE OF PASSAIC
101 MARKET STREET
PASSAIC, NEW JERSEY 07055

CHANCERY OFFICE

November 5, 1981

Mother Paula
Daughters of St. Paul
50 Saint Paul's Avenue
Jamaica Plain, Boston MA 02130

Dear Mother Paula,

On the very happy occasion of the Golden Jubilee of the Foundation of the Congregation of the Daughters of St. Paul in the United States, I am pleased to express the congratulatory sentiments of the bishops, clergy, religious and faithful of the Byzantine Catholic Diocese of Passaic and to include prayerful best wishes for continued growth and success.

The history of the accomplishments by your congregation in the United States is a sterling example of what can be done by just a few people who love God and place their complete trust in Him and His Divine Providence. That faith and love in Him is continually rewarded by the encouragement, reassurance and strength you give countless people through your apostolate in the media of social communication.

As you now celebrate your fiftieth anniversary I pray that God will bless your congregation with many more vocations so that your good work will ever increase in measure and be a source of glory to Almighty God and the salvation of souls.

With the bestowal of my blessing upon you, and the other members of your congregation, I am

Sincerely yours in Christ,

Most Reverend Michael J. Dudick, D.D.
Bishop of Passaic

DIOCESE OF SAN JOSE

December 10, 1981

Mother Paula, D.S.P.
Daughters of St. Paul
50 St. Paul's Avenue
Jamaica Plain
Boston, Massachusetts 02130

Dear Mother Paula,

Congratulations to you and your sisters on the occasion of the Golden Jubilee of your foundation in the United States. Your services of keeping before the People of God the words of our Holy Father and the official documents of the Church have been faithfully and generously performed. I thank God with you that He has called you to carry out your commission and to perform it in the manner to which Paul challenged Timothy:

> "...I charge you to preach the Word, to stay with this task, whether convenient or inconvenient--correcting, reproving, appealing--constantly teaching and never losing patience... As for you, be steady and self-possessed; put up with hardship, perform your work as an evangelist, fulfill your ministry."
> (2 Tim. 4: 2,5)

May God grant you many blessings in this Jubilee year.

Sincerely in Christ,

+Pierre DuMaine
Bishop of San Jose

St. Joseph Center
(415) 967-8670 7600-Y St. Joseph Avenue, Los Altos, CA 94022 (408) 297-2913

October 29, 1981

Dear Mother Paula and Sisters:

Congratulations are certainly due to the Daughters of St. Paul on the forthcoming Golden Jubilee of their Foundation in the United States of America.

For fifty years you have provided an abundance of publications in Sacred Scripture, catechetics, liturgy, papal teachings, Mariology, spirituality, sociology, and children's books which have made God and His Church better known and loved by millions. You have lived up to the mandate of your Founder by the distribution of writings that have enhanced evangelization in our country. You have always done this within the structures of magisterial direction and authority. Your work in Christ's vineyard merits special attention today because of your sustained and increased growth of vocations since Vatican Council II. This must be indicative that where authentic interpretation of the Council's decrees is made there are true fruits in abundance.

For this we ask God to lower His hand in generous blessings over you and your continued work that will embrace countless numbers within the Mystical Body of Christ.

Sincerely yours in Christ,

+ Nicholas T. Elko, Archbishop
Auxiliary of Cincinnati

Mother Paula
Daughters of St. Paul
50 St. Paul's Avenue
Jamaica Plain,
Boston, Massachusetts 02130

DIOCESE OF SAN ANGELO
BOX 1829
SAN ANGELO, TEXAS 76902

Office of the Bishop

Phone 653-2466

Mother Paula Cordero
50 St. Paul Avenue
Jamaica Plains
Boston, Massachusetts 02130

November 6, 1981

Dear Mother Paula:

The fifty years of serving the Gospel and the Church in the U. S.A. through the media of social communication is a cause for rejoicing and thanking God for the dedication of the Daughters of St. Paul. Through your own valiant efforts the Daughters of St. Paul have brought their special apostolate literally from coast to coast. God has blessed your community and its work in serving the cause of Christ in this country.

I am pleased to add my thanks to the large chorus of gratitude that is being expressed to you and the Daughters of St. Paul during the Golden Jubilee celebration. May God bless each of you in a special way.

With prayerful regards and best wishes, I am

Sincerely in Christ,

+ Joseph A. Fiorenza

Most Reverend Joseph A. Fiorenza
Bishop of San Angelo

DIOCESE OF BROWNSVILLE

The CHANCERY

December 3, 1981

Mother Paula
Daughters of St. Paul
50 St. Paul's Ave.
Jamaica Plain
Boston, MA 02130

Dear Mother Paula:

How wonderfully and prophetically the Daughters of St. Paul have served the Church during these last 50 years!

Long before many saw the need for improvement and better use of our communications media, the Daughters of St. Paul launched out into the deep and gave such wonderful example to all the rest of us as to what could be done to make the Gospel message better understood by ourselves and those to whom we are sent.

I have known the Daughters of St. Paul for some 30 years and have so often had the opportunity of witnessing the excellent work you have done. I surely hope that the Lord will continue to bless you and that we Catholics will make every effort to continue to use the excellent service that you provide all of us.

Assuring you of a place in my Masses and prayers, I am

Sincerely yours in Christ,

+John J. Fitzpatrick

(Most Rev.) John J. Fitzpatrick
Bishop of Brownsville

POST OFFICE BOX 2279 — BROWNSVILLE, TEXAS 78520 — (512) 542-2501

DIOCESE OF LINCOLN

Post Office Box 80328

Lincoln, Nebraska 68501

Office of the Bishop

October 27, 1981

Sister Mary Domenica, D.S.P.
Provincial
Daughters of St. Paul
50 St. Paul's Avenue
Jamaica Plain
Boston, Massachusetts 02130

Dear Sister Mary Domenica:

Let me speak for myself and for the priests, religious and Catholic laity of the Diocese of Lincoln and express sincerest congratulations to Mother Paula, to your good self, and to all the Daughters on the occasion of the celebration of the golden jubilee of the foundation of the Congregation of the Daughters of St. Paul in the United States.

The extraordinary growth of your Congregation in numbers during the past fifty years and the phenomenal success of your far-reaching apostolate of communication are evidence of God's special love and blessing and of your zeal in behalf of the Church.

May the Daughters of St. Paul continue to grow in numbers and in zeal for the evangelization of America.

Sincerely yours in Christ,

+Glennon P. Flavin

The Most Reverend Glennon P. Flavin
Bishop of Lincoln

IN DEO CONFIDO

November 14, 1981

Dear Sister Domenica,

Thanks for your fifty years of service to us in the United States. What a special blessing to us your apostolate has been: coming just when it was needed; when it seemed so many of our old standbys were no longer around. May God bless your future.

+ Marion F. Forst

St. Joseph's Home
2223 West Heading Avenue
Peoria, Illinois 61604

FIDE ET FORTITUDINE

November 8, 1981

Sister Mary Domenica, D.S.P.
Provincial, Daughters of St. Paul.

Dear Sister Mary Domenica,

In response to the announcement that your highly esteemed Congregation of the Daughters of St. Paul will soon be celebrating the Golden Jubilee of your foundation in the United States, I join you in thanking God for all that this celebration signifies.

During this rosary of years the experience of your Congregation has been a participation in the joyful, the sorrowful and the glorious mysteries in the life of Our Lord, as you responded to the mission given you by your revered Founder to "become the voice of the Church, of the Pope, of the episcopate, of the clergy" by evangelization with the media of social communication.

Here in the United States, under the inspired leadership of Mother Paul, The Daughters of St. Paul have engaged in that apostolate with great faith, great courage, great sacrfice - and great success.

So it has been for fifty grace-filled years. Please, God, so let it be for all the years that lie ahead.

In union of prayer,

+John B. Franz

Most Rev. John B. Franz, D.D.
Bishop of Peoria (Retired)

DIOCESE OF YOUNGSTOWN
144 WEST WOOD STREET
YOUNGSTOWN, OHIO 44503

OFFICE OF THE VICAR GENERAL

November 4, 1981

Mother Paula and Sisters
Daughters of St. Paul
50 St. Paul's Avenue
Jamaica Plain
Boston, MA 02130

Dear Mother Paula and Sisters:

It gives me pleasure to congratulate the Congregation of the Daughters of St. Paul in the United States on the occasion of the Golden Jubilee of their foundation.

It is heartening to know of and to witness the contribution the Sisters have made and continue to make through their apostolate. Your efforts at Evangelization are highly commendable and your work with the media of social communication are in keeping with the Church's thrust into the future.

I ask God's blessing on your Congregation and that He will continue to bless the Sisters and their work.

With my best wishes, I am

Sincerely yours in Christ,

+ Benedict C. Franzetta

The Most Reverend Benedict C. Franzetta, V.G.
Auxiliary Bishop of Youngstown

DIOCESE OF LAFAYETTE
P. O. DRAWER 3387
LAFAYETTE, LOUISIANA 70502

December 1, 1981

Mother Paula, D.S.P.
Provincial, Daughters of St. Paul
50 St. Paul's Avenue
Jamaica Plain
Boston, Massachusetts 02130

Dear Mother Paula:

To you and all the Sisters of the Congregation of the Daughters of St. Paul, I wish to extend my congratulations on your forthcoming Golden Jubilee.

When I read your brief resumé of the works performed by your Congregation, I was amazed at the tremendous accomplishments in the relatively short time since the formation of the Daughters of St. Paul. So many lives have been touched and perhaps changed by the many years of evangelization through the media. Your Congregation has truly been an inspiration to us all.

I ask God to bless you with many more years of fruitful apostolic work.

With every best wish, I remain

Sincerely in our Divine Savior,

+Gerard L. Frey

+Gerard L. Frey
Bishop of Lafayette

Diocese of
Alexandria - Shreveport

Chancery Office
2315 Texas Avenue
Post Office Box 7417
Alexandria, Louisiana 71306

November 9, 1981

Sister Mary Domenica, D.S.P.
Provincial, Daughters of St. Paul
50 St. Paul's Avenue
Jamaica Plain
Boston, Massachusetts 02130

Dear Sister Mary Domenica:

Thank you for your informative letter of October 20 reviewing the history of the Daughters of St. Paul and their ministry of evangelization in the United States.

I heartily congratulate you and the members of your community on the occasion of your Golden Anniversary in service to the Lord.

Best personal regards in the Lord.

Fraternally yours,

+ William Friend

William B. Friend, Vicar General
Auxiliary Bishop of Alexandria-Shreveport

DIOCESE OF LAFAYETTE IN INDIANA
610 LINGLE AVENUE
LAFAYETTE, INDIANA 47902

30 October 1981

Sister Mary Domenica, D.S.P.
Provincial - Daughters of Saint Paul
50 St. Paul Avenue
Jamaica Plains
Boston, Massachusetts 02130

Dear Sister Mary Domenica:

On theoccasion of the Golden Jubilee of the presence of the Daughters of Saint Paul in the United States, I join you in expressing gratitude to God for the graces He has shed upon your Founder, your American Provincials and on the works of your hands. It is most reassuring that God directed Mother Thecla and Father Alberione to establish the good work of the Daughters of Saint Paul. We are equally grateful for the Provindence of God to direct Mother Paula Cordero to be the leader of your apostolate in the United States. It is most encouraging to realize God's blessings and to appreciate the manner in which you and the members of your Congregation have cooperated with those graces.

It is most providential that in this era of intensified communication that the Daughters of Saint Paul have excelled in the written, spoken and electronically conveyed message, bearing the traditional truth of our Catholic faith to readers, listeners and viewers throughout the United States. It is our grateful prayer to God that the excellence of your efforts will bear rich fruit in defending and preserving the faith in the United States. In realizing the great strides you have made in the past, it is also our prayer that the future will be influenced by increased efforts on the part of the Daughters of Saint Paul to convey the truth and the inspiring message of the Church to more and more people in our country and throughout the world.

Wishing you God's choicest blessings on this occasion and on every day of your future work in behalf of the Church, I remain

Sincerely yours in Christ,

+ Raymond J. Gallagher

RAYMOND J. GALLAGHER
Bishop of Lafayette-in-Indiana

Diocesan Pastoral Office
Diocese of Beaumont
P. O. Box 3948 Beaumont, Texas 77704 (713) 838-0451

IN CORDE JESU
Bishop's Office

October 30, 1981

Daughters of St. Paul
50 St. Paul's Avenue
Jamaica Plain
Boston, MA. 02130

Dear Sisters:

Congratulations on the Golden Jubilee of the Foundation of the Congregation of the Daughters of St. Paul in the United States of America. We have a great history of publishing the written word in this country but no institution has a prouder one than your community. The services it has rendered to the Church over the past half century has been one of dedication to the Truth and dedication to the finest quality in the art of the published word. The Church owes you a debt of gratitude and I wish to join your many friends in expressing my appreciation.

In Corde Jesu,

+ B. J. Ganter

Bernard J. Ganter
Bishop of Beaumont

ARCHDIOCESE OF NEW YORK

AUXILIARY BISHOP

St. Thomas Aquinas
1900 Crotona Parkway
Bronx, N. Y. 10460

212-589-5235

Episcopal Vicar
for Spanish Pastoral
Development for the
Archdiocese of
New York

Most Reverend Francisco Garmendia, D.D.

November 6, 1981

Sister Mary Domenica, D.S.P.
Provincial
50 St. Paul's Ave.,
Jamaica Plain, Boston, Ma.

Dear Sister Mary Domenica,

Thank you for your letter and enclosures. Congratulations on the forthcoming Golden Jubilee of the Foundation of the Congregation of the Daughters of St. Paul in the U.S.

Your resume of the life of the Congregation is brief but it says a great deal. God in His Providence anticipates the needs of the Church and raises up special souls and prepares them for particular fields of labor. Some years back hardly anyone was aware that television, radio, cassettes, audio-visuals etc. would play such an important role in Evangelization, yet your Congregation was being formed and prepared to meet this need.

Please extend to Mother Paula and to each of the Congregation of the Daughters of St. Paul my blessing and warmest congratulations on this very special occasion. May God grant Mother Paula many more years of fruitful service to the Church as she directs her daughters to grow in Christ and trains them to carry out the mandate given by their Founder and Co-foundress to be the voice of the Church, of the Pope, of the episcopate and of the clergy.

Please keep me in your prayers.

Your brother in Jesus and Mary,

Francisco Garmendia

+Francisco Garmendia
Auxiliary Bishop of New York

DIOCESE OF GREENSBURG

723 E. PITTSBURGH ST. • GREENSBURG, PENNA. 15601

December 1, 1981

Sister Mary Domenica, D.S.P.
Provincial
Daughters of Saint Paul
50 St. Paul's Avenue
Jamaica Plain
Boston, Massachusetts 02130

Dear Sister Mary Domenica:

Thank you for your explanation of the scope of your work in communications in the Church in the United States. I am sure the Catholics of the country are grateful for what you do, and what you do is to help in many ways for God's Word to be shared throughout the land. I wish you God's blessings.

With every best wish, I am

Sincerely yours in Christ,

Norbert F. Gaughan

Norbert F. Gaughan
Auxiliary Bishop of Greensburg
Vicar General

DIOCESE OF PROVIDENCE
ONE CATHEDRAL SQUARE
PROVIDENCE, RHODE ISLAND 02903
401-278-4545

OFFICE OF
THE BISHOP

December 9, 1981

Sister Mary Domenica, D. S. P.
Provincial
50 St. Paul's Avenue
Jamaica Plain, MA 02130

Dear Sister:

I am happy to join with other bishops and the Church at large in congratulating the Congregation of the Daughters of St. Paul on the golden jubilee of the foundation of the Congregation in the United States.

During these years, there have been wonderful services rendered to all of us. It is a ministry and apostolate which has been blessed by the Lord and has brought about untold blessings for the people who have been the recipients of this work.

I pray that God will continue to shower His blessings upon the Congregation and all of us who are the beneficiaries of the works you accomplish.

With continued prayers and blessings, I remain

Sincerely in Christ,

+ Louis E. Gelineau

Bishop of Providence

BISHOP'S HOUSE
657 RIVER ROAD
MANCHESTER, NEW HAMPSHIRE
03105

November 2, 1981

Sister Mary Domenica, D.S.P.
Provincial
Daughters of St. Paul
50 St. Paul's Avenue
Jamaica Plain, Boston, MA 02130

Dear Sister Mary Domenica:

Please accept my sincere congratulations on the upcoming Golden Jubilee of the foundation of the Congregation of the Daughters of Saint Paul in the United States. During the last fifty years the dedicated efforts of the Daughters has certainly brought much good fruit to the people of this country. In particular, your twenty-two book and film centers have had, and continue to have, a tremendous influence in making available and promulgating the Faith of the Church.

It is my prayer that God will continue to bless you with vocations and with an even greater and more successful ministry in the next fifty years.

With every good wish, I am

Cordially in Christ,

+ Odore J. Gendron

Bishop of Manchester

THE DIOCESE OF PENSACOLA-TALLAHASSEE

ABYSSUS ABYSSUM INVOCAT

Office of the Bishop

November 6, 1981

Daughters of St. Paul
50 St. Paul's Avenue
Jamaica Plain
Boston, MA 02130

Reverend and Dear Mother Paula:

I wish to extend to you and to all of the Daughters of St. Paul my sincere congratulations on the forthcoming golden jubilee of the foundation of your congregation in the United States. The Church in the United States has been truly blessed by the presence and the apostolic activity of the Daughters of St. Paul. The effectiveness of the service which the Daughters of St. Paul have rendered to the Church in the United States is validated in part, I suggest, by the way in which God has blessed your congregation with vocations. At a time when so many congregations continue to experience a constant loss of members your congregation prospers. I give thanks to God for you and with you.

Asking Our Lord to continue to bless the Daughters of St. Paul and extending to you and all of your sisters an assurance of my continued appreciation and gratitude for all that you are and all that you do for the Church, I remain

Sincerely yours in Christ,

+ Rene H. Gracida

Rene H. Gracida
Bishop of Pensacola-Tallahassee

POST OFFICE DRAWER 17329 • PENSACOLA, FLORIDA 32522 • 1-904-432-1515

November 9, 1981

Mother Paula Cordero,
Daughters of St. Pail,
50 St. Paul Avenue,
Jamaica Plain,
Boston, MA 02130

Dear Mother Paula:

The Golden Jubilee of the establishment of the Daughters of St. Paul in the United States provides many of us with a very welcome opportunity to espress our gratitude for the good work you are doing. In these days when the great media of communication are often used to paganize the world, it is a real comfort to note how well the Daughters of St. Paul use the media to such good purpose to spread God's Kingdom.

May God keep you faithful to your much needed apostolate! I send my blessing.

Sincerely yours,

+ John B. Grellinger
Retired Auxiliary Bishop of Green Bay

Diocese of Sioux City
The Office of the Bishop
1821 Jackson Street
Sioux City, Iowa

November 4, 1981

Sister Mary Domenica, D.S.P., Provincial
Daughters of St. Paul
50 St. Paul's Avenue
Jamaica Plain, Boston, Mass., 62130

Dear Sister Mary Domenica:

I have received your letter of October 20 announcing the forthcoming Golden Jubilee of the Foundation of the Congregation of the Daughters of St. Paul in the United States of America.

I write to express my congratulations to you on this significant occasion and to assure you of my prayers that your Community may continue to grow and to be of service to the Church which Jesus established.

For several years it has been our privilege in this diocese to send copies of your small prayer booklets to every family in the diocese at Christmas time. These prayer booklets are well received and I am grateful to you for making it possible to give such a practical and valuable little gift to our people.

Extending my Episcopal blessing to Mother Paula, to yourself, to all the members of your Province and all your apostolic work, I remain

Devotedly yours in Christ,

+ Frank H. Greteman

Frank H. Greteman
Bishop of Sioux City

CARITAS LEX SUPREMA

BISHOP'S OFFICE
1845 HADDON AVENUE
CAMDEN, NEW JERSEY 08101

November 3, 1981

Dear Sister Mary Domenica,

Congratulations and best wishes on the Golden Jubilee of the Congregation of the Daughters of St. Paul in the United States of America!

Your apostolate of communications and your personal witness to the Gospel of Christ have been of major importance in the Church's mission of Evangelization.

God bless and strengthen you individually and as a Congregation.

Faithfully in Christ,

Bishop of Camden

Sister Mary Domenica, D.S.P.
Provincial
Daughters of St. Paul
50 St. Paul's Avenue
Jamaica Plain, Boston, MA 02130

TELEPHONE (701) 223-1347

DIOCESE OF BISMARCK
420 RAYMOND STREET
POST OFFICE BOX 1575
BISMARCK, NORTH DAKOTA
58501

October 26, 1981

Sister Mary Domenica, D.S.P.
Daughters of St. Paul
50 St. Paul's Avenue
Jamaica Plain
Boston, Massachusetts 02130

Dear Sister Mary Domenica:

I wish to take this occasion to congratulate the Daughters of St. Paul on the Golden Jubilee of the Foundation of the Congregation in this country, and I wish to express my best wishes to Mother Paula for the wonderful work which was initiated in this country under her direction.

For some years I have enjoyed receiving the publications of the Daughters of St. Paul, but I did not realize that you have been exercising this apostolate in this country for 50 years.

Certainly God has blessed your work in this country, and I am pleased that within the past few months a young woman from this diocese has chosen to join your wonderful community.

Asking God to continue to prosper your work in this country and throughout the world, I remain, with best of personal wishes,

Sincerely in Xto.,

+Hilary B. Hacker

Bishop of Bismarck

Bishop's Residence
Post Office Box 1825
St. Thomas, Virgin Islands 00801

February 11, 1982

Sister Mary Domenica, D.S.P.,
Provincial,
Daughters of St. Paul,
50 St. Paul's Avenue,
Jamaica Plain,
Boston, MA 02130

Dear Sister Mary Domenica:

I am very grateful to you for all you do personally for me in sending me your publications. I admire you for the work you do through your apostolate for the bishops of the country, and for the Church throughout the United States.

Father Alberione and Mother Thecla Merlo, and Mother Paula surely had inspired vision in using the media for spreading the Gospel throughout the country. They were so far ahead of the times.

I am happy to see that your zeal and your faithfulness to the religious life has brought you so many vocations, especially in these days when vocations to the religious are so scarce.

May God continue to bless your work of evangelization and send you many young women dedicated to your work and your way of life.

Sincerely ours in Christ,

+Edward J. Harper, C.SS.R.

+Edward J. Harper, C.SS.R.,
Bishop of St. Thomas in the V. I.

DIOCESE OF AUSTIN
AUSTIN, TEXAS 78711

CHANCERY OFFICE

P. O. BOX 13327
CAPITOL STATION

November 6, 1981

The Daughters of St. Paul
50 St. Paul's Avenue
Jamaica Plain,
Boston, Massachusetts 02130

Dear Sisters:

How pleased Father Alberione, Mother Thecla and Mother Paula must be with your half a century of communicating the Gospel. Please accept my congratulations, and know that you have my prayers for the future in your very important ministry.

Praying St. Paul, the Communicator, to obtain continued blessings for the next half century, I remain

Sincerely yours in Christ,

+ Vincent M. Harris

Bishop of Austin

ARCHDIOCESE OF BOSTON
OFFICE OF THE REGIONAL BISHOP
BROCKTON REGION

October 29, 1981

Mother Paula
Daughters of St. Paul
50 St. Paul's Avenue
Jamaica Plain, MA 02130

Dear Mother Paula:

I write to congratulate you and your Sisters on the Golden Jubilee of the Foundation of your Congregation here in the United States of America.

You can look back to difficult days in these fifty years, but God has abundantly blessed your faith in Him and your courage, your patience, your zeal, your obedience, and your hard work.

You will be in my prayers for His continued blessings on you and your Sisters and your apostolate of Evangelization.

Cordially yours in Christ,

+Daniel A. Hart

+Daniel A. Hart

235 NORTH PEARL STREET, BROCKTON, MASSACHUSETTS 02401 · TELEPHONE (617) 588-4000 EXT. 660

THE DIOCESE OF GALLUP
Chancery
P. O. Box 1338
GALLUP, NEW MEXICO 87301

October 29, 1981

Mother Mary Paula
Daughters of St. Paul
50 St. Paul's Avenue
Jamaica Plain,
Boston, MA 02130

Dear Mother Mary Paula:

Congratulations and good wishes on your Golden Anniversary. It is remarkable how much you have accomplished in these years. You are to be commended especially for your orthodoxy and loyalty to the Holy Father, and for making it so much easier for priests and sisters to pray with the CHRISTIAN PRAYER.

I hope you will continue your work in making it easier for the Divine Office to be prayed.

May God grant you many more happy years in His service.

With every best wish, I am

Sincerely yours in Christ,

+ Jerome J. Hastrich

Bishop of Gallup

The Most Reverend Charles H. Helmsing, D.D.

November 6, 1981

Sister Mary Domenica, D.S.P., Provincial
Daughters of St. Paul
50 St. Paul's Avenue
Jamaica Plain, Boston, MA 02130

Dear Sister Domenica,

Congratulations to you, Mother Paul and all the Sisters as you approach the Golden Jubilee of your Foundation in the United States!

A Jubilee is a time of thanksgiving and I join you in gratitude to Almighty God for the many vocations with which you have been blessed and above all for your religious lives of prayer, apostolic zeal and labor to glorify God and work for the salvation of souls through evangelization with the media of social communication.

In the Holy Sacrifice I beg God to bless all of you abundantly and to make your apostolate even more fruitful.

Sincerely yours in Christ,

+ Charles H. Helmsing

Most Reverend Charles H. Helmsing, D.D.

The Cathedral House · Four sixteen West Twelfth Street · Kansas City, Missouri 64105

Diocese of Altoona-Johnstown
Box 126, Logan Boulevard
Hollidaysburg, Pennsylvania 16648

Bishop's Office

January 2, 1982

Sister Mary Domenica, D.S.P.
Provincial, The Daughters of St. Paul
50 St. Paul's Avenue
Jamaica Plain, Boston, Massachusetts 02130

Dear Sister Mary Domenica:

As the Daughters of St. Paul celebrate the Golden Jubilee of establishment in the United States, permit me to extend to the Congregation warmest congratulations and prayerful felicitations. Few mandates have ever been so faithfully, if not miraculously, fulfilled as those of Father Alberione and Mother Thecla back in 1932. For the mustard seed planted here by Sister Paula and her pioneer band has indeed grown into a mighty plant - a tale eloquently unfolded by the statistics of this commemorative book.

The statistics, however, impressive as they are, tell but part of the story. For the Congregation's apostolate has enriched the Church beyond human calculation. For my part, I know of no labor of love that has so effectively promoted the essential mission of Christ's Church. And for that spiritual influence, with so many, I am profoundly grateful to the Daughters of St. Paul.

It is gratifying, though not surprising, to note your vocational growth, the response of clergy, religious and laity to your communications undertakings, the diffusion of your centers. Obviously, the plant grows. And where does one more plainly discern the finger and the favor of God?

To my blessing for you and upon all the Sisters, is added the prayer that the Congregation's apostolate will continue to flourish evermore fruitfully ad multos annos. With prayerful and cordial sentiments of esteem, I am, Sister,

Yours devotedly in Christ,

+ James J. Hogan

Most Reverend James J. Hogan
Bishop of Altoona-Johnstown

BISHOP'S OFFICE
465 STATE STREET
P. O. BOX 6297
ALBANY, N. Y. 12206

November 23, 1981

Sister Mary Domenica, D.S.P.
Office of the Provincial
Daughters of St. Paul
50 St. Paul Avenue
Jamaica Plain
Boston, Massachusetts 02130

Dear Sister Mary Domenica:

Upon the occasion of the 50th Anniversary of the Daughters of St. Paul I wish to take this opportunity to assure you of my prayers for the ever-spiritual renewal of your congregation. Such words of encouragement are surely in keeping with the mandate of the Second Vatican Council on the Renewal of Religious Life:

> If the fruits of the Council are to come to maturity, religious institutes must, first of all, promote a renewal of spirit. Then they should endeavor to effect the renewal and adaptation of their way of life and of their discipline, acting prudently but, at the same time, with energy.

As each of you strives to live the evangelical counsels, be open to the movement of the Spirit in your lives, for this is the source of our hope and joy in service to the Lord.

With every prayerful best wish, I am,

Sincerely yours in Christ,

+Howard J. Hubbard

Howard J. Hubbard
Bishop of Albany

ST. JOHN'S SEMINARY

127 LAKE STREET · BRIGHTON, MASSACHUSETTS 02135 · TELEPHONE: 617-254-2610

OFFICE OF THE RECTOR

December 29, 1981

To Mother Paula and the Daughters of St. Paul on the occasion of the celebration of the Golden Jubilee of your Foundation in the United States:

I want to express my admiration for the courage and zeal that marked the pioneer efforts of Mother Paula and the early Daughters as you struggled to establish the apostolate of evangelization with the media of social communication in the United States. During this Jubilee Year I offer my gratitude for the service you have rendered the Church with such diligence and fidelity. I pray that God may bless you for your life and work in the past and draw you even more to serve the redemptive mission of Jesus Christ in this world.

+ Alfred C Hughes

Most Rev. Alfred C. Hughes
Rector

DIOCESE OF SANTA ROSA
CHANCERY OFFICE
P. O. BOX 1297
SANTA ROSA, CALIFORNIA
95402

PHONE (707) 545-7610

27 October 1981

Mother Paula
Daughters of St. Paul
50 St. Paul's Avenue
Jamaica Plain
Boston, MA 02130

Dear Mother Paula,

It is a great pleasure to greet you and the Daughters of St. Paul on the golden jubilee of the foundation of your congregation in the United States of America. I do so with a great deal of joy and warmth because I know of the good works of your community first hand.

Our Blessed Lord charged His Church with spreading the Word. We know this commandment under the categorical imperative of "evangelization". The use of the modern means of communication and indeed the up to date printing facilities have made your congregation a veritable power house in the fields of both publishing and the printed word and the production of audiovisual materials.

The devotion of your community to the Holy Father and magisterium of the Church has been the lodestar of your work.

I join with your many friends in offering my prayers and congratulations on your golden jubilee. God bless you.

Sincerely in Our Lord,

+Mark J. Hurley
Bishop of Santa Rosa

DIOCESE OF ORANGE
MARYWOOD CENTER
2811 EAST VILLA REAL DRIVE
ORANGE, CALIFORNIA 92667
(714) 974-7120

October 27, 1981

Sister Mary Domenica, D.S.P.
Provincial, Daughters of St. Paul
50 St. Paul's Avenue
Jamaica Plain
Boston, Massachusetts 02130

Dear Sister Mary Domenica:

I am writing to add my congratulations to the Daughters of St. Paul on the occasion of the Golden Jubilee of the foundation of your congregation in the United States. God has blessed the pioneer work of Father James Alberione and Mother Thecla Merlo by the growth of the congregation entrusted to Mother Paula Cordero.

You who are the Daughters of St. Paul can rightly be proud of your many contributions to the Church's growth in the United States. Your noble aims, achieved through use of the social media for purposes of evangelization, serve as a beacon to the many unchurched in our nation. May God continue to bless and prosper your service to the Church.

With best wishes on this occasion and prayerful remembrance of your intentions, I am

Sincerely yours in Christ,

Most Reverend William R. Johnson
Bishop of Orange

UT VITAM HABEANT

That They May Have Life

It is a great pleasure, and an expression of gratitude to the Daughters of St. Paul, and to Mother Paula, to offer ~~my~~ warm and sincere congratulations on the Golden Jubilee of Foundation of the Congregation in the United States.

I know from personal experience, as well as by observation, and by your national reputation, what extraordinary spiritual fruits have been produced by the work of the Congregation. You have been, and are, pioneers in bringing the Word and the grace which accompanies it, to millions of souls in our beloved country!

May God bless and multiply your members, your works, and your fruits for generations to come.

+ Robert F. Joyce
Retired Bishop of Burlington

(Nov. 5, 1981)

BISHOP'S RESIDENCE
29 QUEALY PLACE
ROCKVILLE CENTRE, NEW YORK

OFFICE OF THE BISHOP

December 3, 1981

Sister Mary Domenica, D. S. P, Provincial
Daughters of St. Paul
50 St. Paul's Avenue
Jamaica Plain
Boston, Massachusetts 02130

Dear Sister Mary Domenica:

On the joyous occasion of the Golden Jubilee of the Foundation of the Congregation of the Daughters of St. Paul in the United States, I ask our loving Father to bless the members of your Congregation with the choisest of His Blessings.

May His Holy Spirit of Wisdom continue to inspire your efforts as you serve to lead all to Christ.

Yours sincerely in Christ,

+ Walter P. Kellenberg

Most Rev. Walter P. Kellenberg
Retired Bishop of Rockville Centre

DIOCESE OF JUNEAU

419 Sixth Street Juneau, Alaska 99801

Phone: (907) 586 - 2227

October 29, 1981

Sister Mary Domenica, D.S.P.
50 St. Paul's Avenue
Jamaica Plain,
Boston, MA 02130

Dear Sr. Mary Domenica,

Since first receiving the documents of the second vatican council published by the daughters of St. Paul your community has been one I have held in esteam and gratitude.

You are rendering the church of today a singular service in making available so many publications relative to the faith in life of the Catholic in the twentieth century. This is a truly anage of the media. Your book stores and film centers located all over the United States are a great blessing to us all.

May I extend therefore blessing and heartfelt words of gratitude to all of the sisters of your community as you celebrate you Golden Jubilee. May God continue to Bless you in your invaulable apostolate.

Sincerely yours in Christ,

+Michael H. Kenny
Bishop of Juneau

P.S. Thank you very much for sending along with the letter anouncing your Jubilee a copy of a collection of papal addresses by the three most recent Pope's.

DIOCESE OF SALINA
421 Country Club Road - P. O. Box 999
SALINA, KANSAS 67401

OFFICE OF THE
BISHOP

November 19, 1981

Sister Mary Domenica, D.S.P.
Provincial
Daughters of St. Paul
50 St. Paul's Ave.
Jamaica Plain
Boston, MA 02130

Dear Sister Mary Domenica:

I am pleased and honored to write these few words of appreciation on the occasion of the Golden Jubilee of the Daughters of St. Paul. The work accomplished by your Community has been nothing short of phenomenal. In your founders and in Mother Paula you have beginnings firmly rooted in faith -- a faith that has overcome many obstacles and blossomed out into the thriving Community that you are today.

As one member of the hierarchy in the United States, I express my gratitude for the many services the Daughters of St. Paul provide the Church in the area of evangelization and the use of the media. We are all the richer for it, and so I pray that all your works may prosper for the good of God's kingdom and that you may continue to have abundant vocations to carry on your great work of spreading the good news of salvation.

With best wishes,

Sincerely yours in Christ,

(Most Rev.) Daniel W. Kucera, OSB
Bishop of Salina

Diocese of Springfield — Cape Girardeau
200 McDaniel Building
Springfield, Missouri 65806

March 3, 1982

Sister Mary Domenica, D.S.P.
Provincial
Daughters of St. Paul
50 St. Paul's Avenue
Jamaica Plain
Boston, Massachusetts 02130

Dear Sr. Mary Domenica:

Please let me congratulate you on the GOLDEN JUBILEE of the Foundation of the Congregation of the Daughters of St. Paul in the United States of America. The work of the Daughters of St. Paul in disseminating the teaching of the Holy Fathers is tremendously impressive. The crucial area of communication has been enhanced by the dedication and zeal of your Congregation.

Asking God to bless you in all your endeavors, I am,

Devotedly yours in Christ,

+Bernard F. Law

Bishop of Springfield-Cape Girardeau

Diocese of Savannah

OFFICE OF THE BISHOP

225 ABERCORN STREET
POST OFFICE BOX 8789
SAVANNAH, GEORGIA 31412

November 3, 1981

Sister Mary Domenica, D.S.P.
Provincial
Daughters of St. Paul
50 St. Paul's Avenue
Jamaica Plain
Boston, Massachusetts 02130

Dear Sister Mary Domenica:

On the occasion of the forthcoming Jubilee of the Foundation of the Daughters of St. Paul in the United States, I am pleased to send to you and your Community my most heartfelt and prayerful congratulations.

Your Community's apostolate in the field of communications has indeed been abundantly blessed with results that only the Lord could measure. May He continue to favor your work with continued success. I wish to single out in particular, among your many projects, your making available in such attractive and accessible form the timely teaching and rich messages of the Holy Father.

With renewed greetings and anniversary good wishes, I remain

Sincerely yours in Christ,

+Raymond W. Lessard

Bishop of Savannah

VICAR GENERAL
ARCHDIOCESE OF PHILADELPHIA

November 9, 1981

Mother Paula, D.S.P.
Daughters of St. Paul
50 St. Paul's Avenue
Jamaica Plain
Boston, Massachusetts 02130

Dear Mother Paula:

I offer my felicitations and best wishes to you and your distinguished Congregation of Daughters of St. Paul on the golden jubilee of the foundation of your Congregation here in the United States.

Our city is blessed to have a St. Paul Catholic Book and Film Center here in Philadelphia, and we appreciate the diligent work your Sisters at the center are doing here to spread the gospel. We appreciate, too, the quality of your publications.

God be with you in the years to come. May the second fifty be even more fruitful than the first.

Devotedly yours in the Lord,

+ Martin N. Lohmuller

Most Reverend Martin N. Lohmuller
Auxiliary Bishop of Philadelphia

222 NORTH SEVENTEENTH STREET • PHILADELPHIA, PA., 19103 • (215) 587-3555

UKRAINIAN CATHOLIC
DIOCESE OF STAMFORD

November 25, 1981

Rev. Sister Mary Domenica, D.S.P.
Provincial Superior,
50 St. Paul's Avenue,
Jamaica Plain, Boston, Massachusetts 02130.

Reverend and dear Sister Provincial:

After preaching, the spreading of the Good News of Our Saviour by means of writing is in time the second apostolate which appeared in the history of the Church. The name which you chose for your institute, that of the first Christian writer, St. Paul, is most appropriate. His desire to reach through his letters the many whom he could not meet in his body, has been the inspiration of your saintly Founder in adopting the apostolate of the printed word as the noble task for his spiritual daughters.

In the first half century of the existence in this country of the Congregation of the Daughters of St. Paul, you have splendidly fulfilled the sacred task to which each of you has devoted her life. Your coming to the United States at the moment in history in which it happened, must be considered providential. When your community had grown just to the right size, the Ecumenical Council of Vatican II resulted in an intensive need for an apostolic endeavor, organized on a permanent basis, and wholly dedicated to serve the purpose of the Magisterium of the Church, as is yours.

You have fulfilled the expectations of the bishops and of the faithful of this country in a splendid measure. You and your sisters deserve the thanks of all Catholics of the United States and the most abundant rewards of God.

With my heartfelt congratulations and my sincere wishes that your Congregation may be permitted not only to continue but to expand even more its apostolic activity for the good of the Church, I pray for God's choicest blessings upon you.

Sincerely yours in Christ,

+Basil H. Losten

Most Reverend Basil H. Losten
Bishop of Stamford

BISHOP'S CHANCERY 161 GLENBROOK ROAD STAMFORD, CONNECTICUT 06902 (203) 324-7698

CHRISTUS PAX

OFFICE OF THE EPISCOPAL VICAR October 29, 1981 **URBAN REGION**

Sister Mary Domenica, D.S.P.
Provincial
Daughters of St. Paul
50 St. Paul's Avenue
Jamaica Plain
Boston, Massachusetts 02130

Dear Sister Domenica:

The unique and irreplaceable pastoral ministry of the Bishop of Rome is the hallmark of Catholic Tradition. Through the Servant of Servants, the Church is preserved and strengthened in unity and the clarity of the message of the Gospel is passed on from generation to generation. Given this critical pastoral role of the Holy Father, the apostolate of the Daughters of St. Paul is also a unique and irreplaceable service of truth within the Catholic Faith.

On the occasion of the Golden Jubilee of the Daughters of St. Paul in the United States, then, I want to take this opportunity to congratulate you and to thank you for being a constant resource for papal teaching and reflection. Please extend to Mother Paula my sincerest appreciation for the efforts of evangelization carried on by the Daughters of St. Paul.

To each and every Daughter of St. Paul, I pray that the Spirit give the wisdom and courage He alone can give.

Peace,

Most Reverend James P. Lyke, O.F.M., D.D.
Auxiliary Bishop of Cleveland

CLEVELAND - THE CATHOLIC CENTER
CATHEDRAL SQUARE 1031 SUPERIOR AVENUE CLEVELAND, OHIO 44114

ARCHDIOCESE OF WASHINGTON
OFFICE OF THE REGIONAL BISHOP
ROUTE 7 - BOX 42L
WALDORF, MARYLAND 20601

November 3, 1981

Mother Paula
Daughters of St. Paul
50 St. Paul's Avenue
Jamaica Plain
Boston, Massachusetts 02130

Dear Mother Paula:

It is a joy to join with so many others in extending congratulations to you and the Daughters of St. Paul on the occasion of the Golden Jubilee of the Foundation of the Congregation.

The vision of the Founders and the zeal and trust in Providence which has characterized your efforts and those of your Sisters has been a great blessing for the Church.

May Our Lord continue to bless the Daughters of St. Paul and your efforts to bring His Word to all.

Sincerely yours,

+Thomas W. Lyons

Most Reverend Thomas W. Lyons
Auxiliary Bishop of Washington

Diocese of Scranton
300 Wyoming Avenue
Scranton, Pennsylvania 18503

December 29, 1981

Mother Paula Cordero, D.S.P.
Daughters of Saint Paul
50 Saint Paul's Avenue - Jamaica Plain
Boston, Massachusetts 02130

Dear Mother Paula,

On the occasion of the Fiftieth Anniversary of the Foundation of the Congregation of the Daughters of Saint Paul in the United States, I am pleased to extend to you my heartfelt congratulations and best wishes.

The extent to which your apostolate has grown in this country and the number of vocations your Community is attracting indicate the providential role which God has given to the Daughters of Saint Paul in the evangelization of our people.

Your Congregation's devotion to the Holy See is exemplary. I pray it will remain steadfast and thus assure the fruitfulness of your zeal for the Church in the years ahead.

Asking God to bless you and all your Sisters, I am, with every good wish,

Sincerely yours in Christ,

+J. Carroll McCormick

Most Reverend J. Carroll McCormick, D. D.
Bishop of Scranton

OFFICE OF THE VICAR FOR EDUCATION

DIOCESE OF PITTSBURGH

111 BOULEVARD OF ALLIES
PITTSBURGH, PENNSYLVANIA 15222
(412) 456-3100

November 11, 1981

Sister Mary Domenica, D.S.P., Provincial
Daughters of St. Paul
50 St. Paul's Avenue, Jamaica Plain
Boston, Massachusetts 02130

Dear Sister Mary Domenica:

On this Golden Jubilee of the Foundation of the Daughters of St. Paul, I write to express my thanks and congratulations. The Lord has been good to your Community these past fifty years and through the Community all of us have received countless blessings.

I again thank you for all the personal favors shown me. The books, brochures, and pamphlets which I have received are special, useful, and treasured gifts. They are also a reminder of the good work which the Sisters do day after day.

May the Lord continue to bless you with many more vocations so that your work of evangelization may prosper in the future as it has in the past.

My prayers of thanks are for you, and joined to your own.

Gratefully yours in Christ,

+ John B. McDowell

Most Reverend John B. McDowell, D.D., Ph.D.
Auxiliary Bishop - Vicar General
Vicar for Education

Diocese of Reno - Las Vegas
515 COURT STREET - P. O. BOX 1211
RENO, NEVADA 89504

THE CHANCERY

January 14, 1982

Mother Paula Cordero, D.S.P.
Daughters of St. Paul
50 St. Paul's Avenue
Jamaica Plain
Boston, Massachusetts 02130

Dear Mother Paula:

Fifty years of apostolic service to the Church in the United States! I congratulate you and your Sisters in the fullest sense of that phrase: "I rejoice together with you."

It is truly a time of rejoicing -- and of thanksgiving -- for you, Daughters of St. Paul, and for us, your brothers and sisters in the Family of God, who have been enlightened, encouraged and strengthened by your promulgation of the Word through the instruments of communication and by your daily witness to the Gospel in your generous lives.

God has indeed blessed your beginnings -- the expansion of your Book and Film Centers throughout the United States, the prodigious output of your publications and programs, are remarkable achievements. But we know that they are only the beginnings. The response of the Daughters of St. Paul to God's graces over the past half century assures us that the Church in America will be blessed by even greater accomplishments down the years as you continue your loving and dedicated service to God's Word.

All of you are in my fond and grateful prayers.

Sincerely in Christ,

+ Norman F. McFarland

Most Reverend Norman F. McFarland
Bishop of Reno-Las Vegas

AS ONE WHO SERVES

150 EAST SUMMIT STREET
MUSKEGON HEIGHTS, MICHIGAN 49444

November 10, 1981

Dear Sister Mary Domenica,

Jesus Christ is Lord!

I thank God and rejoice with you in these fifty years of heralding the Good News about Jesus. "By their fruits you will know them." Your fruits indicate that the Father wants to say to you what He said to Jesus, "You are My beloved daughters. In you I am well pleased."

Sincerely in the Lord Jesus,

+ Joseph C. McKinney

Most Rev. Joseph C. McKinney
Auxiliary Bishop of Grand Rapids

Sister Mary Domenica, D.S.P.
Provincial
50 St. Paul's Avenue
Jamaica Plain, Boston, Ma.
02130

The Chancery
Diocese of Buffalo
35 Lincoln Parkway
Buffalo, New York 14222

(716) 883-1372

October 27, 1981

Mother Paula,
Daughters of St. Paul,
50 St. Paul's Ave.,
Boston, Massachusetts 02130

Dear Mother Paula,

My prayerful good wishes on the Golden Jubilee of the service of your Community to the people of the United States.

The expansion of your Community, and the tremendous amount of work you have done to spread the word of God are testimony of God's approval.

May God continue to bless and prosper you that you may continue your all important apostolate.

With every good wish, I am

Respectfully yours in Christ,

+ Bernard J. McLaughlin

Most Rev. Bernard J. McLaughlin,
Auxiliary Bishop of Buffalo

Office of the Bishop
524 East Lawrence Avenue
Post Office Box 1667
Springfield, Illinois 62705

Area Code 217
Telephone 522-7781

December 22, 1981

Mother Paula, D.S.P.
Daughters of St. Paul
50 St. Paul's Avenue
Jamaica Plain
Boston, Massachusetts 02130

Dear Mother Paula,

It is a privilege to join with all admirers of you and your Community in extending my prayerful congratulations on the Golden Jubilee of the Foundation of the Daughters of St. Paul here in the United States. How privileged our nation has been to receive the services of your zealously energetic Community.

Your apostolate has touched millions of my fellow Americans, and we are all the richer for it. At a time when there are divisive forces within the Church, it is a pleasure to work with a Community so totally dedicated to Christ and so wholeheartedly loyal to the Holy See.

It was a privilege for me, during my years as an Auxiliary Bishop in the Archdiocese of St. Louis, to assist you in finding a suitable location for your now very successful Center. What a joy it was to introduce you and the Sisters to the outstanding laymen who have been strengthened in faith by working with your Sisters.

Knowing you personally, dear Mother Paula, and seeing your faith and confidence in God, easily explains the spirit and the success of your Community. On this happy occasion, I pray that God will continue to bless you and all of the Daughters of St. Paul. Your work is more needed now than at any time since you first came to the United States of America.

May Mary, our loving and courageous Mother, strengthen your heart and the hearts of each of these great women who are the Daughters of St. Paul in our midst.

Sincerely yours in Christ,

+ Joseph A. McNicholas

Bishop of Springfield in Il

202 North Seventeenth Street
Allentown, Pennsylvania 18105

November 10, 1981

Mother Paula Cordero, D. S. P.
Daughters of Saint Paul
50 Saint Paul's Avenue
Jamaica Plain
Boston, Massachusetts 02130

Dear Mother Paula:

To you in particular I wish to express congratulations on the glorious occasion of the

GOLDEN JUBILEE

of foundation of the Congregation of the Daughters of Saint Paul in the United States of America.

Sister Paula, you began your mission of faith the same year I began the mission of my priesthood, some fifty years ago. Those early days, in the depths of the depression, were extremely difficult. But now they point out in your own labors to guide the Daughters' foundation here in the United States how strong faith and persevering diligence merit God's support and blessing. I admire you and the Daughters for what you have meant and accomplished for souls here in America, and I pray that God will continue to prosper your work in this part of His vineyard.

With renewed felicitations and looking forward to the Golden Jubilee celebration next June, I remain

Cordially yours,

+ Joseph McShea

Bishop of Allentown

Diocesan Office
for Apostolic Ministry / Alcala Park

November 6, 1981

Daughters of St. Paul
50 St. Paul's Avenue
Jamaica Plain
Boston, Massachusetts 02130

My beloved Daughters of St. Paul:

I greet you in the joy and peace of Our Lord Jesus Christ. I rejoice with you and extend my congratulations to you and all those whose generosity and dedication have brought you to this Golden Jubilee of the founding of the Congregation of the Daughters of St. Paul in the United States.

From the early days of Mother Paula to today the Daughters of St. Paul have witness to a deep faith, heralds of hope, messengers of the Good News, and true workers for justice. Seriously undertaking the call of evangelization, your sisters have made the message of Christ heard through the media of social commitments.

In San Diego we are grateful for the witness and the service of the Daughters of St. Paul and offer our sincere congratulations, and assure you of our prayers that God will continue to bless your congregation and your beautiful ministry.

Sincerely in Christ,

+Leo T. Maher
Bishop of San Diego

Post Office Box 80428, San Diego, California 92138 / Telephone (714) 298-7711

Chancery Office
Diocese of Stockton
1105 North Lincoln Street
P. O. Box 4237
Stockton, California 95204

Telephone
(209) 466-0636

To Reconcile God's People

October 29, 1981

Sister Mary Domenica, D.S.P.
Provincial
Daughters of St. Paul
50 St. Paul's Ave.
Jamaica Plain, Boston, MA 02130

Dear Sister Mary Domenica:

I am pleased to learn that the Daughters of St. Paul will be celebrating their Golden Jubilee of the Foundation in 1982.

I am pleased to join your many friends in extending my sincere congratulations upon reaching this milestone in your service of God and Church. Your tremendous evangelization efforts over the years have borne great spiritual fruit, and continue to bring forth even more fruitfulness for the spread of the Kingdom of God.

Your role in using modern means of communication to proclaim the gospel is a most commendable one and I ask God to bless and reward all of you for your evangelical energy and commitment.

May the next fifty years continue to be ones of great zeal and fruitfulness for the entire Church.

Please be assured of my very special prayers especially during the time of your Jubilee.

With kindest personal regards, I am

Sincerely yours in Christ,

+ Roger Mahony

Most Reverend Roger Mahony
Bishop of Stockton

Archdiocese of Louisville

212 EAST COLLEGE STREET • P.O. BOX 1073 • LOUISVILLE, KENTUCKY 40201

THE CHANCERY

November 13, 1981

Sister Mary Domenica, D.S.P.,
Provincial
Daughters of St. Paul
50 St. Paul Avenue
Jamaica Plain
Boston, Massachusetts 02130

Dear Sister Mary Domenica:

I received your letter of October 20 announcing the forthcoming Golden Jubilee of the Foundation of the Congregation of the Daughters of St. Paul in the United States of America.

In response I take advantage of the occasion to congratulate you and your Sisters and to let you know that I join you in expressing heartfelt thanks to Almighty God for the truly marvelous wonders He has worked in this country through your apostolate of communication.

With prayerful best wishes for God's special blessing on a joyous celebration of this Jubilee, I remain

Yours sincerely in Christ,

+ Charles G. Maloney

Auxiliary Bishop.

ARCHDIOCESE OF NEWARK
OFFICE AND RESIDENCE:
131 East 4th Avenue - Roselle, N.J. 07203
(201) 245-3233

MOST REV. DOMINIC A. MARCONI
Episcopal Vicar for Union County

October 29, 1981

Mother Paula Cordero
Daughters of St. Paul
50 St. Paul's Avenue
Jamaica Plain, Boston MA 02130

Dear Mother Paula:

I would like to extend my sincere congratulations to you and the Daughters of St. Paul as you observe the Golden Jubilee of the Foundation of your Congregation.

Certainly, the past fifty years of service to the Church in the United States, through the media of communication, have been fruitful and rewarding.

May God continue to bless you with new vocations, and increase your apostolate of evangelization for His glory and the salvation of souls.

Sincerely yours in Christ,

+ Dominic A. Marconi

Most Rev. Dominic A. Marconi
Episcopal Vicar-Union County

BISHOP'S OFFICE
351 NORTH AVENUE
BURLINGTON, VERMONT 05401

November 2, 1981

Mother Paula
Daughters of St. Paul
50 St. Paul's Avenue
Jamaica Plain
Boston, MA 02130

Dear Mother Paula,

It is joyful news to learn that the Congregation of the Daughters of St. Paul will be celebrating the Golden Jubilee of their foundation in the United States of America in 1982. On behalf of the priests, religious and laity of the Diocese of Burlington, I wish to express our heartfelt congratulations and gratitude for the good works that you have accomplished the past fifty years on behalf of the Church in our country in the communications field.

Your achievements have been extraordinary. Coming to the United States in the midst of a severe depression with little or nothing by way of material resources, your trust in God and dedication to His service have resulted in the establishment of media centers from coast to coast.

Although your accomplishments have been great and our compliments are most sincere, I am sure that you find the favor of God to be still more encouraging. I refer, of course, to the remarkable number of professed Sisters, novices and postulants, who have been drawn to your Congregation by God's grace even at a time when vocations to the religious life have been dwindling.

It is our prayer that the Lord God will continue to bless your Congregation, which so effectively communicates God's Word to His people, with numerous vocations and with an ever greater capacity to make Him and His teaching known to the world.

Gratefully and devotedly yours in Christ,

+ John A. Marshall

(Most Reverend) John A. Marshall
Bishop of Burlington

St. Helena's Rectory
6161 North Fifth Street
PHILADELPHIA, PA. 19120

January 7, 1982

Sister Mary Domenica, D.S.P.
Daughters of St. Paul
50 St. Paul's Avenue
Jamaica Plain
Boston, Massachusetts 02130

Dear Sister,

May I take this opportunity to congratulate you, the Daughters of St. Paul, on the Golden Jubilee of the foundation of your Congregation in our country. You have reaped a rich harvest during these past fifty years in spreading the Kingdom of Truth through your communications apostolate. It is my fervant prayer that God will continue to bless your mission of evangelization with the media of social communication and that the years ahead will be as replete with His graces as the past has been resplendent with His glory.

With warmest personal regards and prayerful best wishes that God will favor you with His every special grace, I remain

Sincerely yours in Christ,

+ John J. Graham

Most Reverend John J. Graham, D.D.
Auxiliary Bishop of Philadelphia

The Diocese of Cheyenne

Hubert M. Newell, D.D.
Retired Bishop of Cheyenne
P.O. Box 1117
Torrington, Wyoming 82240
(307) 532-5933

October 28, 1981

Sister Paula
Daughters of St. Paul
50 St. Paul's Avenue
Jamaica Plain
Boston, MA 02130

Cordial felicitations to you and your sisters on the fiftieth anniversary of the establishment of the Daughters of St. Paul in the United States. May this be a time of rich and abundant blessings for you and your community.

How generous the Lord has been to your congregation! Begun in the trying and difficult days of the 1930's, your apostolate in the field of social communications has flowered in a manner that bespeaks the aid of Divine Providence.

May God continue to bless and prosper your work and may the admirable devotion of your sisters to the Church be an inspiration to religious everywhere.

Renewed good wishes and prayers for all your needs.

Faithfully in Christ,

+ Hubert M Newell

Retired Bishop of Cheyenne

2400 TWENTY-FIRST AVENUE, SOUTH-NASHVILLE, TENNESSEE 37212-615/383-6393

November 4, 1981

Sister Mary Domenica, D.S.P.
Provincial
Daughters of St. Paul
50 St. Paul's Avenue
Jamaica Plain
Boston, Massachusetts 02130

Dear Sister Mary Domenica:

Greetings, grace, joy and peace be with you and your Congregation as you look forward to your Golden Jubilee of your foundation in the United States of America.

Congratulations on having been entrusted by God with such an important apostolate as is yours in our country. You have proven yourselves worthy of his trust.

We are grateful for your generous cooperation with God's grace and for the great fruit that has come forth to thousands because of your dedicated and gifted ministry.

Now as you look forward to your Golden Jubilee and the desire to grow even more in your service to God and his people, I pray that God's blessings will be with you even more abundantly in all your needs, in all things and in all the days ahead.

Joyfully yours in Christ,

+James D. Niedergeses

James D. Niedergeses
Bishop of Nashville

MILITARY VICARIATE
1011 First Avenue
New York, New York 10022

Office of the Vicar General

December 28, 1981

Sister Mary Domenica, D. S. P.
Provincial
Daughters of St. Paul
50 St. Paul's Avenue
Jamaica Plain, Boston, Mass. 02130

Dear Sister Mary Domenica:

Although I have been a bishop but a brief period of time, I have been deeply gratified by the historic and continuing contributions of the Congregation of the Daughters of St. Paul in the United States. While the work of the Daughters of St. Paul had been known to me through catechetical publications, it was not until I was ordained a bishop and assigned by the Holy Father to my current responsibilities that I became intimately familiar with the extent and the breadth of the Congregation's efforts and the significance of these efforts for the Church in the United States.

I have been privileged to have my own modest little work on war and peace published by the Daughters of St. Paul, and because of this to develop a more personal association than might otherwise have been the case. To have been able to visit the publishing house in Jamaica Plain, Boston, and to have spoken personally with the sisters, observing their work at first hand, and being inspired by their prayerful spirit and very obvious commitment to their apostolate, I feel a special gratitude for the half century that they have been with us.

Obviously, no one could express his appreciation for the Daughters of St. Paul, without simultaneously "canonizing" Mother Paula. It's difficult to imagine that any religious could have accomplished more than Mother Paula has accomplished in the unique mission entrusted to her. To know her is a singular privilege; to have her in our midst is a singular blessing.

Permit me to join with the enormous numbers expressing their warmest congratulations and gratitude on the occasion of your Golden Jubilee.

You will continue in my prayers and Masses for all the years to come.

Faithfully in Christ,

+ John J. O'Connor

+ John J. O'Connor
Vicar General and
Auxiliary Bishop

DIOCESE OF PORTLAND
THE BISHOP'S OFFICE
510 OCEAN AVENUE, PORTLAND, MAINE 04103

October 30, 1981

Sister Mary Domenica, D.S.P.
Daughters of St. Paul
50 St. Paul's Avenue
Jamaica Plain
Boston, MA 02130

Dear Sister Domenica:

I am happy to share in the spirit of joy and thanksgiving that marks the Golden Jubilee celebration of the foundation of the Congregation of the Daughters of St. Paul in the United States. I salute you, Mother Paula and all the Daughters of St. Paul and join you in thanking Our Father for the blessings of a half-century in this country. True to the tradition of your Patron, St. Paul, and your Founders, you asked the Holy Father September 2, 1981 at Castel Gondolfo, "Please pray for us, that we may always be faithful." Indeed, you have been faithful in promoting God's glory and serving His people, after the manner of St. Paul, through evangelization with the media of social communication these past fifty years in our country.

God bless you and with my personal good wishes, I am

Sincerely yours in Christ,

+ Edward C. O'Leary

Bishop of Portland

PLENITUDO LEGIS DILECTIO

BISHOP'S
HOUSE

November 9, 1981

Sister Mary Domenica, D.S.P.
Provincial
Daughters of St. Paul
50 St. Paul's Avenue
Jamaica Plain, Boston, MA 02130

Dear Sister Mary Domenica:

On the occasion of the forthcoming GOLDEN JUBILEE of the foundation of the Congregation of the Daughters of St. Paul in the United States of America, I wish to convey my warmest greetings and congratulation to all the members of the institute.

I am aware of the tremendous task you have undertaken, and in large measure achieved, of spreading the salvific message of the Son of God far and wide through a vigorous and expert use of the media of social communication: press, radio, films and TV.

More than anything else I wish you to know that as a shepherd of souls I greatly appreciate the fact that you have undertaken to evangelize in intimate union with those endowed with the teaching office in the Church.

I pray to God that the Daughters of St. Paul may never give in to the temptation of pleasing the ear; that your task be always performed in perfect consonance with the Magisterium.

I send you my pastoral blessing, and remain

Sincerely yours in Christ

+ Fremiot Torres Oliver

Fremiot Torres Oliver
Bishop of Ponce

General Phone 419-255-1670
Development 419-255-1270
Communications 419-255-1935

DIOCESE OF TOLEDO
CHANCERY
2544 Parkwood Avenue
Toledo, Ohio 43610

December 31, 1981

Sister Paula
Daughters of St. Paul
50 St. Paul's Avenue
Jamaica Plain, Massachusetts 02130

Dear Sister Paula and Daughters of St. Paul:

Congratulations to you and all members of the Community as you mark your Golden Jubilee. I join you in offering a word of thanks and praise to God who has been so gracious to you in the important apostolate which is yours.

I also wish to offer you a word of thanks for the current evangelical and catechetical materials which you presented as a gift. I look forward to the opportunity to read the books and to keep them available for reference.

May the Lord continue to bless all of your undertakings.

Only good things to you,

Sincerely yours,

James R. Hoffman
Bishop of Toledo

ARCHDIOCESE OF NEW ORLEANS

7887 WALMSLEY AVENUE

NEW ORLEANS, LOUISIANA 70125

OFFICE OF THE VICAR GENERAL

November 9, 1981

Sister Mary Domenica, D.S.P.
Provincial
Daughters of St. Paul
50 St. Paul's Avenue, Jamaica Plain
Boston, Ma. 02130

Dear Sister Mary Domenica:

Greetings! And heartfelt congratulations to you and to all the Daughters of St. Paul in this Country on the happy occasion of your Golden Jubilee of the Foundation of your Congregation.

I rejoice with you, the Sisters, and your many friends here in the United States. I view your apostolate as ever more vital and important to Christ and His Church as you endeavor to bring the good news of Redemption to our people.

You have many opportunities and you face many challenges in this New Advent of the year 2000, as the Holy Father describes our age. Be assured of my continued friendship, support, and prayers. May Jesus, the Good Shepherd, bless all of you!

Yours in Christ,

+Stanley J. Ott

Stanley J. Ott, Vicar General
Auxiliary Bishop of New Orleans

BISHOP'S HOUSE
505 S. ARTHUR ST. P.O. BOX 967
GRAND ISLAND, NEBRASKA 68801

October 28,1981

Ven.Sister Mary Domenica D.S.P.
Provincial Superior
Daughters of St.Paul
50St.Paul Ave.
Jamaica Plain
Boston,MA. 02130

Dear Sister Domenica:

It is a source of genuine joy to me to be able to extend to the Daughters of Saint Paul and to Mother Paula my warmest congratulations and cordial good wishes on the occasion of the Golden Jubilee of the Foundation of the Congregation of the Daughters of St.Paul in the United States.

It is obvious to all who have eyes to see that Almighty God has blessed your community and its members in a very special way.As the Latin has it: "digitus Dei est hic."The Church in America has been blessed by your coming to our shores.

I pray Heaven's choicest blessings upon your Congregation and its noble apotolate for the years to come.May the future be even more glorious than the past.

With every kind wish I remain,
Devotedly yours in Christ,

John L. Paschang

John L.Paschang
Retired Bishop of Grand Island

OFFICE OF THE BISHOP

THE CHANCERY
DIOCESE OF CLEVELAND
CHANCERY BUILDING, CATHEDRAL SQUARE
CLEVELAND, OHIO 44114

November 1, 1981

Mother Paula Cordero
Daughters of St. Paul
c/o 50 St. Paul's Avenue
Jamaica Plain
Boston, Mass. 02130

Dear Mother Paula:

My sincere congratulations to you and to the Daughters of St. Paul on the occasion of the Fiftieth Anniversary of your congregation. Your work of evangelization with the media of social communication is such a need in today's world.

Be assured of my personal best wishes and of a remembrance in my prayers for all the Daughters of St. Paul.

Sincerely in Christ,

+Anthony M. Pilla

Most Reverend Anthony M. Pilla
Bishop of Cleveland

DIOCESE OF PORTLAND
OFFICE OF THE AUXILIARY BISHOP
510 OCEAN AVENUE
PORTLAND, MAINE 04103

November 10, 1981

Sister Mary Domenica, D.S.P.
Provincial Superior
Daughters of St. Paul
50 St. Paul Avenue
Jamaica Plain
Boston, Massachusetts 02130

Dear Sister Domenica:

The Golden Jubilee of the Foundation of the Congregation of the Daughters of St. Paul in the United States is certainly an occasion for great rejoicing and thanksgiving. Your Congregation's evangelization efforts through the media of social communication these past fifty years have brought the Good News of Salvation to untold thousands of people hungering for spiritual nourishment.

May the Lord continue to bless your endeavors in the years to come and keep the Daughters of St. Paul in His love always.

Sincerely,

+Amedee W. Proulx

Auxiliary Bishop of Portland

THE CHANCERY Diocese of Sacramento

October 28, 1981

To the Daughters of St. Paul:

It is my pleasure to send Mother Paula and all of you my heartfelt congratulations on the occasion of the Golden Jubilee of the Foundation of the Congregation in the United States.

It must be a source of great joy for all of the Daughters to look back on fifty years of dedicated service to the Church in the United States. To work for the glory of God and for the salvation of souls through the use of the press, radio, films, and television, is a noble apostolate.

I am a grateful for your ministry among us, and I am looking forward to your continuing assistance in spreading the Good News.

With my choicest blessings for the success of your Communications Ministry, I am

Sincerely in Christ,

+ Francis A. Quinn

Francis A. Quinn
Bishop of Sacramento

1119 K STREET :: P.O. BOX 1706 :: SACRAMENTO, CALIFORNIA 95808 :: TELEPHONE (916) 443-1996

Diocese of Norwich

Office of the Bishop

201 Broadway
Norwich, Connecticut

January, 1982

Mother Paula
Daughters of St. Paul
50 St. Paul's Avenue
Jamaica Plain
Boston, Massachusetts 02130

Dear Mother Paula,

Congratulations to you and all the Daughters of Saint Paul on the observance of the Golden Jubilee of your order's establishment in the United States. I join with my brother bishops, priests, and all men and women religious, and all God's People in praising the Lord for the abundance of His grace and favor He shares with us through you.

The Daughters of Saint Paul are known across our country for their work in bringing the Good News of Jesus Christ to all people through the media. What you do is so successful because of who you are. For in you we see women of faith, like Mary, the Mother of God, whose lives magnify the Lord. Strengthened by prayer, and the Sacraments, you witness to the redemptive love of Jesus Christ by making known His Gospel and teaching His Truth. In uttering your own "fiat" to the Lord, you have allowed his Word to mold and shape your lives so that you can serve Him in all your brothers and sisters.

Today we rejoice for the blessings that the Lord has shared with you over these past fifty years. I pray that your apostolate will continually be blessed with success and that many will be inspired by your commitment, dedication and zeal to follow the Lord as the life of a religious.

Asking God to bestow His choicest gifts on you, Mother Paula, and all the Daughters of Saint Paul, as we observe this Golden Jubilee, and praying that the Lord will fill you with His special grace for many, many years, I am

Sincerely yours in Christ,

+ Daniel P. Reilly

Most Reverend Daniel P. Reilly
Bishop of Norwich

MOST REVEREND LAWRENCE J. RILEY, S.T.D.
AUXILIARY BISHOP OF BOSTON

MANE NOBISCUM DOMINE

OFFICE OF THE REGIONAL BISHOP
GREATER BOSTON REGION
43 MAPLE STREET
HYDE PARK, MASSACHUSETTS 02136

October 27, 1981

Sister Mary Domenica, D.S.P.
Provincial
Daughters of St. Paul
50 St. Paul's Avenue
Jamaica Plain, MA 02130

Dear Sister Mary Domenica:

I write to offer my heartfelt congratulations on the occasion of the 50th Anniversary of the coming of the Daughters of St. Paul to the United States.

Here in our country the amazing progress of your community and the incalculable amount of good which has been done for the honor of God and the sanctification of souls through your apostolate of evangelization will always be associated with Mother Paula's half century of tireless zeal.

From one end of this nation to the other she has been instrumental in bringing the word of God to countless millions. No obstacle has ever prevented her from pursuing undeviatingly the goal that has motivated her whole life: to make Jesus Christ better known and better loved.

The influence that Mother Paula has had, especially on young girls whom God has called to the religious life, has been truly extraordinary. At close range they have experienced her ability and resourcefulness and industriousness and determination. But far more important,God has given to them in her a model of what a genuine religious should be: a woman of the loftiest ideals, totally consecrated to the work of God and the Church, uncompromisingly faithful to the teaching of the Church, and unswervingly loyal to the Vicar of Christ on earth.

In congratulating Mother Paula and all the members of your Community on your fiftieth anniversary in the United States, I pledge a constant memento at the altar. May Almighty God, through the intercession of His Immaculate Mother, and of St. Paul, your patron, continue to bless abundantly you and your labors in the immensely important work of evangelization through the media of social communication.

Asking an occasional remembrance in your prayers, and with every best wish, I remain

Sincerely in Christ,

+Lawrence J. Riley

Most Reverend
Lawrence J. Riley, S.T.D.

THE ARCHDIOCESE OF MIAMI

FROM THE RISING TO THE SETTING OF THE SUN IS THE NAME OF THE LORD TO BE PRAISED

December 3, 1981

Mother Paula Cordero, D.S.P.
Daughters of St. Paul
50 St. Paul's Avenue
Jamaica Plain
Boston, Massachusetts 02130

Dear Mother Paula:

Each anniversary of a religious consecration is an occasion to be thankful for the grace and perseverance given to us.

Your 50 years of fidelity to your vows and generous donation of self to the work of the Church entrusted to you are an inspiration to all of us.

May the Lord bless you and grant you good health and many more years of fruitful prayer and service in His Kingdom.

Sincerely yours in Christ,

+ Agustín A. Román

Agustín A. Román
Auxiliary Bishop

cc: Sister Mary Domenica, D.S.P.

6301 BISCAYNE BOULEVARD • MIAMI, FLORIDA 33138 • TELEPHONE (305) 757-6241

PER MATREM DEI

1503 MICHAEL ROAD
RICHMOND, VIRGINIA 23229

November 12, 1981

Dear Daughters of St. Paul:

Congratulations on the Golden Jubilee of your foundation in our beloved country. I join you in thanking God for His blessing on you Sisters for this half century, and on your successful and important apostolate of evangelization through press, radio, films and T.V.

He has also blessed you beyond other religious communities so that now there are 154 Daughters of St. Paul working together for the glory of God and the salvation of souls.

It has been my happiness through the years to receive and ready many of your books and pamphlets with great interest, edification and information and I am confident that your forty million productions have reached and aided innumerable souls.

Offering holy Mass for your intention and with all good wishes, I am,

Gratefully yours in Our Lord,

+ John J. Russell

John J. Russell
Former Bishop of Richmond

ROMAN CATHOLIC DIOCESE OF HONOLULU
CHANCERY OFFICE 1184 BISHOP STREET HONOLULU, HAWAII 96813

30 October 1981

Sister Mary Domenica, D.S.P.
Daughters of St. Paul
50 St. Paul's Avenue
Jamaica Plain
Boston, Massachusetts 02130

Dear Sister:

I am happy to be included in this Golden Jubilee Commemorative Album honoring the Daughters of St. Paul and the labors of Mother Paul Cordero during the past decades.

The courage and vision which Mother Paula brought to the United States in 1932, and the subsequent growth and spirit of dedication of all of the Sisters who have embraced the religious counsels of Father Alberione, have been a boon to the Church in America. I salute Mother Paula and all of the Daughters of St. Paul, and I wish them every success in the very modern apostolate of the media.

With renewed congratulations, and with all good wishes, I remain

Sincerely in Christ,

+JOHN J. SCANLAN
Apostolic Administrator

Maris Stella Rectory
4912 DUNE DRIVE
AVALON, N. J. 08202
(609) 967-3746

November 2, 1981

Sister Mary Domenica, D.S.P.
Daughters of St. Paul
50 St. Paul's Ave.
Jamaica Plain
Boston, Ma. 02130

Dear Sister,

Congratulations on your forthcoming Golden Jubilee. Your work has been a real service to our beloved church in America.

I also thank you for the book, "To the Church in America".

God love you.

Sincerely in Christ,

+ James L. Schad

Most Rev. James L. Schad,
D.D., V.G.

Most Rev. Alphonse J. Schladweiler, D.D.
Retired Bishop of New Ulm
415 North German Street
New Ulm, Minnesota 56073

Telephone
Area 507-354-5032

October 31,1981

Mother Paula
Daughters of St. Paul
50 St. Paul's Avenue, Jamaica Plain
Boston, MA 02130

Dear Sister Paula,

The regularity with which books and pamphlets worth hundreds of dollars arrived at my door from the Daughters of St. Paul when I was bishop of New Ulm, and even since in my retirement, makes it a joy and a matter of decency that I congratulate the Daughters on the Golden Jubilee of their work in the United States.

Mother Paula, you have guided your flock well and with an understanding of the Church's needs especially since the Second Council of the Vatican. The Golden Jubilee must be a time of rejoicing and of gratitude to God that He inspired the work of the Sisters and that our people appreciated their efforts.

May God continue to prosper the work of the Daughters of St. Paul and may you, dear Mother Paula, enjoy God's special blessing and also good health.

Sincerely yours in Christ,

+Alphonse J. Schladweiler
Bishop of New Ulm, Retired

Post Office Box 550
Marquette, Michigan 49855

November 5, 1981

Dear Mother Paula,

I wish to extend my prayerful congratulations to you and all the Sisters on the occasion of the forthcoming Golden Jubilee of the Foundation of the Congregation of the Daughters of St. Paul in the United States.

I am sure you can look back with much joy upon your beautiful apostolate especially in regard to evangelization with the media of social communication. Small wonder that God continues to bless your congregation with many vocations. May His blessings remain with you forever.

Sincerely yours in Christ,

+Mark F. Schmitt

Most Reverend Mark F. Schmitt
Bishop of Marquette

Mother Paula, D.S.P.
Daughters of St. Paul
50 St. Paul's Avenue
Jamaica Plain
Boston, Massachusetts 02130

ARCHDIOCESE OF DETROIT
1234 WASHINGTON BOULEVARD
DETROIT, MICHIGAN 48226

November 12, 1981

Dear Sister Mary Domenica,

I want to extend my sincerest congratulations and best wishes on the forthcoming Golden Jubilee of the Foundation of the Congregation of the Daughters of St. Paul in the United States of America.

Although the Daughters of St. Paul are not in the Archdiocese of Detroit, I am well aware of their untiring work in the field of Catholic Book and Film Centers. "By the fruits of their labor, you shall know them." This can truly be said of the Daughters of St. Paul.

The Community's work with the press, radio, films, and TV in the field of evangelization is a beautiful tribute of their witness of the Gospels.

I know God will continue to bless your endeavors as you continue to bring the Word of God into many lands and communities with your various apostolates.

I pray for God's continued blessing for you, and your Community for many, many more years to come.

Yours in the Lord Jesus,

Walter J Schoenherr

Bishop Walter J. Schoenherr
Auxiliary Bishop of Detroit

Sister Mary Domenica, D.S.P.
Provincial
Daughters of St. Paul
50 St. Paul's Avenue
Jamaica Plain, Boston, MA. 02130

MOST BLESSED SACRAMENT PARISH
1325 SMELTER AVENUE
BLACK EAGLE, MONTANA 59414

October 27, 1981

Dear Sister Mary Domenica:

Please accept my prayerful congratulations on the occasion of the GOLDEN JUBILEE of the Foundation of your community in the United States. For many years your congregation has been a shining light both by word and personal example of the religious life in America. Frequently, I have occasion to give thanks to God for your providential apostolate which is sorely needed in our day. Your publications are always a joy, even my grand-neices and nephews look forward to "MY FRIEND"! May Our Lord richly bless you, Mother Paula, and all the Daughters of St. Paul during the Jubilee Year and always.

Devotedly yours,

+ Eldon B. Schuster
Most Rev. Eldon B. Schuster
Former Bishop of Great Falls

Sister Mary Domenica D.S.P., Provincial
Daughters of St. Paul
Boston, Ma. 02130

ARCHDIOCESE
OF MILWAUKEE
345 NORTH NINETY FIFTH STREET • P.O. BOX 2018 • MILWAUKEE, WISCONSIN 53201 • PHONE 414/476-2101

OFFICE OF THE AUXILIARY BISHOP

November 9, 1981

Sister Mary Domenica, D.S.P.
Provincial
Daughters of St. Paul
50 St. Paul's Avenue
Jamaica Plain
Boston, Massachusetts 02130

Dear Sr. Mary Domenica,

Sincere congratulations on the occasion of your Golden Jubilee of foundation in the United States of America. The Church is grateful for your dedication to the dissemination of truth and solid piety. May you continue to grow in the spirit of faith and freedom so courageously articulated by the apostle whose name you bear, and may you be a constant witness to the Resurrection in our age.

Sincerely,

+Richard J. Sklba

Most Reverend Richard J. Sklba
Auxiliary Bishop of Milwaukee

CATHOLIC CENTER
ARCHDIOCESE OF BALTIMORE
320 CATHEDRAL STREET
BALTIMORE, MARYLAND 21201

OFFICE OF THE URBAN VICAR

(AREA CODE 301)
547-5452

November 30, 1981

Daughters of St. Paul
c/o Sister Mary Domenica, Provincial
50 St. Paul's Avenue
Jamaica Plain
Boston, Massachusetts 02130

My Dear Sisters in Christ,

With deep joy I congratulate you on the occasion of your Golden Jubilee of Foundation in the United States.

In 1975, Pope Paul VI, of Blessed Memory, gave the world his own vision of the Gospel task in Evangelii Nuntiandi. This six-year old document gave Christians another call to go teach all nations. It is with pleasure we see this task slowly but surely moving forward in our diocese and through our parishes.

To the Daughters of St. Paul, this is no new task. Your Community has persevered in this task quietly for 50 years. It is to the credit of your American foundress, Sister Paula, that in the midst of an economic depression in this country, she should follow the call of Jesus to proclaim that the "Kingdom of God is at hand."

The ministry of your Community to spread the Gospel Message by printed and visual media is certainly a timely one. More and more people are using film and television to communicate the Word of God. Certainly books and pamphlets are bombarding society on every side. To write, to teach, and to produce these materials in the spirit of your patron, St. Paul, is a choice that will not outgrow its usefulness.

I thank the Lord with you for all the efforts already put forth. I pray that the blessing of God may continue to show itself in your ventures.

Sincerely yours in Christ,

+ J. Francis Stafford

Most Rev. J. Francis Stafford
Auxiliary Bishop of Baltimore

December 3, 1981

The Daughters of St. Paul
50 St. Paul's Avenue
Jamaica Plain, MA 02130

Dear Mother Paula and Sisters:

I am happy to send my congratulations on the occasion of the *Golden Jubilee* of the foundation of the Congregation of the Daughters of St. Paul in the United States of America. How God has blessed you in your fifty years of service as you work to extend His kingdom here on earth! The greatest blessing, of course, comes from the increase in professed Sisters and the work that you do as apostles in His vineyard.

You have taken upon yourselves a service program of reaching-out into the lives of many, many people. Your monthly magazine, *FAMILY*, speaks to all of our people and especially to those who have the responsibility of educating the young. Your other monthly magazines, *STRAIN FORWARD* and *MY FRIEND*, as well as the many books, pamphlets, cassettes, records and filmstrips, make available the authentic teachings of the Church in a way that our people can respond and receive the benefits of our Catholic faith.

You have truly carried out the mandate of your founder, Fr. James Alberione: *"Become the voice of the Church, of the Pope, of the episcopate, of the clergy. That same voice is then to be multiplied and reinforced by you as if by an amplifier, so as to reach everyone."*

It is my prayer that God will continue to bless you and your work and give you the encouragement and help that you need.

Sincerely yours in Christ,

James S. Sullivan
Auxiliary Bishop of Lansing

DIOCESE OF LANSING, 300 West Ottawa Street, Lansing, Michigan 48933

DIOCESE OF BATON ROUGE
BISHOP'S OFFICE
BATON ROUGE, LOUISIANA 70821

November 30, 1981

Reverend Mother Paula Cordero, D.S.P.
Daughters of St. Paul
50 St. Paul's Avenue
Jamaica Plain
Boston, Massachusetts 02130

Dear Mother Paula:

On the occasion of the forthcoming Golden Jubilee of the foundation of the Daughters of St. Paul in the United States, permit me to express my sincerest congratulations and prayerful best wishes to you and to your Congregation.

In 1932, when you and your young companion began your mission of faith, in the United States of America, at the direction of your Founder, The Reverend James Alberione and your Co-foundress, Mother Thecla Merlo, you came without any human means but only with faith, hope and love of God. With these supernatural virtues, together with your obedience to your Founder and Co-foundress, you were able to go through many difficult and trying times. Your Congregation, blessed by Almighty God and spurred on by your zeal, expanded from that small beginning from coast to coast establishing twenty-two Centers of light in fifteen states. Your fidelity to the Church and to the Magisterium, your loyal obedience to legitimate authority, has been blessed by Almighty God. Contrary to the experience of many other congregations after Vatican II, your Congregation has seen a growth in vocations. This is surely a sign from God that He is pleased with the manner of your ministry.

Your work in the Diocese of Baton Rouge at the St. Paul Catholic Book and Film Center has been a source of light and a focal point of orthodoxy and faith for our Catholic people in the diocese. I consider the Daughters of St. Paul a most important arm of my teaching apostolate. Your aim of the glory of God and the salvation of souls through evangelization with the media of social communication is most important in this day of the media; it is essential that the media be utilized in the proper way for the spread of the Catholic Faith. Only God knows the tremendous good that you have done and will do.

Therefore, on this joyful occasion of your Golden Jubilee, I extend to you my gratitude, my congratulations and my prayers that you may continue to be a beacon of light and an instrument of the Holy Spirit in the spread of the Catholic Faith in today's world.

With my blessing and prayerful best wishes, I am

Faithfully yours in Christ,

+ Joseph V. Sullivan

Most Reverend Joseph V. Sullivan, S.T.D.
Bishop of Baton Rouge

1011 FIRST AVENUE
SUITE 1357
NEW YORK, NEW YORK 10022

November 30, 1981

Sister Mary Domenica, D.S.P.
Provincial
Daughters of St. Paul
50 St. Paul's Avenue
Jamaica Plain, Massachusetts 02130

Dear Sister Mary:

This is just a little note of prayerful congratulations on the forthcoming Golden Jubilee of the Foundation of your Congregation. Our Divine Lord and His dear Blessed Mother have certainly blessed your efforts down through the years. There is no measuring all that you have been able to accomplish, particularly through your Catholic Book and Film Centers, of whom many of us have been the recipients of many valuable books.

To my little note of congratulations I add the prayer that Our Divine Lord and His dear Blessed Mother will continue to bless the work of you and your Congregation in every way.

With every prayerful best wish,

Cordially yours in Christ,

Edward E. Swanstrom

DIOCESE OF ST. PETERSBURG
OFFICE OF THE AUXILIARY BISHOP

OFFICE
6363 NINTH AVENUE NORTH
ST. PETERSBURG, FLORIDA
(813) 344-1611

MAILING ADDRESS
POST OFFICE BOX 13109
ST. PETERSBURG, FLORIDA 33733

November 17, 1981

Sister Mary Domenica, D.S.P.
Daughters of St. Paul
50 St. Paul's Avenue, Jamaica Plain
Boston, Massachusettes 02130

Dear Sister Mary Domenica:

I acknowledge receipt of your recent letter regarding the forthcoming Golden Jubilee of the Foundation of the Congregation of the Daughters of St. Paul in the United States of America and the enclosed copy of "To the Church in America".

Since the establishment of your Community in Miami, I have not only made frequent visits to your book store but used the facilities offered. We are blessed with the presence of your Community in Florida.

I assure you of my continued prayers for you and the Daughters of St. Paul.

With cordial regards and every best wish, I am

Sincerely yours in Christ,

+ J. Keith Symons

Most Reverend J. Keith Symons
Auxiliary Bishop

DIOCESE OF PUEBLO
OFFICE OF THE BISHOP
1426 North Grand Avenue
Pueblo, Colorado 81003
303 — 543-5575

November 6, 1981

Sister Mary Domenica, D.S.P.
Provincial
Daughters of St. Paul
50 St. Paul's Avenue
Jamaica Plain, Boston, MA 02130

Dear Sister Mary Domenica:

I am pleased to learn that the Daughters of St. Paul will be celebrating their Golden Jubilee next year. Congratulations!

I have always admired your work to keep the Church of the United States informed regarding papal teaching. Your role is a very important one since the communications media has grown so tremendously.

I will remember you, the Sisters and your work in my prayers as you celebrate your 50th Anniversary.

Sincerely yours in Christ,

+Arthur N. Tafoya

+Arthur N. Tafoya
Bishop of Pueblo

THE DIOCESE OF CHARLESTON

119 BROAD STREET

CHARLESTON, SOUTH CAROLINA 29401

OFFICE OF THE BISHOP

November 3, 1981

Dear Sisters:

Peace and greetings in the Lord!

In the United States, you have demonstrated for fifty years a special witness to the life of Our Blessed Lord and His Mother. This witness embraces an authentic response to the rhythm of the paschal mystery within the Catholic Church and in your religious community. Indeed, you have been pioneers in the area of Communications. Contemporary society is attuned to the media of Social Communications in all its dimensions. As a religious community of women, you commit yourselves to evangelization through the media. You reach out to our nation which has been blessed because of your presence and mission in the United States.

We, the Catholics of South Carolina, rejoice with you as you celebrate your Jubilee year. You have our congratulations, our finest wishes and prayers.

Asking a special blessing upon your community, I beg to remain

Sincerely yours in Christ,

+ E. L. Unterkoefler

Most Reverend Ernest L. Unterkoefler
Bishop of the Diocese of Charleston

Sister Mary Domenica, D.S.P.
Provincial
Daughters of St. Paul
50 St. Paul's Avenue
Jamaica Plain
Boston, Massachusetts 02130

Diocese of Birmingham in Alabama
BISHOP'S OFFICE
P. O. BOX 2086
BIRMINGHAM, ALABAMA 35201

8131 4TH AVENUE, SOUTH
TELEPHONE 205-833-0171

November 12, 1981

Sister Mary Domenica, D. S.P.
Provincial
Daughters of St. Paul
50 St. Paul's Av. Jamaica Plain
Boston, MA 02130

Dear Sister Mary Domenica:

The Diocese of Birmingham joins me, Bishop Joseph G. Vath, in congratulating the Sisters on the Golden Jubilee of the Foundation of the Congregation of the Daughters of St. Paul. The Daughters adherence to the magisterium and zeal for the spread of God's word has been a credit to the Congregation.

May God continue to bless the apostolic work of the Daughters of St. Paul and Mother Paula.

Sincerely in Christ,

+Joseph G. Vath

Most Reverend Joseph G. Vath, D. D.
Bishop of Birmingham in Alabama

BQ.

St. Walter Parish
117 West Maple Avenue
Roselle, Illinois 60172

November 11, 1981

Sister Mary Domenica, D.S.P.
Provincial,
50 St. Paul's Ave.
Jamaica Plain,
Boston, Ma. 02130

Dear Sister Domenica,

I am aware of the Golden Jubilee of the Foundation of the Daughters of St. Paul in our United States and take this opportunity to extend my sincere congratulations to you, your Community and to Mother Paula. The disclosure of your accomplishments is most impressive and outstanding. All of us are so very proud of what you have been able to do and we thank God and your Congregation on behalf of all the people of God whom you have served so well. Your dedication and tireless work are strong inspiration for all of us who are witnesses.

May God bless all of you in a special way and increase your numbers among us.

Cordially yours in Christ,

+ R. J. Vonesh

Most Rev. R. J. Vonesh,
Vicar General,
Aux. Bishop of Joliet, Illinois

ARCHDIOCESE OF SEATTLE
907 TERRY AVENUE
SEATTLE, WASHINGTON, 98104

+

Dear Sister Domenica and Daughters of St. Paul:

I am happy to know that you are taking note of your Golden Jubilee and that, through your announcement of October 20th, you are inviting the friends you have in this country to share with you the joys of such an observance.

Your work in the field of communications' media, - press, radio, films, and television, is well known and the approach you take to it is widely appreciated. The very fact that you now have a history of fifty years in the United states is in itself evidence of the acceptance of your apostolate and, at the same time, proof of God's reward for having proclaimed Him so faithfully to the poeple of this country.

I am especially appreciative of the loyalty and respect the Daughters of St. Paul have shown for the Vicar of Christ. Your fifty years have been glorious testimony to your commitment to the Holy Father. The witness of fidelity to him has impressed me, and your dedication to the mission of Christ which he directs has constantly made me grateful to you, to your founders, and to your associates.

May God bless you always, and may Mary, the Star of Evangelization, continue to intercede for you as you look for new ways of spreading the Gospel!

Your Brother in Christ
Nicolas E. Walsh, V. G.
Auxiliary Bishop of Seattle

October 30, 1981

DIOCESE OF SPOKANE
POST OFFICE BOX 1453
SPOKANE WASHINGTON 99210
WEST 1023 RIVERSIDE AVENUE

BISHOP

November 4, 1981

Sister Mary Domenica, D.S.P.
Provincial, Daughters of St. Paul
50 St. Paul's Avenue
Jamaica Plain
Boston, MA 02130

Dear Sister Mary Domenica:

Thank you for the good news informing me of the upcoming Golden Jubilee of the Foundation of the Daughters of St. Paul. Congratulations, and thank you for the contribution you make to the Church in the United States and around the world.

As per your request, I add here a short note for publication in your anniversary album:

> Dear Daughters of St. Paul,
>
> Let me take this opportunity to wish you God's blessings on the occasion of your golden anniversary. Surely He has been good to you during these past fifty years. Thank you for the contributions you have made to the work of the Church, particularly your reprints of papal documents and ecclesial statements. I am sure that many bishops and the People of God find such a service helpful in building a Church in the likeness of Christ and the spirit of Vatican II.

Devotedly yours in Christ,

+ Lawrence H. Welsh

The Most Reverend Lawrence H. Welsh
Bishop of Spokane

Diocese of Arlington

Chancery Office

SUITE 704
200 NORTH GLEBE ROAD
ARLINGTON, VIRGINIA 22203
(703) 841-2500

January 1982

Dear Daughters of Saint Paul,

It is a privilege to join many other grateful beneficiaries in offering words of congratulation on the Golden Jubilee of the Foundation of the Congregation of the Daughters of Saint Paul in the United States.

As I write these words the Diocese of Arlington awaits the official beginning of your latest Catholic Book and Film Center. We see this as a grace to benefit our catechetical efforts and a presence of great value for the whole area. We are delighted that four of our young ladies have already joined your ranks and we are sure there will be more.

That these fifty years have all been stamped by the apostolic zeal and wisdom of Mother Paula is truly an amazing gift of God to your Community and to all of us. May the next fifty years be as fruitful in the work of evangelization and as the Holy Father said, "May God sustain you in your generous service of the Gospel, the great task of helping to spread Christian doctrine."

Sincerely yours in our Lord,

+ Thomas J. Welsh

Most Reverend Thomas J. Welsh
Bishop of Arlington

CHANCERY OFFICE
P.O. Box 36 Dyker Heights Station
Brooklyn, New York 11228-0036

8120 - 15th Avenue
Brooklyn, New York 11228-0036
(212) 259-9200

DIOCESE OF ST. MARON - U.S.A.

November 4, 1981

Sister Mary Domenica, D.S.P
Provincial
Daughters of St. Paul
50 St. Paul's Ave,
Jamaica Plain
Boston, MA. 02130

Dear Sister,

It is with great pleasure and gratitude that I congratulate you, Mother Paula, and the entire community of the Daughters of Saint Paul on the occasion of your Golden Jubilee.

Your community has done so much in the area of evangelization through publication and the media of social communication. It is for this reason that the Lord has blessed you with success and vocations. May He continue to bless you and your work as you toil to expand His Kingdom. May your labors become more and more fruitful and your numbers increase for the service of his glory.

Be assured of my prayers for your entire community. I remain

Sincerely yours in Christ,

+Francis M. Zayek

+FRANCIS M. ZAYEK
BISHOP OF ST. MARON

Congratulatory Messages

From Major Superiors of Religious Women

FRANCISCAN SISTERS OF CHICAGO
1220 MAIN STREET
LEMONT, ILLINOIS 60439
•
PHONES 257-7776 OR 257-7777

March 18, 1982

Daughters of St. Paul
172 North Michigan Avenue
Chicago, Illinois 60601

Dear Sisters,

I want to take this opportunity to thank you for your kind invitation on the occasion of the Golden Jubilee of the founding of the Daughters of St. Paul. I wish to congratulate Mother Paula, Foundress, and all of the members of your Congregation on this happy occasion. I thank our God for each of you and I continue to say that you are God's gift to the Archdiocese of Chicago and the entire Church.

May you continue to experience God's Love, Peace and Joy today and always, as you minister to each of us in your Christ-like way.

Sincerely in Christ,

Sister Mary Antonissima

Sister Mary Antonissima
Assistant Superior General

Saint Cecilia Convent

NASHVILLE, TENNESSEE
37208

OFFICE OF
THE MOTHER GENERAL

Friday, March 5, 1982

Mother Paula, D.S.P.
50 St. Paul Avenue, Jamaica Plain
Boston, Ma. 02130

Dear Mother Paula

Almost two weeks ago we enjoyed the privilege of celebrating with your Community the golden anniversary of the foundation of the Daughters of St. Paul in the United States.

It was truly a memorable occasion, Mother, as well as an inspiration to have seen the evidence of God's abundant graces showered upon you and your Sisters these fifty years.

Of course, God's most significant visual signs of His

approval were the many young women around you. Truly, yours is an oasis in a desert land of vocations!

Your apostolic work is surely the work of the Church in the modern world! You are true to the charism of your patron, Saint Paul, bringing the Word of God to the People of God.

We congratulate you on the house that you have built "upon a rock." God has blessed your labors, the fruit of which reflects honor on your Congregation and upon the Church, as well as glory upon your patron, that tireless Apostle. Mother, we think his sandals fit your feet pretty well!

Thank you for your warm and generous hospitality. If I sent an Airline ticket would you come and visit us? I could take you to visit Mother Angelica's TV studio.

Sincerely in Christ,
Mother Assumpta, O.P.

Rosary Hill Home

Hawthorne, New York 10532

February 24, 1982

Dear Mother Paula and Sisters

It is a pleasure and a privilege to congratulate you on your fiftieth anniversary in our country and to offer our heartfelt thanks for the fruitful offering you have made to God in your apostolate of the printed word.

God always fills the need of the times and He has done this in setting you in our midst to counteract the evil that is daily thrust before the public through the news media. Saint Paul continues his missionary work through you, it cannot fail.

May God continue to bless your loving labors in His vineyard, bless you with vocations to His work and fill your hearts with His love and peace and grace.

Please accept the enclosed gift. We are also having a novena of Masses offered for your Golden Jubilee.

In the Sacred Hearts of Jesus and Mary

Mother M. Bernadette and Sisters

50

Magnificat...

anima mea...

Dominum...

OUR

Spiritual Bouquet on the

Golden Anniversary:

Holy Mass

will be offered in our CHAPEL

in gratitude for your loyal service in U.S.A.

Our dear

DAUGHTERS of ST. PAUL,

Hearty

Congratulations!

May God abundantly reward you for sowing the seeds of good in U.S.A. – all for His glory. Many more blessings on your path of the next half-century.

1982
Our Lady of the Angels Province
Enfield, Connecticut, 06082

Mother Bernarda Mary, CSSF
Provincial Superior,
and ALL Felician Sisters

THE FELICIAN SISTERS, O.S.F.
36800 SCHOOLCRAFT ROAD
LIVONIA, MICHIGAN

March 3, 1982

Mother Paula, D.S.P.
Daughters of St. Paul
50 St. Paul Avenue
Jamaica Plain, Boston, MA 02130

Dear Mother Paula and Daughters of St. Paul,

We extend our sincere congratulations, wishes, and prayers upon your golden milestone. Though as Church communities go, you are still a young institute, yet you have accomplished much in these past fifty years for the Church through the proclamation of the Word. Your community has responded to this special call to evangelization with generosity and effectiveness.

As teachers in Catholic parochial schools, we are grateful to the Daughters for the wealth of media materials in the field of religious education. The numerous publications and various teaching aids are invaluable in conveying the truths of the faith to the minds and hearts of the young.

All religious, too, are indebted to you for your service in keeping up with the most recent pronouncements of the Holy Father and the Sacred Congregation for Religious. We find your publications a rich resource for knowing the mind of the Church. The Daughters of St. Paul are noted for their unswerving loyalty to Christ's Vicar on earth and in this way contribute to the unity of Christ's family, the Church.

The Felician Sisters stand firmly with you in this loyalty to the Holy Father and the teaching of the Magisterium. As we congratulate you today for all your accomplishments achieved in these past fifty years with the grace of God, we pray that your years and numbers will be multiplied a thousand times for the greater glory of God and His Church.

Sincerely in Christ,

Mother Mary Clarentine, CSSF

Mother Mary Clarentine, CSSF
Provincial Superior

NOTRE DAME INSTITUTE FOR ADVANCED STUDIES
IN
RELIGIOUS EDUCATION

MIDDLEBURG, VIRGINIA 22117

A PONTIFICAL
CATECHETICAL
INSTITUTE

March 1, 1982

The Daughters of St. Paul
50 St. Paul's Ave.
Jamaica Plain
Boston, Massachusetts 02130

Dear Mother Paula, Sister Domenica, Sister Concetta and Community,

Fifty years ago in 1932 - the year the writer received the holy habit of the Sisters of Notre Dame - a courageous Junior Professed Sister came with her companion to the shores of the United States. In retrospect, we can only thank and praise God for that day because she persevered in the mission God had given to her for His Holy Church.

Mother Paula, we thank God and we are deeply grateful to you for cooperating with the overwhelming graces which our Heavenly Father has bestowed upon you. You accepted the challenge, received that special charism which characterizes your Community, and you persevered in leading your Sisters along uncharted paths in the area of communications and the media. God knew how much you loved Him with a love so strong that you had the power to face obstacles, accept them with faith and overcome them with supernatural courage.

Today the Daughters of St. Paul in the United States constitute a mighty army of courageous women religious, dedicated to one of the most important contemporary apostolates in the Church. You have a vision and a goal which makes your community an inspiring example of happy paradoxes.

The Daughters of St. Paul are strong, yet humble; prayerful, yet industrious; supernaturally agressive, yet delightfully unassuming; self-effacing, yet self-fulfilling; vocal, yet reticent; knowledgeable about the things that really matter in life, yet open to all changes which might better life and draw others closer to God.

Your loyalty to the Holy See has made it possible for millions to hear the "Voice of Peter" in the United States during the past fifty years. You have thereby kept them in the Roman Catholic Church where, if they are faithful to Her Teaching, they can be assured of an eternity in heaven with their Creator, their Redeemer, their Sanctifier, and their Heavenly Mother.

As a Sister of Notre Dame whose Congregation is primarily committed to the education of youth, I thank you for the many authentic and orthodox books and pamphlets which you have made available to us.

May God continue to bless and reward the Daughters of St. Paul in their apostolate of communicating the Living Word of God.

Your grateful and devoted,

Sister Mary Elise S.N.D.

Sister Mary Elise, S.N.D.

SISTERS OF ST. JOSEPH
OF CLUNY
91 Washington Street
Newport, R.I. 02840

March 10, 1982

Dear Sister Paula,

Thank you, first of all, for being instrumental in bringing the Consortium to Boston and, secondly, for the great contribution you and your Sisters made, in all areas, to ensure the success of the proceedings.

I am sure all would agree that the highlight of the week-end was our visit to your Provincialate. That was truly an inspiring experience your accomplishments in the short space of fifty years are indeed overwhelming, and together with your flourishing Novitiate, the tangible evidence of the good Lord's response to your undaunted trust in Him. May He continue to show you His favor as you carry on your very worth while Apostolate.

Sister Eucharia S.J.C.

Notre Dame Educational Center
13000 Auburn Road
Chardon, Ohio 44024

February 28, 1982

Dear Mother Paula, Sister Domenica
and Sisters All:

A word of CONGRATULATIONS is in order as you commemorate the Golden Anniversary of your first foundation in the United States! When the young Sister Paula and her companion stepped off the ship and onto the pier in the New York Harbor in the year 1932, neither they nor any one of the many people around them had any idea of what the future had in store for the first two Daughters of St. Paul who had come to the "Land of the free and the home of the brave." A loving Father in Heaven knew - He had great plans but He kept them a secret.

Now, fifty years later, we have seen how the two pioneers and all the "Daughters" who have followed them, cooperating with His grace, have brought His plans to fruition. The pioneers have doubled and tripled and quadrupled many times and today, the community numbering almost two hundred can look back on 50 years of consecrated service to God and to His Church using "the means of social communication" to spread the Word of God.

Like the sower in the Gospel the Daughters of St. Paul have sown seed in many parts of the United States - seed that has brought forth fruit thirty, sixty and hundred fold. This you have done through the powerful media of communication -- press, radio, T-V, films, slides, records, cassettes, music, song.

The opportunity, recently, to visit your media center helped many sisters to understand more fully the breadth and depth of your apostolate. That God has blessed your work is evident, not only in the growth of your community during the past fifty years, but also in the joyful, dedicated spirit that permeates the atmosphere of your convent home and working areas.

May God continue to bless you AD MULTOS ANNOS! And in the words of Pope John Paul II -

> "May God sustain you in your generous
> service of the Gospel,
> in the great task of helping to spread
> Christian Doctrine."

I pray that "through your apostolate 'the word of the Lord may speed on and triumph'."

In the love of Our Lady, Queen of Apostles, I am

Your grateful,

Sister Mary Florice, S.N.D.

Franciscan Sisters
of the Immaculate Conception
Province of Saint Clare of Assisi

11306 LAUREL CANYON BOULEVARD
SAN FERNANDO, CALIFORNIA 91340
(213) 361-2703

February 27, 1982

THE DAUGHTERS OF SAINT PAUL
50 St. Paul's Avenue
Jamaica Plain
Boston, MA 02130

Dear Sisters:

It is with love and appreciation that we extend our congratulations to you on the occasion of the Fiftieth Anniversary of your Congregation's first foundation in the United States of America.

During the Consortium Perfectae Caritatis meeting in Boston we came to know first hand the beautiful religious spirit that your Sisters brought to our beloved Country. For this we are most grateful.

We join with you in thanking Almighty God for this Anniversary and we pray that our Nation be always blest with your presence.

Yours sincerely,

Sister Imelda Marie, O.S.F.

Sister Imelda Marie Gallegos, OSF
Provincial Superior

J. M. J. T. (213) 289-1353

CALIFORNIA PROVINCE OF THE MOST SACRED HEART
CARMELITE SISTERS
920 East Alhambra Road, Alhambra, California 91801

February 25, 1982

Sister Mary Domenica, D.S.P.
Provincial Superior
DAUGHTERS OF ST. PAUL
50 St. Paul's Avenue
Jamaica Plain, Boston, Massachusetts 02130

My dear Sister Mary Domenica:

Congratulations on your 50th Anniversary of dedicated service in the Church. It was a remarkable experience for us to have toured your printing presses which publish such fine books, periodicals, and other facets in the media of social communication. We join you in thanking our Lord for the fruitful 50 years of evangelization in the United States. We pray that the wonderful work you are doing now will continue to bear much fruit.

Please keep us in your prayers that we too may continue to work for His greater honor and glory; we must add that your publications have been a great asset and help to our own Sisters in their various apostolates.

With personal esteem, I remain

Sincerely yours in Christ,

Sister Josephine OCD

Sister Josephine, O.C.D.
Provincial Superior

Sisters of the Divine Master
43 West St – Boston, Mass. 02111
Tel: (617) 482-0978

March 1, 1982

Mother Paula
Daughters of St. Paul
50 St. Paul's Avenue
Jamaica Plain, MA 02130

Dear Mother Paula,

We would like to warmly congratulate you on your 50th Anniversary of your life in this our country.

We have always admired the great work that you are doing with the grace of God.

We also feel rewarded because of the will of our Founder to assure you - and all the Pauline Family - of our contribution of prayer and perpetual Adoration.

We wish and pray that you may succeed in spreading God's Word with all the means of communication, and that it may be efficacious to make a better world.

In Our Divine Master,

Sister Disciples of the Divine Master

1932 50 1982

Zealous

Communicators

of

Christ's Love

discover the Joy of bringing

God's word to the people of U.S.A.

Hearty Congratulations to you, dearest

Daughters of St. Paul, on the

50th Anniversary of your great

Apostolate in the U.S.A.

God's richest bounties for today
and for
many more years of evangelizing His word!

Ad Multos Annos!

Mother Mary Viterbia,
Provincial Superior,
and FELICIAN SISTERS

Lodi, N.J.
1982
Immaculate Conception Province

J. M. J. + A. T.

The root of religious life, of its peace, quiet, even of its sanctity, is humility.

Father Gillet

Dear Mother Paula,

May the peace of Christ be with you!

The Twentieth Assembly of the Consortium will live in my memory! The contributions of your community were truly appreciated. "Thank you" seems so inadequate for expressing all the gratitude of my heart.

I shall offer a Novena of Masses in thanksgiving for your fidelity to God and His Church during these past "Fifty Years", and ask God's continued blessings on the future community, your youth! They truly inspired me by their love, joy and humility.

The enclosed stationery is one small way we try to spread the spirit of our saintly founder, Father Gillet. Our novice designed it and we had it printed.

God bless you, dear Mother, and all your dear Sisters of St. Paul! I am in Mary's Immaculate Heart,

Lovingly and gratefully,

Sister Mary William, HOM

February 23, 1982

Feast: St. Polycarp

Daughters of St. Paul

IN MASSACHUSETTS
50 St. Paul's Ave., Jamaica Plain, Boston, MA 02130; **617-522-8911; 617-522-0875**
172 Tremont Street, Boston, MA 02111; **617-426-5464; 617-426-4230**
IN NEW YORK
78 Fort Place, Staten Island, NY 10301; **212-447-5071**
59 East 43rd Street, New York, NY 10017; **212-986-7580**
625 East 187th Street, Bronx, NY 10458; **212-584-0440**
525 Main Street, Buffalo, NY 14203; **716-847-6044**
IN NEW JERSEY
Hudson Mall — Route 440 and Communipaw Ave., Jersey City, NJ 07304; **201-433-7740**
IN CONNECTICUT
202 Fairfield Ave., Bridgeport, CT 06604; **203-335-9913**
IN OHIO
2105 Ontario St. (at Prospect Ave.), Cleveland, OH 44115; **216-621-9427**
25 E. Eighth Street, Cincinnati, OH 45202; **513-721-4838**
IN PENNSYLVANIA
1719 Chestnut Street, Philadelphia, PA 19103; **215-568-2638**
IN VIRGINIA
1025 King St., Alexandria, VA 22314 **703-683-1741**
IN FLORIDA
2700 Biscayne Blvd., Miami, FL 33137; **305-573-1618**
IN LOUISIANA
4403 Veterans Memorial Blvd., Metairie, LA 70002; **504-887-7631; 504-887-0113**
1800 South Acadian Thruway, P.O. Box 2028, Baton Rouge, LA 70821 **504-343-4057; 504-343-3814**
IN MISSOURI
1001 Pine Street (at North 10th), St. Louis, MO 63101; **314-621-0346; 314-231-1034**
IN ILLINOIS
172 North Michigan Ave., Chicago, IL 60601; **312-346-4228 312-346-3240**
IN TEXAS
114 Main Plaza, San Antonio, TX 78205; **512-224-8101**
IN CALIFORNIA
1570 Fifth Avenue, San Diego, CA 92101; **714-232-1442**
46 Geary Street, San Francisco, CA 94108; **415-781-5180**
IN HAWAII
1143 Bishop Street, Honolulu, HI 96813; **808-521-2731**
IN ALASKA
750 West 5th Avenue, Anchorage AK 99501; **907-272-8183**

IN CANADA
3022 Dufferin Street, Toronto 395, Ontario, Canada
IN ENGLAND
128, Notting Hill Gate, London W11 3QG, England
133 Corporation Street, Birmingham B4 6PH, England
5A-7 Royal Exchange Square, Glasgow G1 3AH, England
82 Bold Street, Liverpool L1 4HR, England
IN AUSTRALIA
58 Abbotsford Rd., Homebush, N.S.W., Sydney 2140, Australia

MEANING OF THE PAULINE EMBLEM

The emblem enlightens the Pauline spirit and life:

—In the upper part of the emblem shines the HOLY HOST, which sheds light and warmth upon the whole. It is Jesus Christ, the Divine Master, Way and Truth and Life. Born of the Eucharist, we must always live It.

—After the divine nourishment, the divine light—the BOOK, the BIBLE. It enlightens the whole human being. It is the number one book to be reproduced and diffused.

—The PEN is the first instrument of social communication and indicates the whole series of other instruments.

—The INSCRIPTION on the book (Eph. 3:10) indicates our position as children and humble servants of the Church, which is the guardian and teacher of the wisdom revealed by God.

—The SWORD has a twofold meaning. The first: St. Paul, victim of his zeal, died by the sword. The other meaning: St. Paul says that the Word is a two-edged sword which divides and separates man from the spirit of the world and from slavery to evil.

—ALBA has a twofold significance. The first is the origin of the Pauline Family in Alba (Piedmont, Italy), on August 20, 1914. The other significance: the letters ALBA are abbreviations of the Latin names for the symbols of the Evangelists: A = Angel (St. Matthew); L = Lion (St. Mark); B = Ox (St. Luke); A = Eagle (St. John).

—GLORY TO GOD AND PEACE TO MEN. These are the goals, the same ends for which the redemption was carried out.

—The FRAME OF THE EMBLEM indicates the defense of the various symbols included therein, and shows how the Religious must guard their spirit and fulfill their special mission.

IHS

That through the Church the manifold wisdom of God might now be made known.

GLORY TO GOD PEACE TO MEN

A L
B A